How Shall We School Our Children?

How Shall We School Our Children?
Primary Education and Its Future

Edited by

Colin Richards
and Philip H. Taylor

FALMER PRESS
Taylor & Francis Group

UK   Falmer Press, 1 Gunpowder Square, London, EC4A 3DE
USA   Falmer Press, Taylor & Francis Inc., 1900 Frost Road, Suite 101, Bristol, PA 19007

First published in 1998

A catalogue record for this book is available from the British Library

ISBN 0 7507 0781 X cased
ISBN 0 7507 0780 1 paper

Library of Congress Cataloging-in-Publication Data are available on request

Jacket design by Caroline Archer

Typeset in 10/12 Garamond by
Graphicraft Typesetters Limited, Hong Kong

Printed in Great Britain by Biddles Ltd., Guildford and King's Lynn on paper which has a specified pH value on final paper manufacture of not less than 7.5 and is therefore 'acid free'.

Every effort has been made to contact copyright holders for their permission to reprint material in this book. The publishers would be grateful to hear from any copyright holder who is not here acknowledged and will undertake to rectify any errors or omissions in future editions of this book.

Contents

Contents

Acknowledgment

The structure of this book owes much to Alan Blyth's categories of 'promoters', 'producers', 'providers', 'professionals', 'parents' and 'pupils' which he employed in a paper, *'The Changing Nature of Primary Education: Today and Tomorrow'*, given to the first Primary Schools Research and Development Group and University of Birmingham Joint Conference in 1994, and though he is not responsible for its contents, except for his own contribution, he does bear a considerable responsibility for the influence he has exercised over many years on how we think and feel about primary education. We are pleased to acknowledge this influence and to thank him for the ideas which helped us create this book.

Colin Richards
Philip Taylor
January 1998

Preface

'Well begun, is half done', is an adage as true today as it ever was and is especially true of primary education. The foundations in learning, thinking and feeling which it provides are essential for what comes later not only in schooling but also in life. Too often the achievements of primary education are swallowed up in secondary, further and higher education despite the evidence of the critical importance of learning and understanding the 'basics' (which go well beyond literacy and numeracy) to later success in schooling. This book is being both a corrective of the taken for granted view of primary education and an audit of its qualities as the century comes to an end. Both may help everyone — parents, teachers, Government, local authorities and the public at large — to reflect on what steps to take as they seek to improve the education of young children in the first half of the twenty-first century. Their education underpins their future and society owes it to them to equip them to deal with its problems and possibilities. It is to this end that this book is addressed most especially to the teachers and to their pupils some of whom as primary teachers themselves will contribute to the further development of primary education as the twenty-first century unfolds.

Colin Richards
Philip Taylor
January 1998

Part 1

Changing Perspectives

1   English Primary Education: Looking Backward to Look Forward[1]

Alan Blyth

This first chapter looks backward, over half a century. Social trends in their effects on English primary education develop gradually rather than abruptly, so that it is possible for this elderly observer and participant to detect, from his own necessarily limited perspective, at least some of the trends in the recent past which may continue to influence the future.

The years immediately after 1945 appear, in retrospect, to have been largely an attempt to recreate and continue rival versions of the best of pre-war England. Then, the early 1950s saw gradual social and technological changes which set this country, stripped of its influence and crippled in its economy, on a course which has been characterized by recurrent changes unimaginable to most people who had just survived the Second World War. An integral part of this process, responding to major social changes, has been the widening of the scope and complexity of primary education in England.

I shall consider the trends affecting post-war English primary education under these headings: provision of primary education; the public image of primary education; the clients of primary education (parents and children); the primary curriculum; primary teaching; and research and study in primary education. The selection of headings is mine, but I think they are comprehensive, related to social change, and relevant to children's future schooling.

Provision of Primary Education

For a century before 1945, the adjective 'primary' had been spasmodically used to refer to the education of children below about the age of 10 or 11 in elementary schools. It applied both to the publicly financed 'county' schools and to the various rate-supported voluntary schools, mostly Roman Catholic or Church of England, the two categories comprising the 'dual system' hitherto perpetuated throughout the century by successive Education Acts. Consequent upon the redefinition of 'secondary' (or 'post-primary') education as a stage above 11 for everyone, rather than as a type of education for some, the term 'primary' also came officially to denote the earlier stage: schooling 5–11. It was in turn sub-divided into nursery (before 5), infant(s) 5–7, and junior 7–11, although the Consultative Committee of the Board of Education itself had rather confused the new terminology by calling its 1931 Report on the 7–11 years *The Primary School*. However, the term 'elementary' remained in official parlance until the Butler Act superseded it in 1944. Even after that, it survived in folk usage, especially when associated with traditional buildings. For until 1960, or even later in some downtown or rural areas, children still spent their entire school life in what came to be known as 'all-age' primary schools: the elementary schools, 'council schools' or 'church schools', which had been known locally for generations.

In any case, primary schools were rarely regarded as equally important as secondary schools, for two main reasons. First, the 1944 Act defined 'primary pupils' as those below 12 years, while in 1945 building regulations were drawn up, assuming that juniors needed less floor space, and less current expenditure, than secondary pupils. Then again, because of the machinery of education involved at that time in the tripartite secondary structure, the newly designated primary schools soon became generally regarded as seedbeds for the selective breeding of primary pupils for different kinds of secondary education rather than as arenas for common social experience. Where there were substantial population changes, for example through slum clearance schemes, some airy new junior elementary schools (and also senior elementary schools with various designations) were built before the Second World War, to be supplemented after 1945 as part of post-war reconstruction especially after the blitz. But it was not until the leaving age for 'post-primary' education was raised, as the 1944 Act required, first to 15 in the late 1940s and then, 20 years later, to 16, that primary education could fully develop in its own right.

By then, the movement to abolish selection for secondary education had acquired momentum. Ironically, just as selection had exercised a backwash effect on primary schools, so did the movement to abolish it. For full secondary education with a wide range of possibilities for everybody required facilities which only the selective schools had previously enjoyed. Since it was impossible to find the resources needed to build a whole range of new schools, some local education authorities considered accommodating their new pupils by raising the entry age instead. Meanwhile experiments with later transfer were being undertaken for more 'educational' reasons by a few LEAs such as the former West Riding of Yorkshire. In 1967 a later age was recommended by the last of the major reports on primary education, Plowden for England and Gittins for Wales: in Scotland and many other countries, primary education already continued until 12. So middle schools, preceded by first schools, sometimes in a 5–9–13–16 but usually in a 5–8–12–16 system, began to appear in about one-third of England though only once in Wales. The second pattern was preferred 'on balance' by Plowden and was popular with most LEAs because *all* the middle-school pupils, 8–12, were 'deemed primary' and so cost less: in 9–13 schools the pupils over 11 were, and are, almost always 'deemed secondary'.

First and middle schools might have developed more widely had it not been that some of the largest LEAs found it cheaper, after all, to stick to 11 as the transfer age and to make do with other expedients such as split-site schools as their way of managing their plans for a non-selective secondary sector. Then, unexpected changes in the numbers of children in primary schools justified their policies. So the middle-school tide turned during the seventies, and now only a relatively few areas retain them, in spite of the educational advantages which were sometimes attributed to them by Plowden and others, of whom I was one. Unfortunately the Key Stages of the National Curriculum (5–7–11–14–16) now make the surviving middle schools appear still more anomalous (although in fact a good case could be made for *not* allowing the end-of-Key-Stage assessment procedures to coincide with transfer to a new school).

Meanwhile attempts have continued to solve the perplexing problem of adjusting buildings and teachers to the numbers of children in an age-group, and to do so in the face of population moves caused by economic change and facilitated by private-car commuting. More recently, changes in the control of schools and their budgets have quite substantially affected many primary schools, placing heavy burdens especially on the smaller ones as they struggle to 'deliver' the now obligatory curriculum.

Technically, that responsibility now rests with the governors. Since the 1960s, primary schools as well as secondary schools have governors, not managers as previously. The new title does raise the status of primary schools, although the financial and other responsibilities now laid upon the governors means that they have to do more managing than managers did. Their tasks are likely to become no easier, though they are often remarkably well discharged. Meanwhile the other big administrative change in recent years, the movement of some schools from local authority control to grant-maintained status, now to be supplanted by foundation status, has not yet made a great impact upon the primary sector.

During the past half-century, the education of some 90 per cent of English children of primary-school age has been provided in the institutions already mentioned. The others have been catered for in three very different ways; in various kinds of independent fee-paying schools; in schools for those with different kinds of special educational needs; and a comparatively small number 'otherwise' than at school, as the 1944 Act put it. Each of these sectors has retained its proportionate share fairly steadily. Yet the first and sometimes the third have at different times met with political encouragement or opposition. As for the special needs provision, the emphasis since the Warnock Report and the Education Act of 1981 has moved away from the earlier terminology of 'handicap', but it is still the focus of a different kind of controversy, about how far children with the more severe learning difficulties or physical or behavioural problems should be segregated from, or 'mainstreamed' into, primary schools, and which children should, in yet uglier terms, be 'statemented', or merit 'dis-application' from the National Curriculum. To those directly concerned, these are *the* issues in education during the primary years; but in this brief survey they cannot receive more than passing mention.

Alan Blyth

The Public Image of Primary Education

Primary education has usually responded to social and educational change, rather than initiating change. One reason for this unflattering concept of primary education can be traced to the continuing influence of its elementary and preparatory origins.[2] Both represented something limited and also something already almost too familiar: instruction in the basic skills and rudimentary information which seemed to be within anybody's intellectual capacities, combined with a sub-stratum of more controversial civic/religious values on which, none the less, everyone had an opinion. Even R.H. Tawney, considered in Labour circles as a major prophet of education, regarded it as essentially preparatory in nature. True, as long ago as 1931 the Hadow Report had boldly, if inconsistently, challenged this conception, but it was not until the 1960s, the Plowden decade, that a 'developmental' view of primary education, and the more prestigious image which it implied, began to make a real impact. For that was a time when, perhaps uniquely, education as a whole enjoyed increased respect.

More than that: primary education was well placed to share in the current fashion for newness (now consciously recaptured by New Labour). It was seen as new and exciting rather than something old and hackneyed. New buildings and a generally new atmosphere became essential, if only because demographic changes made them necessary. New schools, embodying (and responding to) new open-plan designs, were built for the newly developed estates and commuter villages characteristic of the sixties and seventies. To their surprise, visitors from elsewhere, especially from the Untied States, found these new schools stimulating and exciting. So, from being a humble handmaid, English primary education, or at least one conspicuous part of it, became a showcase for exportable ideas; and this itself conferred higher status. Meanwhile, with less publicity, the majority of the older primary schools were also brightened up. Fortunately, this growing sense of newness was not quenched by the external appearance of some of the older buildings, the worst of which were declared unsuitable as workplaces for secretaries, though apparently not for teachers or children. Some still are.

That was in the 1960s and 1970s. Since then, English primary education has experienced two contrary influences. On the one hand its importance has been generally recognized, first when compared with the outcomes of overseas systems and especially those of the 'tiger economies' of the Pacific Rim. The outcome of such comparisons has tarnished the image of primary education established in the 1960s and 1970s. In the search for results, the transmission or input–output model of education has regained much of its previous dominance, and in the process the handmaid role of the primary school, preparatory or even elementary, has been reinstated. Moreover, this latest image of primary education has given rise to a demand for official control of what goes on, culminating in the establishment of OFSTED and its challenge to the autonomy and thus to the professional status of primary education itself.

Control has been asserted not only over the curriculum, as will be seen later, but also, though less successfully, over the ethos of primary schools, with an attempt to revive some form of civic/religious consensus in what has now become a much more pluralist society. So this dominant view looks toward reimposing traditional roles on primary teachers.

Yet at the same time the rapid growth of information technology has generated another image of primary education in which traditional roles are totally superseded. In this other image, children are put in touch with new sources of information such as the Internet and virtual reality and left largely to develop their own learning. This contrasting image is still something for the future rather than the present, but it does show that current thinking is not all moving in the same direction. And in the end, the two images could be complementary, balancing individual learning with social control.

The Clients of Primary Education: Parents

Parents are one category of clients of primary education, whose undeniable importance has recently been emphasized as part of political rhetoric. Yet as late as the 1960s parents were only just being recognized as partners in the educative process. Before that, primary teachers, and headteachers in particular, were respected especially in stable communities for their pedagogical skills, and sometimes feared from one generation to the next for the ferocious but effective discipline with which they achieved their results. And nobody doubted that those results were what everybody needed. So when the Plowden Report actually devoted a chapter to parent–teacher relations, this was seized upon as a significant departure.

At that time, the emphasis was on how parents and teachers could co-operate in the education of their younger children. As the primary curriculum evolved, so parents became less able to help their children with work which they themselves had never undertaken. New approaches to the arts, science, mathematics and humanities, revealed in equally unfamiliar displays on class-room and corridor walls, were welcomed by most parents for their stimulus, but left them aware of their inability to help their children except in co-operation with teachers.

There were other new parent–teacher relations too. The sixties saw the large-scale development of planned new towns and peripheral estates, in which primary schools, as in pre-war days, were often placed at the hub of neigh-bourhoods. Young parents who moved out to towers and maisonettes away from the close social networks of the slums found that the schools, especially the primary schools, now provided the most obvious everyday support institu-tions. Headteachers and their staffs came to know families and their needs, and sometimes to visit their homes. Then parallel developments took place towards town and city centres and, in a different mode, in suburban areas. Village schools had always known this function, but they were changing in the opposite way, as the composition of the rural population was weighted away from traditional occupations towards commuters with wider social networks less intimately linked with their villages and village schools, whose numbers were in any case declining. Meanwhile, in schools of all kinds, there was increasing cooperation through parent–teacher associations with their notable fund-raising capacities, and through parent representation on the new governing bodies.

In the different political climate of the 1980s, there has been a further change in the meaning of parent–teacher relations. Instead of these forms of mutual cooperation in curriculum and social process, the emphasis has come to be placed on parents' rights. As schools compete for pupils, parents equip themselves with league tables and prospectuses and make what they believe to be informed choices. So, instead of seeing teachers as their partners in caring for children's development, parents have been encouraged to assume that teachers ought to be primarily agents of traditional formal learning, requiring criticism if they failed in the Gilbertian task of pushing each child faster than each other one. Of course the older relationships still persist in many places, as do others which reach back still farther; but the general climate has changed.

The Clients of Primary Education: Children

Despite the title of the Plowden Report — Children and *their* Primary Schools — it is still unusual to think of children themselves as being clients. Usually it is assumed that they are only there to be taught and influenced and restrained. Only rarely, in particular schools and classes, have they been allowed some official say in their own education and self-assessment. Yet, as teachers and indeed writers of fiction well know, children even in the primary years do in fact exercise enormous collective power over what goes on in schools. There is a culture of childhood, as well as a culture of adolescence, and a large part of it relates to what happens secretly in the playground and all too openly in the classroom.

This general shared culture in turn influences sub-cultures in each school and class, increasingly so because, itself influenced in turn by national and global media, it supersedes local characteristics. And those national and global media themselves reflect, and accelerate, supranational change in a way that was not consciously realized in earlier generations. Two centuries ago, the arrival of the travelling fair was the principal source of excitement from beyond the parish. Now, everyone goes to Disneyworld.

At this point it would be only too easy to indulge in a trite mixture of reminiscence, sentimentality and prejudice about cultural change and the abolition of childhood. Many do. Journalists and even social scientists claim to identify trends in the culture of childhood which others dispute. Here are some which I regard as important.

First, advances in technology, from television to CDs, computer games and now digital TV and the Internet, have placed in young children's hands new possibilities which not only increase their own powers but quite often leave both parents and teachers less well equipped than the children are. Consequently, traditional respect for the wisdom of elders is weakened, while towards the 'nerds' among their own number it is, perhaps reluctantly, increased.

Then again, the processes of maturation have been artificially as well as naturally accelerated and complicated. The primary children's world is no longer as simple as when I first wrote about it in the 1960s. Those footages of newsreel from the 1940s and 1950s now legitimated within the History National Curriculum show evacuees and their successors up to the age of 12 or even 13 equipped with such archaisms as school caps and badges, plimsolls, satchels, frocks, and short trousers. Now it is acceptable to start adult-style jeans and anoraks and soccer 'strips' in the infant years, while school identity is expressed in sweatshirts, that is, until it becomes 'cool' to affect designer clothes and footwear. And adults have to concur, while nervously allowing amounts of pocket money on a scale far beyond what is accounted for by inflation since 1950. Other adult perceptions of children also make their impact. In long-term reaction against soulful Victorian and Edwardian sentimentality, young children, especially boys, are smiled upon if they are cheeky, comic and cute.

The social and ethnic composition of primary school populations has become more diverse, widening the range of social experience for many children. Some have confidently welcomed this diversity. Others, including those from ethnic minorities, have encountered some degree of rejection and so have been more wary and defensive, sometimes behind a shield of aggressiveness. Adult attitudes, in parents and teachers, have influenced children, while teachers themselves have not always known how to handle the relationships involved.

More generally, young people in post-Imperial, post-modern Britain seem to have nourished a culture in which almost everything inherited is post-something, ripe for deconstruction. In such a climate, when even officialdom remains undecided about values, pop music and sport remain legitimate grounds for keen and even excessive loyalty and enthusiasm. But where institutions and values are concerned, it is more fashionable, and often assumed to be more mature, intelligent and 'cool' to criticize and ridicule, to scoff at warnings about tobacco, alcohol and drugs as clumsy attempts at repression, rather than to accept and perpetuate. This culture of derision is essentially an adolescent phenomenon, but primary-age children soon aspire to emulate it. So now, when the public image of primary schools is itself frequently belittled, if not for its vices, then for its virtues, it is hardly surprising that some primary-age children are more prone than any of their predecessors to challenge the authority and values of parents and teachers alike.

But this point must not be unduly generalized. For one thing, the virtual elimination of the 11+ and the reduction of rigid streaming (as distinct from setting) has removed one source of divisiveness and resentment — which might reappear if selection were reintroduced. Meanwhile many primary schools, especially voluntary schools and others in self-contained communities or standing for specific values, have retained a distinctive ethos. And others in what seem the least likely places have developed, largely through the efforts of their staffs, a much more positive set of values which still command the loyalty of most if not all of their children, even the oldest.

That reference to age difference serves as a reminder that cultural change, however widespread, affects children differently as they become older. Its impact alters as the partly socialized individuals in the reception class grow towards the self-sufficient groups and nascent puberty of 11-year-olds. What is sometimes surprisingly overlooked is the now accelerating mechanism by which that impact takes place, in neighbourhoods and to some extent in schools. Children at each age-level try to prove their own growing powers by learning the culture of the more powerful level above. Meanwhile they also dominate the one below, whose members in turn copy the culture of their elders in order to convince themselves that they too are growing. I now consider that the term 'peer group' is strictly misleading here, for much social learning comes from the group next above the peer level. Meanwhile it *is* among peers that children learn to become boys, or girls, as their culture expects. In the process, even among the youngest, some can be cruelly stereotyped and bullied, a process once overlooked or denied but now so obvious that adults have to take it seriously.

The Primary Curriculum

From the very beginning of the twentieth century, schools were informed that they had freedom to design their approach to curriculum. 'Suggestions' came to exercise more influence on the curriculum than the infamous 'Codes'. No longer were teachers told how or even what to teach; but the basic assumption remained that any curriculum would follow an input–output model in which instruction was given, information provided, and suitably educated persons would result. The various year-levels, still sometimes anachronistically called standards, were associated with particular kinds of work, and often in any one school, for years on end, with the same teacher. There were some striking additions, mostly initiated by powerful headteachers: conservatism modified by idiosyncrasy. But for the most part the curriculum was handed down from generation to generation, with parents and teachers and children all knowing what to expect in the higher classes, where their elder siblings were already farther up the same enduring ladder inherited from the elementary past.

Meanwhile another approach to the primary curriculum, originated in the eighteenth and nineteenth centuries mainly in Europe and later in the USA, was beginning to gain attention. This was the counterpart of the 'developmental' view of primary education already mentioned (p. 6). The basis of this approach was not so much what children *should* learn as how they *did* learn. Many English teachers and others suspected it as being too foreign, too intellectual and probably ineffective in practice. But to the growing number who espoused this approach, it became a matter of faith to spread it.

Its first important official mention was in the Hadow Report of 1931, where it influenced the general chapters though not the treatment of individual subjects: it was still assumed that the primary curriculum would in practice be subject-based. The high watermark of official recognition followed in 1967 with the publication of the Plowden Report, though there too the subject tradition remained firmly represented. The relation between subjects and children's learning has preoccupied thinking about the primary curriculum especially since Plowden, and has unsurprisingly generated a very substantial body of professional literature.

During the 1980s, there was a revival of concern in the possibility of an official curriculum in England and Wales, and in Northern Ireland. It became evident that many other countries (though not Scotland) had one, and it was now widely believed that the *laissez-faire* curriculum fashioned by professionals in a 'secret garden' concealed from the public would no longer do what was needed. Eventually this newer thinking led to the Education Reform Act of 1988 which put in place a National Curriculum and system of assessment. It reasserted a traditional subject approach to curriculum more firmly than at any previous time. Three subjects (English, mathematics, and now, with an eye to world markets, science, expanded far beyond the 'nature study' of post-war years) were accorded core status. Six 'other foundation subjects' (technology which unsurprisingly superseded 'craft', history, geography, art, music and PE) were also admitted, with the controversial RE as part of the 'basic' but not the 'national' curriculum. In Wales, Welsh was added, but with core status only in the Welsh-speaking areas. Modern languages were introduced as a status required only in the secondary school, while other subjects were excluded. In addition, a doubtfully practicable and frequently counter-productive daily act of 'broadly Christian' worship, based on practice in the 1944 Act and before, was prescribed. Curricular practices, such as topic work, were not actually prohibited; indeed a possible place was later found for them outside the statutory framework itself, through what became known as cross-curricular themes, dimensions and skills. All of this was a typical political compromise, achieved by different pressure groups at the expense of practicality. For the individual subject programmes of study reflected what subject specialists though every child should learn, and preferably enjoy, on the road to educated citizenship, rather than what all children themselves could readily understand on the road to maturity. The totality appeared burdensome, largely inappropriate, and bureaucratically imposed.

So the closing years of the century have been devoted to attempts to reduce the burden of this overweight curriculum on teachers and learners alike. In 1995 it was overhauled and reduced, with more emphasis on the basic skills and with the cross-curricular elements quietly dropped. A similar operation will mark the millennium; for the curriculum, like the House of Commons, is now to be reshaped every five years. It remains to be seen what will happen to the rest of the primary curriculum; even to science. Some aspects seem likely to remain outside: others may yet join them, while the claims of a modern language for inclusion in the primary curriculum are increasingly heard. Perhaps it will again be the relative power of different interest groups, rather than the relative needs of children, which will determine the outcome.

Primary Teaching

Irrespective of variations in numbers due to changes in birth-rate and in public financial policies, more teachers work in primary schools than anywhere else. In 1945 it was still widely assumed that the old elementary curriculum was self-evident and that teaching was only a humble vocation consisting of instilling, with the aid of discipline, the elements of the basic skills and morality, with a few optional extras, just as it had been in the later years of the previous century. For this, two years in a non-graduate training college, even if improved as the McNair Report in 1945 advocated, would suffice. It was some advance, not universally approved, when after the war a basic salary scale for all teachers, men and women, primary and secondary, was established. It may be interesting to note that the new basic scale began at £300 pa, with an annual increment of £15. The graduate allowance was a further £60. I remember, because that is where I started.

The prevalent assumption in the post-war years, and long afterwards, was that secondary teaching, especially in grammar schools, was more important and so more worthy of graduates, who should not 'waste' their degree expertise on the under-11s. This assumption was likely, as long as education was conceived according to the old elementary image and the input–output model of curriculum. The only reversal of this correlation of pupil age with teacher status was at the lowest extreme, or in the field of what was then called special education, where it was accepted that the psychology of very young children, or of slow learners or those with disturbed behaviour, was a legitimate field of study and practice for graduates.

Gradually, the idea spread that professional preparation of this kind, reinforcing the vocation of teaching with the study and understanding of children and their education, could be extended across primary education as a whole. It was linked with the newer conception of primary schooling as set forth in the Plowden Report, in which children should organize and pace their own learning, in a controlled environment, with the teachers as designers and supervisors of this learning process, rather than as instructors and assessors of individual progress. This approach was logically combined, as was recognized in the 1960s by the Robbins Report, with a need first for three-year training and then for an all-graduate profession (BEd, or other degree with postgraduate certificate) and for expansion of further professional development and higher study. These developments coincided with a big expansion in primary training, the first since the post-war boom, and with an updating of non-graduates to 'in-service BEd' degrees. In 1972 the James Report proposed a modification, but not a reversal, of these developments. The new pedagogic orthodoxy was never as widely dominant as some opinion formers have suggested. But where it was established, it was vigorously propagated, and sometimes, it must be said, reinforced among students by means far removed from the permissive approach advocated for them to use with children.

A further feature of primary teaching, and its possible consequences, has often been noted. Class teachers, and especially those employed in infant schools, have been predominantly female. This has been partly because primary teaching with its distinctive pattern of terms and holidays but limited remuneration has tended to suit women rather than men, and partly because of established stereotypes of employment and of the 'nurturing' role of women. The result has been a limitation of adult role models not only for boys but also for girls. With the more rapid social maturation of both girls and boys, this issue has become more acute during the half-century since 1945, and there is little sign that any change in this respect is likely. Among headteachers and other 'postholders', however, men have been more substantially represented.

In the post-Plowden years, the general reaction against the more extreme forms of child-centredness in primary education has been reflected in widespread and sometimes ill-informed criticism of all primary teacher education, and even of educational studies and research. A series of steps, culminating in the establishment of the Teacher Training Agency, has been quite widely acclaimed, in spite of (or even because of) its challenge to the claims of primary teacher education to stay, together with all other professional education, within higher education as a whole.

Research and Study in Primary Education: A Brief Comment

Ironically, some of the justification for this intervention has itself been based on a growing volume of academic study of primary teaching by Robin Alexander and others. For there has been a remarkable post-war development in scholarship and research in primary education. When in 1948 I enquired about the possibility of a higher degree specializing in primary education, I sometimes met with incomprehension. Indeed the literature about primary schools was then scanty, much of it avuncular advice to teachers, and for the rest limited to such matters as intelligence testing and psychological observation. Now, there is a huge accumulation of research and writing about English primary education, some of it very good and some rather less so, much of the best being dependent on grants from major research foundations. The most important publications alone now fill a bookcase, while the number of University professors of primary education now represents a significant part of the total scholarship in education. First and higher degrees in primary education are now commonplace. There is an Association for the Study of Primary Education, a series of journals devoted to primary education or to aspects of the field, including *Education 3–13* (whose title recalls the middle-school days), while many articles in all the major educational journals relate to the education of younger children. The very nature of the remaining chapters in this book illustrates the extent of the changes since the 1940s.

The study of primary education today ranges over child development, the social psychology of the classroom, aspects of sociology of education, the history and philosophy of primary education, international comparisons, the primary curriculum, pedagogy and teaching style, the nature and status of primary teaching, and primary school management, these various aspects being thrown into prominence as circumstances change.[3] In the process, the importance of primary education and its enhanced image has become more firmly established. Current attacks on primary education as a field of study, some of them gratuitously conducted by specialists in other fields, should not be allowed to impede this process.

Meanwhile, as in other fields, most writing now adopts a necessarily neutral stance, combined with a post-traditional interest, in multicultural Britain, in newer scientific theories and, in compensation for previous bias, in different religious and political sources of values. That represents a marked change from the mid-century climate in writing about primary education. (As a believing ecumenical Christian uneasy about any barriers of denomination or style, I may now look like a septuagenarian relic; though that is certainly not how I see myself.)

Conclusion

My backward look has indicated some trends in English primary education in the second half of the twentieth century. I have already suggested how one or two of these may develop. For the rest, I cannot foretell which of these will continue to affect how we — more correctly, you — will school the children of our country as the new millennium begins. Some at present appear likely to continue. Structures should persist in some form, though we cannot yet be sure whether the 'ages and stages' will continue as they are, or whether primary schools themselves will have their roles and images radically recast in the new information society. Independent schools, provision for special educational needs, and 'education otherwise' are likely to continue. Indeed, with homeworking jobs more widespread, and access to the Internet more available to parents undertaking such work, maybe this last sector will expand; though only if parents master the art of teaching and also enable children to socialize in other ways. Primary teachers, still the backbone of the education of most young children, are likely to be less important as purveyors of an input–output curriculum than as facilitators of resources and as students and managers of people. By this last point I mean that they will need not only to understand and organize children and to know something about the society in which they are likely to live, but also to bring adults representing parts of that society into schools and to help them, sometimes, as partners in the educative enterprise, to interpret the world to young children. The clients of primary education, parents and children alike, will probably appreciate teachers more in these new extended roles which, at their best, will embody both vocation and profession. Society will no doubt continue to make big demands on primary teachers, and perhaps to need fewer of them, but will almost certainly be obliged to accord them higher professional status and to reward them more, without saddling those who are fully prepared with lifelong debts incurred during their student days. In any case primary teaching will continue to be the focus of productive study and research, all the more so in a new technological environment, and this will in turn provide the basis for a self-critical but self-confident profession scarcely dreamed of in 1945.

Here then are a few attempts at looking forward at primary education through looking backward. All of these attempts are based on trends which can be detected, in some measure, in the recent past. Some readers of these pages will perhaps be among those who, in 2050, will be able to say how far these attempts are accurate.

Acknowledgment

I am grateful to Penelope Harnett and to the editors for their help and advice in the preparation of this chapter.

Notes

1   References to individual authors and books have been largely omitted from this chapter, for any necessary list would be intolerably long: but see note 3.
2   I used the terms 'elementary', 'preparatory' and 'developmental' in 1965, to denote three different traditions in English primary education (see my *English Primary Education*, vol. 2, Routledge and Kegan Paul). This terminology has been quite widely used since then.
3   Some of the major contributors to this expansion are among the authors of other chapters in this book. Others include Robin Alexander, Neville Bennett and Charles Desforges on children's learning, Robert Dearden on the philosophy of primary education, Wynne Harlen on primary science, Jennifer Nias on teachers' careers, Ann Lewis on special educational needs, Peter Mortimore on school effectiveness, Christine Pascal and Kathy Sylva on young children's development, Alistair Ross on social studies, and Brian Simon on the recent history of primary education. Even so, any such list must be provisional, with other well-known names claiming inclusion.

References

ALEXANDER, R. (1995) *Versions of Primary Education*, London: Routledge.

ALEXANDER, R. (1997) *Policy and Practice in Primary Education*, 2nd edition, London: Routledge.

BENNETT, N. et al. (1984) *The Quality of Pupil Learning Experiences*, Hove: Lawrence Erlbaum Associates.

CAMPBELL, R.J. (ed.) (1993) *Breadth and Balance in the Primary School Curriculum*, London: Falmer Press.

CENTRAL ADVISORY COUNCIL FOR ENGLAND (1967) *Children and their Primary Schools, (The Plowden Report)* 2 vols, London: HMSO.

CUNNINGHAM, P. (1988) *Curriculum Change in the Primary School since 1945: Dissemination of the Progressive Ideal*, London: Falmer Press.

GALTON, M. et al. (1980) *Inside the Primary Classroom*, London: Routledge.

GALTON, M. (1989) *Teaching in the Primary School*, London: David Fulton.

GAMMAGE, P. (1986) *Primary Education: Structure and Context*, London: Harper and Row.

MARRIOTT, S. (1985) *Primary Education and Society*, London: Falmer Press.

POLLARD, A. (1985) *The Social World of the Primary School*, London: Holt Education.

POLLARD, A. (ed.) (1987) *Children and their Primary Schools*, London: Falmer Press.

RICHARDS, C. (1980) *Primary Education: Issues for the Eighties*, London: A and C Black.

RICHARDS, C. (ed.) (1982) *New Directions in Primary Education*, London: Falmer Press.

THOMAS, N. (1990) *Primary Education from Plowden to the 1980s*, London: Falmer Press.

Also the series of 'ASPE papers' published for the Association for the Study of Primary Education by Trentham Books.

2   From the Good Old Days to a Brave New World? Aims and Purposes of Primary Schooling

Peter Cunningham

National Aims and Purposes

'Traditional' v 'progressive'. Fierce and simplistic debates have raged around teaching methods and school effectiveness, overlooking and even obscuring the fact that at root these are conflicts about aims and purposes. The debate has remained remarkably polarized, though a broad spectrum of positions has been identified by Alexander (1995).

Where can we look for an official statement of aims? There is a taken-for-grantedness about aims and purposes. Statutory pronouncements and administrative edicts are not eloquent about a rationale for the provisions they make. In this lack of clarification lies a great deal of difficulty, for significant differences of view surround the fundamental purposes of education. Drafters of legislation avoid the kind of value-laden preamble that would rouse obstructive debate and opposition, so, on the whole, we look in vain to official documents for clarification of aims and purposes.

The historic Education Act of 1944 began by defining an administrative structure for the education system, and it was only in section 7 that some hint of 'aims and purposes' emerged in the duty laid upon local education authorities to 'contribute towards the spiritual, moral, mental and physical development of the community' by securing efficient education to meet the needs of the population of their area. It was this section too which defined the organization of schools in three progressive stages, the first of which was to be known as 'primary' education. In the 1988 Education Reform Act this list of implicit aims and purposes is promoted to section 1, enhancing the powers of central as against local government. Now, in section 1, the duty of the Secretary of State in respect of every maintained school, becomes:

to secure a balanced and broadly based curriculum which
(a) promotes the spiritual, moral, cultural, mental and physical development of pupils at the school and of society and
(b) prepares such pupils for the opportunities, responsibilities and experiences of adult life.

Already two significant additions to aims and purposes have appeared in 1988 compared with 40 years earlier. They are the 'cultural development' of pupils and of society and 'preparation of pupils for adult life'. The law of education does, then, offer a brief and general description of aims for the education system, which will be adopted as a framework later in this chapter.

Section 2 of the 1988 Act goes on to specify requirements for religious education and the National Curriculum, in that order. In pursuance of the Act, the Secretary of State appointed working parties of educationists and academics to draw up detailed programmes of study in each curriculum subject. Drafting the original set of National Curriculum orders, the working parties produced a careful rationale for each of their subjects, published in the consultative documents, but these statements were significantly missing from the orders as placed before Parliament. So, for all its prescriptiveness about curriculum content, the state has not committed itself to elaborating an explicit set of aims.

Despite this reluctance, the state acknowledges the importance of primary education by its investment of £9.6 billion annually in a massive system throughout the UK, comprising 23,000 schools, 211,000 teachers and five million pupils. (These figures include Scotland and Northern Ireland.) Primary education, establishing basic attitudes and skills as a foundation for future learning, is seen as crucial to securing political stability and economic security for the nation. With a century-long tradition of universal provision, compulsion and high attendance rates, the underlying rationale fails to be articulated. Contrast the situation of developing countries, or those where industrialization and economic development are more recent. There, conflicts between 'Westernization' and the defence of traditional culture are ever present in debates about policies for elementary education, where English medium on the one hand might be seen as the key to economic progress for individuals and for society, while regional languages remain central to maintaining the identity and stability of local communities. Their limited public finances also impose heavy constraints on the scope of basic education and force debate on aims and purposes.

International comparisons have informed public debate about our own approach to primary education. For example, the restricted curriculum and regimented methods of teaching prevalent in the 'tiger economies' have been identified as a key to industrial competitiveness. But the inferences drawn can be superficial and wrong. Even whilst these educational practices have been presented as models for educational reform in our own country, so Korea and the Pacific Rim nations are concerned about the failure of their own school systems to generate creators and innovators, and are looking to more 'progressive' Western methods as a way forward. Moreover, economists' views can be remarkably short-term, and already the prospects for continued economic growth in these newer economies have been questioned, casting doubts after all on the efficacy of the educational methods on which their apparent economic success appeared to be based.

Local Aims and Purposes

At a local level through their school prospectuses, governors have the opportunity to make statements of aims and purposes which allow school policy to reflect the particular character of its immediate community. The publication of these documents became mandatory 10 years ago and has resulted in some admirable expressions of intent by governing bodies. Since the onset of more rigid inspection procedures a shift can be detected towards lists of aims carefully drafted as much to satisfy OFSTED requirements as a genuine expression of aspirations by local people for their children and their primary education. That is one example of the tyranny which over-prescriptive central direction can exert.

One inner-city maintained primary school in 1991, after the launch of the National Curriculum but before the inauguration of OFSTED, endorsed a published statement of aims that had been produced by the LEA, and proceeded to set out its own distinctive aims and objectives under four categories as set out in Figure 2.1.

Figure 2.1

Treatment of the Child:
City-Centre C.P. aims to
- give each child equal opportunities
- give parity of esteem to all pupils
- ensure that pupils' knowledge and skills progress at the right pace through e.g. project based work
- encourage children to participate
- help pupils develop lively enquiring minds through learning, solving by trial and error and exploring a variety of ways of expressing themselves
- contribute to the emotional, physical and social growth of each pupil, enabling them to develop and test their own personal values and attitudes.

Parents and the Community:
City-Centre C.P. aims to
- project the school as part of the local community and accept its share of responsibility
- keep an open door policy which welcomes and values the contributions that parents and others can make and ensures the existence of a comfortable and open atmosphere
- respect the contribution which every member of staff makes to the community
- offer help and support to all families of pupils who require it

School Ethos:
City-Centre C.P. aims to
- provide a welcoming and supportive atmosphere for all its activities
- give full support to pupils in times of crisis
- provide the resources to enable each child to realize their potential
- recognize that children are entitled to high quality, well planned and well organized teaching throughout their education
- help pupils respond to a changing society
- regularly monitor the progress of each individual child
- help pupils to develop and experience success
- encourage reflection and self-evaluation
- build on the ethnic diversity in the school
- value bilingualism

Figure 2.1 Continued

Learning Aims:
City-Centre C.P. aims to ensure that each child
• has the opportunity to learn through first hand experience
• is able to communicate confidently and clearly
• learns how to record and apply knowledge with accuracy and understanding
• acquires some knowledge and understanding of the world and its peoples
• develops the capacity to become a contributing member of the community
• is encouraged to develop self motivation, self regulation and self confidence
• learns to work individually and as part of a group

In a spirit of dialogue, the governors and staff invited comments and suggestions from parents and other interested members of the community. Clearly the main emphasis throughout this list of aims was on the social development of the pupils and the social role of the school within the community. Learning aims were as much about experience and attitude as about skills and knowledge.

A neighbouring Church of England school, with a similarly multiethnic population, was more succinct in its statement of aims, published in 1996 with an OFSTED inspection imminent.

In this list, values and relationships were still well to the fore. Inspectors' findings were that the aims of the school were well met, resulting in an ethos which demonstrated 'good attention to pupils' moral, social and cultural development', integrating 'children from a wide range of backgrounds into a cohesive and inclusive community'.

However, comparing the two statements from 1991 and 1996 is instructive. A tightening of definition in key phrases and a shift of nuance reflects government priorities and the prevailing tone of official discourse: 'High quality teaching' is replaced by 'effective teaching'; 'equal opportunities' becomes 'equal access to the school curriculum'; 'self-motivation, self-regulation and self-confidence' are transformed to 'self-control' and 'self-discipline'.

Different emphases in some schools' declared aims, have followed the prioritizing of core subjects in public debate, so that the 1997 statement of one rural county primary school runs as follows:

> At primary school level, it is important that a child becomes literate and numerate. We aim to help children acquire knowledge, skills and practical abilities, and to develop qualities of mind, body, spirit, feeling and imagination to prepare them for a changing world. Teaching will adhere to the National Curriculum. . . .
>
> All children will study these subjects and attainment targets and progress will be monitored. Assessments will identify the child's strengths and weaknesses and will help ensure that continuity and the right level of assistance is given in the appropriate way at the right time.
>
> We hope that these learning experiences will give the children confidence and reassurance to express themselves. We also feel it is important that children become aware of participating in a caring and sharing community.

Figure 2.2

Aims of St. C.E. School
1   To provide stimulating and effective teaching which will result in each child reaching his/her potential.
2   To develop relationships between children and adults based on honesty, respect, friendship and self-control.
3   To provide a calm, secure, caring, environment through the development of self-discipline and established routine.
4   To teach children to value their own and others' efforts and achievements.
5   To help the children develop enquiring and creative minds, an awareness of their environment and the ability to adjust to a changing society.
6   To develop respect for, and an understanding of, religious and moral values and tolerance of different behaviours and attitudes.
7   To ensure that all children have equal access to the whole school curriculum.
8   To maintain and develop the school's role as part of the community.

This statement of aims is more obviously dominated by National Curriculum requirements although a description of the intended ethos of the school did go on to describe a happy, safe and caring environment, valuing individual worth, open and welcoming to all sections of the community (see Figure 2.2).

Schools' statements of aims and purposes must inevitably reflect their individual character, and in the British system that will mean not only the locality but also religous affiliation in the case of voluntary schools. Thus, the recently published aims of a rural voluntary controlled school reflect National Curriculum priorities, together with a strong denominational emphasis:

Statement of purpose
The purpose of rural Church of England controlled primary school is to provide the highest quality of education within a Christian context for children living within the area of the parishes . . . and also for children from a wider area whose parents apply for admission to the school.
Aims
To achieve this purpose we aim:
1   to encourage all children, whatever their talents and abilities, and including those with special needs, to reach their full potential through the implementation and delivery of the National Curriculum;
2   to introduce children to the Christian faith, to promote their spiritual and moral development and to make the teaching of religious education and collective worship an important part of their daily lives;
3   to encourage firm links between school, home and the wider community;
4   to create an environment in which children's sense of curiosity and excitement is stimulated, their confidence and self-esteem is built up and their respect for, and understanding of, other people is developed.

Interest Groups

Locally and nationally, statements of aims and purposes reflect dialogue, debate and conflict between, and within, different interest groups, debate which often flows from a clash of ideologies. Most newsworthy over the last decades have been conflicts triggered by changing conditions and crises of one sort and another, real or invented. Child abuse and literacy standards provide two examples, or 'failing schools' like William Tyndale in 1976 and Morningside, Hackney in 1996. Key interest groups are the professionals, the politicians and parents; this sequence is not one of priority, but arises from the course of recent history and the list excludes children, perhaps the most important interest group of all, but one which has had no independent voice or political power.

Professionals

For 25 years after 1944, the aims of the primary school may fairly be said to have been left to the teachers. Following the Government's quite deliberate abdication of its responsibility for curriculum back in 1926, decisions about what and how to teach had been largely left to the professionals, at school or even classroom level, with uneven measures of guidance from LEAs. Given the historical and political circumstances it was unjust subsequently to accuse teachers of maintaining a 'secret garden' around the curriculum. It is true that responsibility for curriculum development became a matter of professional interest and pride; when, from the mid 1970s this aspect of teachers' authority came under attack, it was a blow to professional self-esteem.

One myth that flourished in the subsequent heated atmosphere was that teachers' aims and purposes had been universally coloured by, at best, permissiveness and, at worst, subversion. Alexander's research into 'curriculum associated discourse and pedagogy' in primary schools has identified 'powerful continuities' in teachers' approaches to their work. A basic conservatism may well inform their practice. The motivation for primary teaching is preeminently care and concern for young children which implies a fundamental 'child-centredness' of aim, a consequent resistance to the more utilitarian purposes embodied in the National Curriculum may be understood in this light. Teachers have much collective wisdom and classroom experience to contribute to the debate on aims. Strong headteachers have been shown to be critical in setting and maintaining the ethos of the school.

Politicians

Over the last quarter of this century, the state has struggled to regain the initiative in formulating educational aims. Political parties stake their educational concern on the economic future of the country, on entitlement and justice as well as on costs to the public purse. Their aims and purposes are about maximizing opportunity, generating the wealth-producing skills, and realizing the ambition of parents to improve their children's life chances. As elected representatives politicians have claimed to speak for disappointed and disillusioned parents, though ambition and career can influence their stance.

The politicians' platform is the mass media, however, and soundbites and stereotypes have been a major obstacle to clear thinking about aims.

Raising public consciousness about the importance of primary education has been one achievement of politicians in recent years, and some sense of a shift from the dogmatic to the pragmatic in very recent times offers some hope, though the White Paper of 1997 still conveys a disappointingly narrow view of the purposes of primary education.

Parents

The parental voice is now more powerful in educational policy than it was half a century ago. Movements such as civil rights, pressure group politics and consumerism have effected change across the spectrum of social policy and primary schooling is no exception. This voice is often articulated by a wide range of well-informed and politically well-organized groups, as Secretary of State John Patten discovered at the cost of his career, when policies premised on parental dissatisfaction were in fact scuppered by parental resistance.

The disillusioned parent stereotyped by politicians and journalists is far less typical in fact than the silent, compliant majority who appear to trust the teachers of their own children. In many cases lack of participation in school affairs may also indicate a willingness to let professionals run the show. But parental aspirations should strongly influence the enunciation of aims and purposes through representation in governing bodies and through public meetings.

Children

Parents are the consumers of education on behalf of their children. Children are not consulted formally on fundamentals like 'aims' and 'purposes', though their rights are acknowledged, often in a token way, through devices like 'school councils' which play a small part in the day-to-day management of some primary schools. It may be seen as impractical or unrealistic for primary school children to contribute to policy-making, but their views can be gathered and can inform policy through research. Teenagers, as recent recipients of primary schooling, might be consulted long before they become parents. Children's voices are destined to be heard more and more into the next century.

Aims and Purposes for the Twenty-first Century

As we pass the millennium, so the 'great reform' of 1988, compromised and modified as it may be, will still be the statutory root of our education system. Accepting this fact, we might adopt the wording of section 1 as a framework for our aims and purposes. What can our primary schools reasonably aim to achieve under each of these headings?

Spirituality

Least tangible but most holistic of our aspirations for young children must be the development of their spirituality, however defined. Cultivation of the soul, of self-knowledge, of the higher faculties must be as devoutly wished as it is difficult to define. OFSTED inspectors look for evidence of 'awe and wonder' (often, apparently, in vain). Awe and wonder might be inspired by the hugeness of the universe, the ineluctable processes of nature, the mysteries of creation or evolution, the complexity of the mind or the amazing achievements of human beings. An ever accelerating advance in frontiers of knowledge and technology appears set to characterize the next century and our children will need the inner resources of the spirit to cope with the demands this progress makes.

What this means in practice, and how it is to be achieved in school, remains contentious and hugely challenging, but plurality of answers and solutions must itself be an aim for education. Our primary schools must embrace the cultivation of traditional faiths alongside the continuing search for new resolutions to questions of self and identity.

Morality

The promised scientific and technological progress will in turn pose moral dilemmas for individuals and society in the twenty-first century. Biological engineering, globalization of communication and trade, military conflict and the movement of peoples on an unprecedented scale, climatic and ecological change all have moral implications. One aim of the primary school must be to equip our children to deal with these big issues as well as with the more local problems of interpersonal relations and relationships within the community.

Research on the cerebral processes of interaction between reason and emotion offers one new signpost. Daniel Goleman's enormously popular work suggests strategies for the learning of 'emotional intelligence'. Primary schools must provide a secure environment in which morality can be practised. Examples can be set, but children must also experience some degree of control, there must be room for experiment and for mistakes to be made as well as for conflicts to be resolved. Primary education must aim not simply to preach but to provide a laboratory for the practical development of moral behaviour.

Culture

Morality can only be developed in practice on a foundation of understanding and knowledge about culture. Societies organize themselves in a fascinating diversity of ways. Family structures and the arrangement of everyday living are a part of culture. Political and legal arrangements are an extension of this, as is organized religion. Symbolic practices such as religion, music, dance and the visual arts express aspects of daily life and belief. Babies from their first days of life are socialized and initiated into the cultural practices of their family and immediate community. Starting school is a rite of passage which formalizes progress into a wider world, and the aim of school must be both to reinforce the cultural development already begun and to extend the horizons of children towards an awareness and understanding of other cultures.

Historically, state schools have served as places of containment where compulsory schooling was a form of control aimed at ensuring political stability. In some sense that purpose is still served by the transmission of a hegemonic culture, but geographical mobility and cultural diversity have presented a new context for this process as our schools enter the twenty-first century. As national boundaries become less relevant, so the concept of 'national culture' becomes more suspect. One aim of the school must be to help children come to terms with a diverse world in which contrasting cultures coexist within the same society. This complex task begins by encouraging curiosity about, and respect for, different cultural practices, a matter of attitude as well as of knowledge.

Mental Development

Literacy and numeracy have been high on the agenda of public and political debate about primary schooling since the 1970s. This concern, sometimes bordering on panic, had its roots in economic recession and an apparent decline in standards. The development of literacy and numeracy is perhaps the most easily identifiable purpose of the primary school, traditional in the sense that it dates back more than a century to the beginnings of state schooling. (Many other factors than formal schooling, however, contributed to the growth of a literate and numerate population, and in the same way declining literacy, such as it is, has a far more complex explanation than just poor teaching or 'failing schools'.)

Few would argue that the promotion of literacy and numeracy remains a central purpose of primary schooling, but we need to explore the rapidly changing contexts in which these skills are deployed as we enter the twenty-first century. The impact of mass media and electronic communication on children's lives means that conventional forms of reading are not the exclusive gateway to knowledge. Visual literacy and computer literacy must accompany the ability to decipher print. In everyday life and in employment, the requirement of language skills is subject to change. The growth in the service sector of our economy and the rise in automation have resulted in an employment sector that requires a higher proportion of literate workers. Bureaucracy and marketing have put a premium on communication skills. Developing oracy remains a crucial purpose of primary schooling. Here, our transition to the twenty-first century in Britain needs to address the ever wider range of spoken languages which children bring to school from home. The purpose of primary school in relation to oracy and literacy remains that of developing confidence and skill in communication, in accurate and imaginative use of language. In numeracy, likewise, the contexts are changing. Vital mathematical skills range far beyond mere numeracy, and the occupational needs for these skills are changing continuously. Continuing rapid developments in information techno-logy imply the need not just for skills in using state-of-the-art software and hardware, but a flexibility of approach and new ways of thinking about the future.

The so-called foundation subjects of the National Curriculum are as sub-ject to change as other aspects of mental development, and impinge on the categories of spiritual, moral and cultural development already discussed. Con-ceptual understanding and information retrieval now have greater priority than the acquisition of 'useful knowledge' and the knowledge deemed to be useful is also changing. The creativity, flexibility and adaptability already identified as desirable objectives of intellectual growth, are qualities likely to be cultivated through the expressive arts.

Physical Development

The physical needs of children aged 5 to 11 are easily overlooked in discus-sions about the purpose of primary schooling. Physical development means so much more than agility and sporting skills, important as these may be to an increasingly sedentary population in the next century. Universal and compuls-ory schooling has turned schools into a convenient agent for intervention in public health, the entire child population being accessible in a way that must be the envy of economically poorer countries. A minimal level of medical and dental inspection is one aspect of this, but personal, social and health educa-tion requires a much broader canvas. Increased awareness and knowledge of child abuse, and the ever younger age at which children become sexually active promise to create a continuing demand for sex education. Needs will vary from one geographical area to another, from community to community. Child poverty is sufficiently widespread for some primary schools having to supplement the diet of needy children and school meals, as in Japan, may become more important as a vehicle of dietary training for the majority.

Preparation for Adult Life

'Preparation for adult life' a distinctive aim, in the terms of the 1988 Act, is loaded with ideological significance. 'Understanding the world of work' has been an obsessive aim of legislators for education ever since the Great Debate of 1976. The context then was panic concerning educational effectiveness and economic productivity, against a perceived inclination for teachers to consider primary education as an end in itself, a space for natural development of the individual child rather than a preparation for anything else. The utilitarian response hardened during the Thatcher years, when Sir Keith Joseph advocated schooling as a means of promulgating the principles of free market economics.

Spirituality, morality, cultural, mental and physical development, all add up to a preparation for adult life. We can rest assured that personal fulfillment of the individual and a reflective and tolerant adult society are every bit as important to our future as a healthy GDP. The problem with the latter lies in the need to prophesy. Who will predict with any certainty the employment needs of our current primary children as they enter the world of work c.2010?

Conclusion

The millennium for primary schools is a threat as much as a promise. We have glimpsed already the repressive potential of a brave new world, presented as a scientific solution to the inadequacies and failings of past practice. Centralized curriculum and standardized testing, to be followed in short order by foolproof teaching materials? Small wonder, then, that our aims might be coloured by nostalgia for the good old days. In an idealized past, the child and not the curriculum was at the heart of education, diversity and variety were to be encouraged.

In all forums of debate, national, local, political, parental and professional, the power of the past and fear for the future haunt our discussions. There are personal and political grounds for the stance we adopt, depending on our individual experiences of success or failure in this or that system of schooling on the one hand, and on the other our conception of society and the way it works. We observe and try to see some pattern in developments around us — social, technological, economic and political, and predict what our needs as a society will be.

Hence, detailed prescription for the twenty-first century would require a good mixture of foresight and educated guesswork. More important than getting the details absolutely correct, however, is the way in which aims and purposes are discussed. There are four points to be made.

First, a clear set of aims for primary schooling needs to be made more explicit. Consensus will be elusive, but a heightened consciousness of *purposes*, more open debate and awareness of ideologies embedded in statements of aims is needed. The recent White Paper must be a starting point for study with its insistent emphasis on 'the global economy', 'human capital', 'a dynamic and productive society'. Of course there is acknowledgment of 'wider goals', but not with the balance or priority accorded in section 1 of the 1988 Act. Public debate and consultation should embrace not just the means, but the ends of education, and the latter should be freed from political and professional dogmatism.

Peter Cunningham

Next, we need a *genuine* picture of what parents want for their children. Parents can be consulted and involved at local and at national level; parental representation could be stronger on LEA committees and key bodies such as any future General Teaching Council could include lay membership. Primary schools can benefit from the closer involvement of parents in the earlier years of their children's development, and many do now actively recognize the role of parent as coeducators. Parent governors and public meetings are in place, and home–school contracts are likely to be imposed but these mechanisms should allow too for an open and honest discussion of aims at the school level.

Thirdly, children themselves need to be consulted, and here research is the appropriate medium. Circle times and classroom discussion, school councils and assemblies can provide forums for discussion about aims and purposes within the school environment. On a wider scale, over the years, children's opinions and feelings about their schools have occasionally been researched, but much more needs to be done and more weight accorded to its findings.

Finally professional knowledge, wisdom and experience have an important contribution to make to the formulation of aims. A General Teaching Council offers the possibility of a recognized platform for professional opinion, distanced from the self-interest that has become associated with teacher unions. At the individual level, some teachers at least need the time, space and training to reflect and to engage in fundamental research, an aspect of provision that has been lost in the drive for cost-cutting and more mechanistic reforms.

Aims are not fixed for all time, but change with the times. Our focus should be more on mechanisms for continual review and reflection, than on determining an ideal and definitive set of aims.

References

ALEXANDER, R. (1995) *Versions of Primary Education*, London: Routledge.
ALEXANDER, R. et al. (1996) 'Discourse, pedagogy and the National Curriculum: Change and continuity in primary schools', *Research Papers in Education*, **11**, 1.
CULLINGFORD, C. (1991) *The Inner World of the School: Children's Ideas about Schools*, London: Cassell.
CUNNINGHAM, P. (1988) *Curriculum Change in the Primary School since 1945: Dissemination of the Progressive Ideal*, London: Falmer Press.
DFEE (1997) *Excellence in Schools* [Cm 3681], London: HMSO.
GOLEMAN, D. (1996) *Emotional Intelligence: Why It Can Matter More Than IQ*, London: Bloomsbury.
McFARLANE, A. (ed.) (1997) *Information Technology and Authentic Learning: Realising the Potential of Computers in the Primary Classroom*, London: Routledge.
NIAS, J. (1989) *Primary Teachers Talking: A Study of Teaching as Work*, London: Routledge.
POLLARD, A. (1985) *The Social World of the Primary School*, London: Cassell.

Part 2

*Providers and Promoters:
The State and Its Schools*

3 Primary Education: The State and Its Agencies

Sir Malcolm Thornton

The argument about whether the state, that is to say, the population as a whole, should provide an education service for all children was won more than a century ago. The debate that continues is about the length, content and degree of uniformity that should characterize that provision and the levels at which responsibility and control should be exercised. Two consequential issues relate to resourcing the service and to the formation of judgments about its nature and effectiveness. No central Government and no Parliament could properly abdicate its responsibility for the service but, equally, neither must suppose that the service should be set in stone, identical for each child either at a time or over time. One of the most corrupting myths to excise is that there is one ideal way of doing things. The task is not simply to improve the efficiency of the service but to adapt it to different and changing circumstances. Recent years have seen a much more overt interest by central Government in the detail of the service, notably in seven connections:

(i) the introduction of the National Curriculum for schools and the periodic assessment of children's performance;

(ii) the establishment of OFSTED with the purpose of checking on the effectiveness of individual schools and, now, of local authorities;

(iii) the training of teachers, including the establishment of the Teacher Training Agency and a National Curriculum for teacher training;

(iv) the introduction of the local management of schools and changes in the status and functions of schools and local authorities;

(v) provision for the increased involvement of parents and others locally in the government of schools;

(vi) the increased integration of pupils with special educational needs into mainstream schools;

(vii) provision for the under-5s.

Of course, these things were heralded long before they were enacted; indeed, so far as the last is concerned and despite a long period of public pressure, we have not yet reached the stage of enactment. The Schools Council of the 1960s and 1970s was an attempt to involve teachers, local education authority officials and representatives of the central Government in opening up and modifying the curricula of schools to suit the changing requirements of a modern technological society. The Assessment of Performance Unit, led by the DES but involving many outside it, was designed to report, through sampling, on the capabilities of children particularly in English, mathematics and science. Even that had its predecessor in a series of national surveys of the reading skills of children of 11 and 15 that began in 1948.

It is not often recognized that the House of Commons Select Committee[1] Report published in 1986, *Achievement in Primary Schools*, was highly significant in the introduction of a National Curriculum. It recommended that there should be:

> a change in the law so as to require the Secretary of State to issue from time to time guidance on the curriculum and to introduce a requirement upon local education authorities, governors of county, controlled and special schools to consider the Secretary of State's curricular policy in the process of determining the curricular policy of the LEA or school. (House of Commons Education, Science and Arts Committee, 1986, para 14.50)

The then Secretary of State, Kenneth Baker, came to the Select Committee following that Report to say that he intended to introduce a Bill proposing a National Curriculum. It was not, however, quite in the form that the Select Committee had had in mind. The latter had proposed that the Secretary of State's curriculum proposals should be:

> in broad and simple terms . . . framed to apply to secondary schools as well as to primary schools . . . such that they would not require the Secretary of State, for this purpose, to enter into the more difficult issues of children's performance. Nor . . . require him to establish precise definitions of what should be taught in, for example, history; or how a lesson should be presented; or how a school organized. It does not include a prescription for a timetable. We believe that timetabling and the detailed content of the curriculum are best left to individual schools and their governors. (ibid, para 14.40/51)

The enacted National Curriculum was, and is, very different from what the Select Committee envisaged except that it does not, as yet, prescribe the timetable or school organization. It was, and despite revision still is, far more detailed subject by subject; and it certainly involves the Secretary of State in 'the difficult issues of children's performance'.

Whether one or either view was right is not the main consideration here. What is of interest is that from the first national reading survey of 1948, the central Government was inescapably concerned with what was taught in schools and was, one way or another, influencing what was taught. It was, after all, disappointment with the mean reading scores of 11 and 15-year-olds in the 1970 and 1971 national reading surveys that led to the setting up of the Committee of Inquiry chaired by Sir (now Lord) Alan Bullock into the teaching of English (DES, 1975).

The matters for debate, of which the establishment of a National Curriculum is an illustration, are the extent to which the central Government should:

(i) *define an educational system* that should operate nationwide;
(ii) establish an *accounting system* by which it may learn how well the system is operating, both in terms of its current objectives and in the light of changing circumstances;
(iii) and determine what *resources* are necessary and how they should be provided.

The Definition of the National Education Service

As is clear from the earlier paragraphs, there are a number of aspects to this issue. A first relates to the individuals that the service is to include. So far as this book is concerned, the concentration is on children up to 11 or 12 and it understandably leaves almost entirely to one side children of secondary school age, younger and older adults, though Governments cannot do so. A second concerns the definition of what the children should be taught. A third concerns the establishments through which the service should be provided: for example, to what extent should a school provide for all the children within reach of it without limits on their ages or educational requirements? A fourth raises questions about the delegation of responsibilities within the system: is it necessary to establish only two levels, the central government and individual schools, or are some intermediate structures also required, for what, and in what form?

Who Should Be Included?

It should be remembered that until fairly recently, some children were designated as being ineducable. Now, thankfully, none are and the debate has turned to the question of where children with special needs should be educated, an issue that will be returned to later. For the part of the age range that concerns us here, the running issues are: at what age must children enter the national education system and at what earlier age might they, if their parents wish.

The compulsory starting age of 5 years is early compared with almost all other countries. The only serious proposal to raise the age was by the Plowden Council which proposed a median age of 5 years 6 months, but with nursery provision, part-time for most, available before that. The Council's report (CACE, 1967) is an example of the work of a Government agency, in this case of the Central Advisory Council, set up under the 1944 Education Act. This form of Agency was replaced by specific committees of inquiry such as the Bullock Committee, mentioned earlier, the Warnock (special education) and Cockcroft (mathematics) committees that were set up later. It is worth noticing how often these initiatives were started when one political party was in power and reported under another.

The action arising from reports seldom precisely matches what their authors propose. That is true of the Plowden Report, not least in connection with the provision of nursery education, despite quite intensive and sustained lobbying and a wide acceptance that provision is desirable. The case was accepted by Margaret Thatcher when she was Secretary of State for Education, as is shown by her White Paper, *Education: A Framework for Expansion* (DES, 1972) but was thwarted, among other things, by the oil crisis of the mid-1970s, a point to bear in mind when considering resourcing the system. The debate continues and has been of considerable interest to the Select Committee, which has consistently advocated the expansion of *suitable* provision for under 5s (House of Commons Education, Science and Arts Committee, 1989). Its disquiet has been that an increasing number of under 5s have been admitted to ordinary reception classes without adequate staffing, space or suitable material resources. The Committee has been satisfied that the compulsory age of entry to school-ing should not be lowered. Nor has it challenged the idea that, for the great majority of children of pre-school age, provision should be for only a part of each school week.

The inescapable conclusion is that there is wide agreement, across the political parties and beyond, that it is desirable to provide nursery education for children — certainly between 3 and 5 and possibly from 2 years of age — whose parents/carers wish them to have it. There is continuing debate con-cerning the extent to which that should be embedded within social care so covering more hours and more days per year to provide support for families where the adult or adults are all in paid employment. How much should be paid for from public funds; how much should be provided directly by the state and how much bought in from commercial or voluntary providers? There is another issue that has run through the debate: if it is regarded as impossible to provide for all under 5s — either for the present or for the foreseeable future — should some receive priority? The common view, from the Plowden Report onwards, has been that children living in social deprivation should be the first recipients of provision and that raises the general issue that an expansion of provision may well have to be gradual: too great a leap may make the added cost unacceptable to the population at large and stimulate claims for other kinds of expenditure. Too sudden a leap may also put an intolerable strain on the means of meeting other requirements created by the leap — for example the supply of properly trained staff, or the provision of buildings. Few of us would be satisfied that the Plowden Council's targets for nursery education have still not been met but it should not be supposed that satisfying them is a simple matter of will.

What Should Be Taught and How

The implication of a national education service is that the mass of the popula-tion should be taught something beyond that which people generally could be expected to learn in the course of ordinary family and community life. The questions that flow from that are: to what extent is what should be taught, i.e. the curriculum, the same for everyone; to what extent should the definition of the curriculum be made overt nationally and how far should it be left to common or local practice, unspecified nationally, though possibly with some persuasion from the national Government?

The 1988 Education Reform Act strongly shifted the position from non-specification towards specification. It was not intended that the National Curriculum introduced by that Act should be the whole curriculum of schools, but it soon seemed that there was hardly time for what was included let alone anything else, and the Dearing revision was instigated with the intention of providing more time for local preferences. The Select Committee became concerned very early on with the teaching of reading (House of Commons Education, Science and Arts Committee, 1991) and, later, with the teaching of science and technology in schools, particularly in Key Stages 2 and 3 (House of Commons Education Committee, 1995a). The first note at the end of this chapter draws attention to the importance of consultation in the work of a Select Committee. It is equally important to recognize the importance of prior consultation when a Government embarks on the process of changing the law, whether primary legislation or the various requirements, through Statutory Orders, based upon that legislation. The formal process of consultation that is intended to lead to a new Act of Parliament is triggered by the issue of a White Paper. Of course, it has usually been preceded by, and is followed by, a considerable amount of informal consultation. The questions that have to be answered are whether the purposes are desirable and whether they are achievable by the means proposed. There can be hardly anyone who would not wish to see the education service improved, though there is much more room for debate as to what the nature of the improvement should be. There is certainly room for argument as to whether the current resources are sufficient in volume and kind to carry through the proposed changes. It may not be sufficiently appreciated that the law, as enacted, is as binding on the Government as it is on the rest of the population, and the Government cannot, or at least should not, escape its responsibilities in enabling the system to conform to the law.

It is an open question whether Governments and their agencies, including such activities as the Dearing review, are sufficiently responsive to the results of their consultations. It is a rare change of law that would satisfy everyone, and especially so in such a complex matter as the education of the population. Different sections of the community have different interests and priorities, and that applies even among those employed in the education service: in nursery schools or classes, primary schools, secondary schools, further and higher education of all sorts and between subject interests. Yet the Government has a duty to act in what it understands to be the best interests of the nation as a whole: to do nothing may be the worst solution.

Is that true of methodology and the timetable? It can be very difficult to separate what is taught from how it is taught. For example, if it is agreed that children should be taught to use their initiative, then there is an implication that teaching must go beyond simple instruction. Nevertheless, it is probably true that most politicians would not wish to be very prescriptive about how teachers should do their jobs. Too much depends on the circumstances of the time and the particular attributes of the teacher and children concerned. The Government does have a right to question whether what it intends shall be taught is being taught.

It also has a duty to do all it can to ensure that what it wishes to be taught can be taught. That is the justification and the necessity for, for example, the direct funding of in-service training to improve the likelihood that there would be at least one teacher in each primary school capable of advising his/her colleagues in the teaching of science as defined in the National Curriculum. In intention and in practice, the detail of what such courses should cover is best decided by those with experience in the teaching of young children, including teachers, teacher trainers and inspectors.

The Kinds and Types of Schools: Age Ranges

The issue of the kinds and types of schools that should be provided is more complex and more contentious at the secondary than at the primary stage. For the latter, the issues are about the best age ranges for such schools, about the degree of inclusion of children with special educational needs, and about the degree to which such schools should be 'self'-governing.

So far as the first is concerned, the solution depends as much on location as it does on other factors. For that high proportion of primary schools in villages and small towns, the creation of separate schools for Key Stages 1 and 2, to say nothing of separate pre-schools, would be undesirable in terms of the total sizes of the schools and impractical in terms of the new buildings required. There has been a trend towards combined nursery, Key Stage 1 and Key Stage 2 schools in urban areas, and if the total size is not over-large, or if the separate stages can be given a sense of identity, then the combination has advantages. What would be a pity, nationally, would be if all separate nursery or KS1schools disappeared. In the past and today a good many of these have given the lead in the education of children of the relevant ages, partly because the staff is able to concentrate its attention on the relatively narrow age-range and partly because those especially interested and experienced have been appointed to the senior posts. But decisions about the age-ranges of nursery/ primary schools are much better left to the local community, usually acting through its LEA. Too much depends on local circumstances for the decisions to be taken nationally unless the Secretary of State has to act as an arbiter to decide between local differences of opinion — a role that he or she may have to assume in connection with other local disputes, including some between parents and a school, a school and an LEA, and between parents and an LEA.

Despite taking in a full primary school age-range, a significant minority of schools are small, justifying the appointment of only two, three or four teachers. A good many witnesses to the Select Committee have argued that those numbers are too few, in isolation, to meet the demands of the National Curriculum. Any system of additional support must be specific to the local requirements and should be arranged locally.

The Kinds and Types of Schools: Special Educational needs

Even during recent years, when the central Government was inclined to divest local authorities of some of their duties, the latter have continued to have a particular responsibility for provision for children with special educational needs. During the same period, there has been an increasing agreement that all children should be regarded as educable and that as many as possible, more than formerly, should be educated in mainstream schools. There are part-way arrangements, as for example special units attached to mainstream schools.

Two factors that militate against the admission of all children to mainstream schools are:

(i)   the extent and type of special need(s) may require such special provision (including specially trained staff) that it cannot reasonably be supplied wherever the nearest schools happen to be — the difficulty may be that the special need is relatively rare, or even that it requires hospitalization;

(ii) the extent and type of special need(s) may be such that they would make it difficult to provide reasonable circumstances for the other children in the same teaching space.

The consequences are that a school or unit may have to be provided to meet the needs of children wherever they live in a local authority area or even that a school has to provide for children from a number of local authorities. The central Government must ensure that provision is made and it may need to promote cooperation between local authorities or between them and voluntary or other providers. This role of forging links is no different in principle from that of a school in ensuring that the different classes and departments within it act in accord, or the local authority's role in ensuring that the different schools form a unified system, whether of the same Key Stage or between Key Stages. One aspect of coordination that too often proves difficult at both local and national levels is the establishment of effective policies and arrangements between different departments, for example education and social services.

The Delegation of Responsibility and Local Variation

The previous paragraphs have indicated the case for a national system of education with local variation. Some of that variation is local to a school, some to a local authority and some, for example in the case of a minority of children with special needs, regional. They have also pointed to the need for cooperation between parts of the service which may have to be codified, stimulated and refereed from outside of the parts involved. The delegation of responsibility should reflect those variations, recognize that local knowledge may be more sensitive than a bureaucratic decree, but at the same time make plain the limits within which the sub-groups may operate.

If this argument is right, then it supports the local management of schools, a significant place for local authorities, and a substantial responsibility and overarching function for the central Government.

The important roles of parents were underlined by the Plowden Report (CACE, 1967) and reemphasized and extended by the Taylor Report (DES, 1977). The election of parent-governors has helped to represent their interests and knowledge in the conduct of a school. That is not to say that they will always be the best judges of what the school is doing, and some have been surprised by a contrary view to theirs being formed by visiting teams of OFSTED inspectors: the parents may know too little of what other schools do. Nevertheless, they have undoubtedly brought a new dimension to governing bodies and have as often acted as representatives of schools to parents as vice versa. They may also know rather more than OFSTED inspectors of the long-term practices of a school and its impact upon individual families.

It seems a natural extension of the idea of involving parents that they should have the right to choose the school that their children should attend. It is a principle that has proved difficult to adopt in its totality, and the rights of parents to choose have been balanced by the practice of schools and local authorities to establish criteria by which some applicants are accepted and others not. The criteria have had to satisfy the requirements of the central Government but these have not prevented difficulties in localities where some children have been left unplaced as late as the summer holiday before transfer to secondary school. It is at least arguable that the coordination of transfer from primary to secondary schools, and possibly admission to primary schools, should be overseen by the local authority and not delegated direct, as in the case of grant maintained schools, to the school.

Inherent in this notion of parental choice is that different schools suit different children. It is not and should not be a simple choice between schools that are more or less effective, but also between schools with different characteristics. For example and obviously, are they single-sex or mixed? Does one offer courses in uncommonly taught (though commonly spoken) languages? Is one especially well resourced in the teaching of design and technology? By definition, no individual school can be responsible for providing this variety and local authorities, sometimes in combination, are best placed to encourage the variety under general guidance from the central Government.

One less obvious example of the importance of particular schools developing a special expertise may be in educational provision in some inner city areas. This is an issue that exercised the Select Committee in its 1995 report

(House of Commons Education Committee, 1995b) which drew attention to the local support required by schools in such areas, not only by the education welfare service, and the dangers of allowing a school to slip into a downward spiral. A national cycle of inspections is not sufficient. Nor should it be assumed that all schools in inner-city areas have the same requirements. Some may be in pockets of affluence. Some may cater largely for children from a single language and cultural background, in some places English and in others not. Some may encompass a great mix of languages, religions and cultures. While national guidelines must allow for this variety, the specific response has to be local.

The Accounting System

The accounting process for the education service has a number of aspects, some formal and others more informal.

Children talking to their parents; parents talking to each other and to teachers and their elected representatives all contribute to the accounting system. So do teachers talking to parents, to each other and, usually through their associations, to elected representatives. When Members of Parliament and Prime Ministers interest themselves in an aspect of education, it is as likely to be through the effects of these relatively informal processes as because of any more formal process. It is also true that the media play a part, particularly because they are so often attracted to specific issues that might touch chords in their readers. A danger in the informal system is that the picture formed may well be untypical, and action taken on it alone will have adverse effects on other aspects of the system. Hence the need for more formal arrangements. Currently, the major formal process is that undertaken by OFSTED, with its cycle of inspections of individual institutions. It should not be forgotten that there is also a continuing process of educational research.

In the longer run, increasing self-confidence in all schools to operate under local management may further affect the relationships between schools and local authorities with the effect that the former develop a still stronger sense of independence and the latter greater objectivity about the schools in its area. If that shift does occur, then it may be better if OFSTED were to become a coordinator and stimulator of local authority inspection services on the one hand and, on the other, advisor to the Government on codes of inspection. One important national issue that needs further thought is the balance, in inspection, between exercising judgment of effectiveness and providing advice and support for improvement. There does exist a channel of communication between OFSTED and the Teacher Training Agency on the effectiveness of teacher training institutions, but — especially with the introduction of a National Curriculum for teacher training — more attention may need to be paid to improving the advice on the suitability of national requirements regarding teacher training as the contexts change within which schools work. Educational and possibly other research also has a part to play in this. Whatever views are reached, it is for Parliament to express them in the form of national policies and requirements.

Resourcing the System

Funding

From a Government point of view, the education service is one of a number of competing claimants. Changes of funding can only be obtained through (a) increased revenue from taxes either because rates are increased or as a result of improved general prosperity; (b) shifting resources from one service to another; or (c) shifting resources within a service. The pressure for change comes from a Government's own political stance with regard to education; the pressure and persuasiveness of public opinion; professional feedback about the effectiveness and aptness of the current arrangements. In each of these three groups there are likely to be different opinions about what should be done. Each group has to pay attention to the level of funding, and it is important that the first two, the Government and the public, do not require of schools more than their funding can bear.

One of the Select Committee's jobs is to examine and report upon the expenditure plans of the Government department that it shadows (for example, House of Commons Education Committee, 1995c). In 1994 it also produced a report on the disparity of funding between primary and secondary schools (House of Commons Education Committee, 1994). It listened to evidence from 11 groups or individuals (including twice from DFE) and took written evidence from 139 individuals, schools, local authorities, associations of teachers, and parents' groups. It noted that 'secondary school pupils are funded at 40–50 per cent above the rate for primary school pupils' and concluded that that balance of funding did not properly represent the different requirements of the two sectors. There needed to be a shift in favour of primary schools especially to increase staffing levels so that subject and other coordinators could be given the opportunity, during pupil-hours, to monitor and support the work of colleagues (MAST). The shift should come about by dividing new money coming into the education system unevenly between primary and secondary schools in favour of the former. Some movement has taken place, but there is still a long way to go. A sufficient change will be made only if the political will is strong, for competing claims will continue to be pressed. Indeed, even when the funding balance is redressed, will the extra money be used for the purpose that seemed a priority to the Select Committee? How far should it, or the Government, or a local authority, tie the money it provides to a specific purpose, and how much should be left to a school to decide?

The issue occurs in other forms. It is only comparatively recently that the central Government has earmarked grants for in-service training. How far should it require not only that these funds should be used for in-service training but also what subjects or issues should be covered? How far should the central Government insist that money it calculates is required by a local authority for education must be spent on education? To put it another way, is the present disparity of educational spending from one local authority to another justifiable, having taken special factors into account, for example the extent of social deprivation, the proportion of children for whom English is not their home language, or the scattered nature of the population? The politicians must each fight their own corner, and they can do so effectively only if they are well informed, not simply barracked.

Providing the Teachers

It is no accident that the last Select Committee Report (House of Commons Education and Employment Committee, 1997a) to be produced under the previous Government and the first (House of Commons Education and Employment Committee, 1997b) under the present concern the status, training and recruitment of teachers. The central Government has had an important and direct part to play in the provision of teachers for many decades. It has often, as now, been especially concerned to provide sufficient numbers to replace those leaving and to match the changing numbers of children to be taught. The teacher training institutions have probably experienced more upheavals in their form, status and practices than any other part of the education system. The continuing professional development of teachers has also been subject to change, but principally in the process of growth. New requirements are emerging in the form of qualifications for headteachers and the notion of advanced skills teachers.

Some of the current issues can be dealt with within the education service, as managed by the Government and teacher trainers, both in schools and in institutions of higher education. The National Curriculum for teacher training will need to be adapted as it turns out to be more or less practical and as the context and functions of schools change. The Teacher Training Agency has worked hard at consulting the training and schools communities and that effort needs to continue and become still more effective if suitable teachers are to come into schools. Equally, the profession must look sufficiently attractive to younger and older potential entrants if it is to interest them. Of course, the pay and terms of service must be sufficient, but there is no doubt that teaching has been unfairly diminished by the public statements that have been made about it in recent years. Politicians must accept their share of the blame for that, but so must OFSTED and the media.

We urgently need to improve the status of, and public respect for, teachers by giving proper weight to the good, effective and imaginative work that they do. Perhaps that is as important a task for Government as determining what should be taught, to whom, and how. One possibility is the formation of a General Teaching Council (GTC) through which some control of the membership of the teaching profession is exercised. Quests for a GTC have taken a century and a half, 'a century of aspiration followed by a generation of disappointed initiatives', as noted by the Select Committee in 1990. A GTC would be solely concerned with the qualitative aspects of education. Bargaining over conditions of service and pay, or discussion with Government about current or proposed legislation, would remain the province of the teachers' associations and those representing parents, governors, local authorities and others. The GTC would not of itself, for example, have a view of the curriculum; it would have a view on the competences needed to deliver it and the code of conduct which the public and the teachers themselves would expect. It is to be hoped that this long-overdue reform will soon be achieved.

Note

1   The term *Select Committee* will be used in this chapter to refer to the House of Commons, all-party, back-bench committee that is established by the House to shadow the Government department that has responsibility for the education service. As the Government department's responsibilities change, so its name and the Select Committee's name and responsibilities change; sometimes it has included arts, sometimes science and, currently, employment. A Select Committee chooses its own subjects of enquiry; it invites evidence from anyone with an interest in the subject and seeks additional written and/or oral evidence from whomever it chooses, including the Secretary of State; it makes visits in this country and abroad that seem likely to add to its knowledge before deciding on its report to the House of Commons, including what recommendations it wishes to make. It does not, of course, command what the Government of the day should do; only Parliament as a whole can do that.

References

CENTRAL ADVISORY COUNCIL FOR EDUCATION (ENGLAND) (1967) *Children and Their Primary Schools* (The Plowden Report), London: HMSO.

DES (1972) *Education: A Framework for Expansion* (Cmnd 5174), London: HMSO.

DES (1975) *A Language for Life* (Report of the Committee of Enquiry chaired by Sir Alan Bullock), London: HMSO.

DES (1977) *A New Partnership for Our Schools* (Committee of Enquiry chaired by Thomas Taylor), London: HMSO.

HOUSE OF COMMONS EDUCATION COMMITTEE (1994) *The Disparity of Funding between Primary and Secondary Schools*, London: HMSO.

HOUSE OF COMMONS EDUCATION COMMITTEE (1995a) *Science and Technology in Schools*, London: HMSO.

HOUSE OF COMMONS EDUCATION COMMITTEE (1995b) *Performance in City Schools*, London: HMSO.

HOUSE OF COMMONS EDUCATION COMMITTEE (1995c) *DFE's Expenditure Plans 1995–96 to 1997–98*, London: HMSO.

HOUSE OF COMMONS EDUCATION AND EMPLOYMENT COMMITTEE (1997a) *The Professional Status, Recruitment and Training of Teachers*, London: HMSO.

HOUSE OF COMMONS EDUCATION AND EMPLOYMENT COMMITTEE (1997b) *Teacher Recruitment: What Can Be Done?*, London: HMSO.

HOUSE OF COMMONS EDUCATION, SCIENCE AND ARTS COMMITTEE (1989) *Educational Provision for the Under Fives*, London: HMSO.

HOUSE OF COMMONS EDUCATION, SCIENCE AND ARTS COMMITTEE (1991) *Standards of Reading in Primary Schools*, London: HMSO.

4   The Organization, Management and Culture of Primary Schools

Geoff Southworth

Despite a decade of legislated reforms which have altered the character and tone of primary education, as organizations primary schools remain relatively unchanged. In this chapter I want to argue that primary schools as organizations now need to develop a blend of change and continuity. I will suggest that the class teacher system of primary school organization should be retained because its advantages for pupils continue to outweigh the disadvantages. However, there also need to be some changes in the way schools are managed in order for the disadvantages of the system, both for teachers and pupils, to be overcome. These changes in management and leadership should, in turn, help to develop an organizational culture of achievement which better serves the pupils and better supports the teachers and other members of staff. In outlining these changes I also suggest that the organization, management and culture of schools should reflect three sets of principles — learning, improvement and person centredness.

Primary School Organization

The most notable and important feature of primary schools as organizations is the class teacher system of organization. Under this system the total number of children in the school are divided into classes of pupils. Usually this is done by age, so that children of the same age are grouped together. However, in smaller schools, or those with uneven numbers of children in each year's intake, children are often grouped together in mixed-age classes. In some cases it is school policy to have mixed-age classes. However classes are formed, each is then allocated one teacher who teaches that class for a school year and, in some schools, often for longer. The principle of one teacher per class of children has a long tradition in this country and remains a constant in primary school organization.

The class teacher system has many advantages. The teacher has enough time with the children to get to know them well and they to know the teacher. The majority of children have, until they enter school, experienced a safe, continuous relationship with their parents or guardians and find the continuity of relationship with their teacher reassuring. For those children who have not experienced a continuous relationship with parents, such a relationship with a teacher can, to some extent, provide additional security. Moreover, the teacher can during the school year observe individual pupils' progress across the curriculum and identify their achievements and learning needs. The teacher, being responsible for all the class's work, can directly ensure that the whole curriculum is balanced and that time is used differentially to meet individual children's needs, interests and achievements.

There are also some disadvantages to the class teacher system of organization. If the teacher is generally ineffective or does not get on well with one or more children this can inhibit or impede the children's progress for a school year, or longer. If the teacher is absent then there can be some disruption to the programmes of work the children are following unless very careful arrangements for continuity have been established. The demands of the National Curriculum and the legal requirement for pupils to be taught in 11 subject areas, means that every primary teacher is expected to be knowledgeable in all these subject areas. This is a very heavy expectation. Inevitably no one teacher is equally good in all subject areas of the curriculum. Therefore, the curricular demands sometimes mean that some teachers are teaching a subject in which they do not feel very confident or knowledgeable.

Moreover, the nature of teaching to different age cohorts of pupils also varies. The content, pace and level of challenge needed for teaching a class of 6-year-olds are not the same as those for 11-year-old pupils. As teachers change age groups and gain experience of teaching the full primary pupil age range they must also develop their expertise and knowledge in dealing with the demands and needs of different age groups of pupils. This takes time to achieve and means that some teachers will be working with classes whose learning needs they are still exploring and coming to terms with.

Over recent years the demands placed on class teachers have undoubtedly increased, principally as a consequence of the introduction of the National Curriculum and new assessment procedures at the end of each key stage. Schools have generally responded to these demands not by increasing the number of teachers and reducing class sizes, but by swelling the number of classroom assistants (or learning support staff as they are sometimes called). These helpers are usually not qualified teachers and offer individual help to pupils, particularly those with identified special needs. While such classroom support reduces some of the demands on the teacher they do not alleviate the curricular challenge.

Some schools have supplemented class teaching by introducing other organizational patterns. Setting has been introduced in many schools. Here children of similar ability in a single subject area are grouped together for a teaching session during each day. Such an arrangement is common for mathematics and English. Some schools also make use of specialist teaching by 'buying in' someone to teach science or technology. This may be a limited and partial arrangement, confined to half a term and to pupils in years 5 and 6. Some headteachers also teach particular sets of pupils, such as a more able group of pupils for mathematics or science. It should not be overlooked that much of this supplementary grouping of pupils tends to focus on the core subjects (English, mathematics and science).

An exception to this focus on the core subjects is music. Often the teaching of music is done by a member of the teaching staff who has the ability to play a musical instrument, usually the piano but increasingly guitars and other instruments as well. Often this music teaching involves the teacher visiting other classes to teach them and the class teachers taking charge of the music teacher's class. In this way there is some interclass teaching and the pupils have the opportunity of working with another teacher. For some children there may also be opportunities for additional instrumental tuition if the school chooses to buy-in peripatetic instrument teachers (string or brass instruments being the more common ones) who are employed by the LEA or an agency. Where groups of children work together with such a teacher on, say, learning to play the violin or trumpet, then it is true to say the school sets some pupils for music.

Given its long tradition and enduring nature the class teacher system looks set to continue. Indeed, I think it should. It is the backbone of primary schooling and its advantages are considerable in that pupils are provided with a system of pastoral care, year-long academic support and continuous development of the pupils' learning across the whole curriculum. Yet, if it is to continue, some of its disadvantages for both pupils and teachers should be given greater attention than at present. Furthermore, this attention becomes increasingly important as the drive for school improvement accelerates.

If the class teacher system of organization is to provide high quality teaching and learning and continuous improvement then the way schools are managed has to be reconsidered. In particular, the nature of school leadership should be rethought and the organizational cultures of primary schools refined and developed.

Guiding Principles for School Management and Organization

Before looking at school leadership and culture I want briefly to outline three principles which I think should guide any attempt to redefine primary school management and culture. These principles are:

- learning
- improvement
- person-centredness

The principle of learning means that all organizational structures and processes should contribute to enhancing the learning of pupils and staff alike. Management procedures should be scrutinized to check whether and how they enable learning. Regular evaluations of the use of time, meetings, resources and staff development events should occur to see how far these favour learning. Indeed, management should not be seen as a job in its own right, but as a means to furthering the quality of teaching and learning across the whole school. This includes focusing on and advancing pupils' learning, but it also involves developing the skills of *all* members of staff — teaching staff, support staff, administrative, welfare and cleaning staff and volunteers who contribute to the work of the school. The organization, management and culture of primary schools should strive to make them *learning schools for all*.

The principle of improvement builds upon the principle of learning. Primary schools today are self-managing organizations having their own budgets to manage. They are also expected to be self-improving schools. Of course, schools have always been changing but today improvement has become an imperative. Moreover, improvement has also become both process and outcome oriented. It is no longer sufficient for staff in schools, or the school governors, to claim that the school is getting better. These claims need to be supported and validated in some way. This might be by reference to the targets which the school has set itself and which can be shown to have been met. The school's development plans over a two or three-year period may also show how it has improved aspects of its work, as might the school's post-inspection action plans.

Senior staff also must show that they are tracking levels of pupils' achievement and progress over time. Already many schools are using baseline indicators and year-on-year test data to record how pupils are making progress and to monitor whether curricular initiatives the school has implemented are raising standards of achievement. Primary school management has entered a new phase where staff are beginning to conduct evidence-based analyses of the school's performance and, in the light of them, identify improvement priorities and formulate and implement action plans.

Much of this sounds highly instrumental and hard edged. While a measure of this may not be bad thing, it is important to link it to the first principle of learning. Improving primary schools needs to be understood as a learning process. Schools will not improve unless staff develop professionally themselves The growth of teachers needs to be a major element of school management. Unless teachers and headteachers are growing professionally it is unlikely the school will be improving. Therefore, improvement priorities and action plans need to be aligned with staff development activities so that the school can learn its way forward. Some of this will involve in-service activities and off-site course work. Much, however, will require increased opportunities for learning with and from colleagues *in the school* and where all of this can be orchestrated schools will become learning and improving organizations.

The third principle, person-centredness, celebrates the fact that schools are human and social organizations. Walk around any school and what you see most are people — children, parents, teachers, support staff. Unlike some businesses or factories where you might see machines, computers and technology being operated by one or two persons, in schools you are always confronted with people. Schools are therefore full of subjectivity; feelings and affect abound. In the course of a day in school you encounter laughter, smiles, frowns, worries as well as occasional tears and arguments. Schools are full of people and are loaded with feelings. Schools therefore have to be managed in ways which are sensitive to persons. Children and staff alike must conduct themselves with courtesy, consideration for others and mutual respect.

A recent encouraging feature in many primary schools is the increasing interest in pupil councils where children raise, discuss and seek to resolve the issues and challenges they meet in the school, be it unfair rules, dull playgrounds or poor provision for them when it is a wet playtime or lunchtime. Student councils encourage pupils to participate and to play an active part in managing their own affairs.

At the same time those who exercise leadership need to do so ethically. Schools are not only places where children are taught subjects, they are also places where children learn about living with others in an organized setting. Hopefully they will learn that organizations can be positive settings and that the rules and principles of procedure serve the interests of all, rather than a privileged few. School leaders need to try to ensure that the school is a community which is moral and where the children and the staff work and live in ways consistent with democratic ideals and social justice. The moral and social impact of schools and how they are organized and operating should never be underestimated nor overlooked.

With these three principles in mind I shall now turn to considering leadership and the organizational cultures of primary schools in order to suggest how they might be conceived to better serve primary education and to enable the class teacher system of organization to meet the challenges of today and those of the future.

Leadership

Several studies during the 1990s have shown that one consequence of the educational reforms of the late eighties and early nineties has been an intensification of the work of teachers and headteachers. The task demands of primary heads have increased considerably with the introduction of local management of schools (LMS), open enrolment, increased responsibilities for school governors and the implementation and management of the National Curriculum. All of these changes mean that there is now more to manage at the school site than ever before.

At the same time, the inspection of schools, the publication of school results and the use of league tables to chart schools' levels of performance have meant that headship has become much more visible than formerly with a much sharper sense of school accountability becoming the norm. Schools are no longer closed institutions, they are open to the potentially critical gaze of parents and the community.

The surge in accountability and the increase of management tasks means that many heads feel they have less time to provide the necessary professional leadership of the staff and the school. Many feel they are caught up in chief executive activity at the expense of the time they previously had available to lead colleagues in developing the quality of teaching and learning across the school.

These problems are especially acute in schools of median size (between 150–250 pupils) and in smaller schools. Here budgets are tightly constrained and there are few or no economies of scale. Therefore heads have taken on many of these additional management tasks and responsibilities themselves, largely because there is no one else to delegate them to and not enough money in the school budget to pay for someone else to do them. Yet if heads have taken on more of the chief executive tasks themselves, they have begun to share out some of their professional leadership to others.

The task demands placed on headteachers have caused many, if not most, to involve colleagues more and more in the schools' leadership. This is certainly true in terms of the role of deputy heads. Many deputies see themselves as forming a management partnership with their headteacher and some have been redesignated as assistant heads. In some schools there has also been the introduction of senior management teams (SMT), which have enabled the head, deputy and senior teachers to meet regularly, to review how the school is progressing and to determine what needs to be done.

The involvement of more staff in the management and the leadership of the school helps to develop a stronger sense of shared leadership. Several studies over the past 20 years have shown that the leadership of the headteacher is an important factor in making the school more effective. Yet, in some primary schools heads have remained the sole leader in the school. They have remained pivotal, powerful and proprietal figures in 'their' schools. They may not have been autocratic figures, but they have nevertheless been preeminent and, sometimes, have become a dominating force in the school. Consequently, they have overshadowed their deputies and senior colleagues and inhibited their opportunities to lead.

On occasions and in some circumstances there may still be a case for the head to be the central player and for them to provide strong leadership in such a monopolistic way. However, now that they also have many more things to attend to, it seems unlikely that heads can continue to lead as heads did 20 or so years ago. Nor should we expect heads to lead their schools into the future while facing backwards and trying to lead as heads did in the past. The nature of school leadership needs to be further developed and become more inclusive than formerly.

This means that leadership should be devolved to colleagues and that heads should try to play a less direct role in certain areas, while exercising leadership in some others. Effective headship in this sense means increasing the effectiveness of all the other school leaders.

Subject coordinators today are playing an increasingly important role in managing the curriculum. This is an area of considerable progress in schools and is one which should be sustained and further developed. In particular, coordinators need to offer direct support to their colleagues, draft school policies, ensure there are appropriate schemes of work to guide the work of all teachers and monitor the curriculum in action. Monitoring involves coordinators looking at how the school's policies and schemes of work are being implemented, ensuring that the statutory requirements of the National Curriculum are being met, looking at samples of children's work and reporting back to the SMT and/or headteacher as well as offering to all teacher colleagues a termly or annual progress report on their subject.

In some schools these coordination tasks are undertaken by a pair of teachers working in partnership. This reinforces shared leadership, often allows teachers from key stages 1 and 2 to work together and provides peer support for one another in the pair.

In the light of all this monitoring there should be some evaluation. Monitoring is only the collection of information. What happens when the information has been gathered in is more important. This is one of the key areas where heads and deputies should be directly involved. In a sense this is not something heads should delegate to others. They might wish to share it with others and involve them, but heads should always be party to the analysis and evaluation of curricula and pupil learning data.

Heads will also need to provide the time for coordinators to monitor. Many heads do this by releasing coordinators from class teaching (since almost all coordinators will also be class teachers and some will be coordinators for more than one subject area or aspect of the school's work) and teaching the coordinator's class for them.

However, heads also need to do some monitoring of the curriculum themselves. Many do this informally, as part of their tours of the school, or when they meet informally with teachers after school. I used to advocate that heads undertake MBWA, that is management by wandering about. Today I would redefine MBWA to mean monitoring by wandering about. Several heads I know regard the time between the end of the school day, when the pupils leave and up till 5.30 p.m. as the period when they can go out and talk with teachers about how their day has gone, what the teaching and learning have been like, enquire how certain pupils are progressing and demonstrate a keen and sustained interest in classroom matters.

There are, of course, limits to how much monitoring can be achieved informally and there now should be formal systems for monitoring. Here heads might themselves take in some samples of children's work and see what they can detect about pupils' learning outcomes and progress. They should also show a strong interest in pupils' test results and teachers' reports and use these data to monitor standards, achievements and progress.

The essential point of all this monitoring and evaluation is not to create a climate of fear in the school, nor to imply that teachers are underperforming and need to be checked up on. Rather, it is to try to secure a purchase on what the pupils are actually gaining from all the teachers' hard work and effort. It is intended to show not only what teachers think is happening, but also what can be seen to be happening from examining a range of indicators alongside class teachers' perceptions and professional judgments. Monitoring is the means of collecting various types of evidence to inform analysis and action planning.

There are two other points to highlight about leadership in today's schools and those of tomorrow. First, much of this monitoring will show which teachers are teaching well and in which particular subject areas. A major drawback of the class teacher system and the design of many schools, is that it isolates teachers. Teachers work on their own with their respective classes of children. They may be accompanied by one or more classroom assistants, but they rarely teach alongside another teacher. Therefore, they are independent workers. This often creates the circumstances where teachers do not know what other teachers are doing. Monitoring by coordinators can begin to crack the walls of such private practice and the resulting peer observation can increase dramatically knowledge of how others teach. Where individual teachers are talented and skilled in a particular subject area, or have ideas and approaches worth sharing with colleagues, there is greater likelihood of this happening when staff visit one another and observe each other at work. In other words, monitoring can become a vehicle for increasing awareness about colleagues' professional skills, can be used to reduce the inherent isolationism of the class teacher system in cellular designed schools and can create opportunities for staff to support one another.

Second, in addition to monitoring the curriculum in action and pupils' learning, the quality of teaching should be monitored and evaluated. This seems to me to be a task for the head and the deputy and, perhaps, key stage leaders where they are used. Although heads can and should delegate leadership to many others, I think heads should keep their fingers on the pulse of teaching in the school. They ought to preserve time to observe their colleagues teaching, to talk with them about what they have witnessed, to celebrate the skills and craft of teachers and to consider development opportunities for them. Heads should continue to play a central role in monitoring and evaluating and developing teaching in the school.

Together all of this means that teachers and headteachers will be conducting classroom focused, school-based action research. They will be enquiring into what is actually happening around the school and inside classrooms and all members of the teaching staff have a part to play in this. It will be largely a matter of peer observation and support. The head, deputy and/or SMT may take a lead in collating and analysing some of these data and may report back to all the staff and offer their interpretation of the data. Yet, because much of this monitoring and evaluation involves all the coordinators and, probably, all of the teachers, the process will be an inclusive one. It will also support shared leadership since, over time, everyone will play their part and take a lead. All will be expected, over time, to work outside their classroom and beyond their class group. In this way, knowledge of the school's progress and performance can be shared and everyone can comment and contribute to framing the school's improvement priorities.

While the sharing out of leadership to colleagues adds to teachers' responsibilities, providing these are carefully apportioned they should not become too onerous a burden. For sure, support and time will be needed and heads and governors need to look at this provision each year. However, on balance, the advantages should outweigh the disadvantages. Shared leadership reduces reliance and dependence on the head, increases knowledge and awareness of other colleagues' professional skills and expertise, and creates a context where the talents and ideas of staff can be spread more widely among them. In short, rather than being a collection of individuals who happen to teach alongside one another, the staff become a *combined teaching unit*.

Such a sense of teamwork will better serve the pupils. It will also contribute to establishing and sustaining a particular type of school culture which I want to consider in the next section.

Organizational Culture

Research into the organizational cultures of primary schools shows that when staff are willing to work positively together a culture of collaboration can be established (see Nias et al., 1989). Subsequent research however, shows that while the existence of a collaborative culture is a necessary condition for school improvement, because it creates trust, security and openness, these are not sufficient conditions for school growth. For growth to take place, at the level of either the individual or the school, teachers must also be constantly learning. Therefore, the challenge for staff in primary schools, and for those who support them, is to establish a culture which facilitates teacher collaboration whilst, at the same time, enabling teachers to learn from each other and from courses outside the school. The presence of both these factors will enable professional discourse, sharing and challenge to occur in a climate of trust and openness, thereby ensuring that the risks and discomforts of professional learning are counterbalanced by mutual support and a concern for individuals (see Nias et al., 1992).

Other studies in North America largely support these findings. The characteristics associated with 'moving schools', a notion equivalent to improving schools, include shared school goals and teacher collaboration which, in turn, contribute to higher levels of teacher certainty and commitment and which support teacher learning and pupils' learning. Moving schools are learning-enriched work environments for staff members and such workplace conditions lead to enhanced pupil learning processes and outcomes (see Rosenholtz, 1989; and Fullan, 1991). In other words, where there is a judicious blend of teacher collaboration, a sense of staff unity (but not uniformity), professional enquiry, reflection and evaluation and both peer support and challenge then schools are more likely to improve and prosper.

These findings are not abstract ideals because they are already happening in some schools. From such schools we can learn that in practical terms staff groups need to advance from establishing a culture of collaboration to what might be called a '*culture of achievement*' (see Loose, 1997). A culture of achievement involves staff conducting evidence-based analyses of pupils' achievements and progress and of the quality of their teaching. It means leaders developing systems of monitoring as discussed previously. Indeed, a culture of achievement will embody all that was discussed in the previous section.

However, I want to return to one of the points raised under leadership and amplify it here. This point concerns the idea that headteachers and deputies should monitor the quality of teaching across the school. At present there is little evidence of this happening in large measure in many schools. While currently it is the weakest aspect of monitoring, I believe over the coming years it should become a much stronger emphasis.

Primary school improvement needs to be understood as developing the quality of teaching in classrooms, alongside examining pupils' achievements and progress. Unless monitoring in a school includes an examination of teaching, teachers are unlikely to make many, if any, developments to their classroom practices. Yet, unless teachers develop as classroom practitioners schools are unlikely to improve (see Southworth, 1996). Some schools may apparently improve but perhaps only insofar as they can 'jack up' pupils' test scores. There will not be sustained and real gains in schools' levels of performance unless and until there is a concerted effort inside primary schools to create the workplace conditions and organizational capacity to support and develop pedagogy. In short, improvement efforts in primary schools should focus strongly on developing teachers as classroom practitioners. The development of primary schools hinges on enhancing the knowledge and skills of teachers as *teachers*.

The strong emphasis I am placing upon teaching arises not because I believe primary teaching is poor, but because the teachers' role is challenging and complex. Dealing with 30 or so individual children, for most of the school day and teaching them all of the National Curriculum subjects, plus any number of other social and moral topics, is an immense task. It means knowing and understanding, at conceptual and practical levels, about child development, human learning, individual differences and special needs. It also requires teachers to understand the structure of subjects, the essential features of subjects as disciplines of knowledge and the content to be taught in all subject areas. It also means that teachers have to develop a range of pedagogic skills and a repertoire of teaching strategies. Initial teacher training plays a vital role in preparing teachers but we should recognize, more than we sometimes do, that such training is only what it is described as — *initial and preparatory*. Once teachers embark upon their full-time teaching careers, they must continue to develop as teachers. It is for these reasons that I advocate their continuing pedagogic development as a priority. Moreover, I believe this development of teaching should be more formal, systematic and explicit than previously and that it should largely be school-based.

In terms of the principle of learning discussed earlier this translates into creating learning schools in which teachers learn about their teaching with and from one another, and improve their pedagogy. It means that as part of learning about their teaching, teachers also develop one another's classroom skills, share their craft knowledge and discuss their professional understandings about teaching and learning in primary schools.

While some of this may go on informally and as part and parcel of staff discussions and activities arising from their monitoring, classroom observation and evaluatory enquiries, I now believe the improvement of teaching should be organized and workplace structures and systems developed to ensure that it happens by design rather than by accident. Importantly this means enabling teachers to help one another directly. Peer assistance should not simply be restricted to advice and the trading of teacher tips, it should embrace focused and planned discussions among teachers, the sharing of explanations as to how each teaches a subject and why, and to staff coaching one another.

Peer coaching offers many opportunities for teachers to learn from one another. If a colleague lacks confidence in teaching a subject or wants to improve their skill and understanding in a particular teaching strategy (for example, questioning, use of praise), it makes sense for another colleague, who is experienced in these matters or has a strong interest in them, to work alongside them and help them to develop. Coaching does not necessarily mean telling colleagues what or how to do things, but it does mean developing an enabling partnership which attends to pedagogic concerns and matters.

While some of this goes on informally between critical friends in a few schools, I feel that the time has now come for schools to begin to experiment more systematically with such an approach. With the advent of self-managing, improving schools it seems to make sense that headteachers, senior staff and governors begin to consider how the school as a workplace can be set up for on-the-job coaching and learning about pedagogy. Some of this will need to be nourished by in-service activities and off-site workshops, but first and foremost, the establishment of learning schools needs to incorporate staff learning about teaching. Moreover, the notion of an achievement culture needs to encapsulate teachers achieving more as teachers and for their pupils.

Clearly, an organizational culture should be established and sustained which supports such activities. There needs to be formal and informal teacher interaction and sharing and staff must be able to manage their classroom independence with staffroom interdependence. There will have to be opportunities for teachers to visit one another and observe one another. Increasingly these should be sharply focused on specific aspects of teaching which pairs and groups of teachers want to improve. Sometimes external consultants, advisers and inspectors may be involved to enrich the work or to provide a 'third party' perspective.

When such arrangements take root and blossom in schools so that they become taken-for-granted and professionally natural activities to engage in, then one of the major disadvantages of the class teacher system, namely that teachers not only work on their own, but are left entirely alone and their development as teachers is largely left to chance, will be removed. This, in turn, will mean that pupils will be better taught because their teachers are better supported and better equipped to meet their learning needs.

Conclusions

These ideas while based upon existing practice in a few schools combine to form a new agenda for the development of primary school leadership, management and organization. They build upon some of the valuable developments already under way in schools, but more than this, they will, if implemented, eventually transform the nature of primary school cultures and contribute to the improvement of our schools. The organization, management and culture of primary schools should be restructured so that they become self-managing and improving communities of learners. Learning, both the pupils' and the staff members' professional learning, should be at the very heart, at the core of the organization, management and milieu of primary schools.

References

Fullan, M. (1991) *The New Meaning of Educational Change*, London: Cassell.

Nias, J., Southworth, G. and Campbell, P. (1992) *Whole School Curriculum Development in the Primary School*, London: Falmer Press.

Nias, J., Southworth, G. and Yeomans, R. (1989) *Staff Relationships in the Primary School: A Study of School Cultures*, London: Cassell.

Loose, T. (1997) 'Creating a learning culture', *Managing Schools Today*, **6**, 8, pp. 33–5.

Rosenholtz, S. (1989) *Teachers' Workplace: The Social Organisation of Schools*, New York: Longman.

Southworth, G. (1996) 'Improving primary schools: Shifting the emphasis and clarifying the focus', *School Organization*, **16**, 3, pp. 263–80.

5   Primary Changes

Colin Conner

In our journey into the future, primary schools will have a vital part to play . . . The success of future adults to ride with confidence the waves of continuous change they will undoubtedly experience, will depend to a greater extent than in the past on the nature and quality of their earliest experiences in the schooling system. Our primary schools are a vital key to the future. (Whitaker, 1997)

Introduction

If there is anything that we can say with confidence about the future, it is that we can say very little with confidence. Over 20 years ago, Toffler (1971) suggested that the world was changing at a rate never previously experienced and that if we did not learn to both control and cope with such changes it could lead to the breakdown of society as we know it. More recently, Levin and Riffel (1997) have argued that,

It is a truism to say that we live in a world of change. Indeed we are bombarded with messages about the pervasiveness and importance of changes in our natural, social, economic and technological environments. (p. 6)

If this is true then schools have an even more important role than in the past to prepare children for this world of uncertainty. How far the primary school currently does this, and how far it might be able to do this for future generations is the subject of this chapter. It opens with a discussion of the primary school of the recent past, considers the situation at present and attempts to predict what might be appropriate for the future. Like Ebeneezer Scrooge in Charles Dickens' *A Christmas Carol*, primary education is influenced by the past and the present and this is likely to have a considerable impact on how primary schools respond to the future.

The Ghost of Primary Past

The recent past of primary education is an interesting one as other chapters in this book testify. To many, primary education has been seen as a hotbed of liberalism and to some visitors to this country as a source of inspiration. For example, the American writer, Charles Silberman (1970), described his experience of visiting British primary schools in the late 1960s,

> . . . in schools organized on the basis of informal schooling 'the joyfulness is pervasive'; in almost every classroom visited, virtually every child appears happy and engaged. One simply does not see bored or restless or unhappy youngsters, or youngsters with the glazed look. (pp. 228–9)

There were just as many British advocates for the kind of primary school described here. Alec Clegg, the Chief Education Officer for the West Riding of Yorkshire, identified the characteristics typical of the schools that Silberman would have visited in a pamphlet entitled, 'Revolution in the British primary school', published in 1971.

> In such schools children no longer sit in rows facing the blackboard; the teacher gives formal lessons less frequently; learning is based on experiences rather than subjects; children work at their own pace on topics they choose from 'a range carefully prepared by the teacher' so that the 'integrated day has superseded the day cut up into subject times'; spelling lists and mechanical sums are now rarely used; the teacher encourages pupils to seek knowledge themselves rather than telling everything; there are few set books and more individual books and resources.

In spite of indications to the contrary, Clegg added,

> There is no doubt that the change in English primary schools is a momentous one. Our primary schools at their best, are models of the kind of social communities in which we would all wish to live.

It was this spirit of optimism and enthusiasm that was captured and advocated by the Plowden report of 1967 with its famous dictum that 'at the heart of the educational process lies the child'. Subsequent research, however, suggests that this supposed enthusiasm for child-centred practice was some way from reality and that primary schools tended to be rather traditional places and therefore that the potential of primary schools to change in the light of circumstances was limited.

In 1972, Bealing surveyed a sample of primary teachers in two local education authorities in the Midlands. This study provided some evidence of teachers adopting and adapting some of the ideas associated with progressive primary practice, but also found that the teachers still retained a relatively tight control over the curriculum and class teaching was still the dominant strategy. Bealing concluded,

> Some of the results . . . question widely held beliefs about the 'primary school revolution'. Despite the relatively informal classroom layouts adopted by the vast majority of teachers there was so much evidence of tight teacher control

over such matters as where children sit and move that it seems highly doubt-ful that there is much opportunity for children to choose or organise their own activities in most classrooms. (p. 235)

These findings were confirmed by subsequent research, in particular, the ORACLE (Observational Research and Classroom Learning Evaluation) project based at the University of Leicester from 1975–80. An important outcome of the project was the extent to which.

> . . . teaching was found to be largely didactic in character. The promotion of enquiry or discovery learning appeared almost non-existent . . . Collaborative group work or enquiry was also found to be seldom realised . . . Further, as regards the content of education, a major emphasis on 'the basics' was found. One-third of normal teaching sessions was devoted to number work, or mathematics, one-third to language (the great bulk of which time was spent on writing), and one-third to general subjects, topic and project work, art and craft and science . . . Certainly there was little evidence of any fundamental shift either in the content of education or in the procedures of teaching and learning, in the sense that didacticism still largely prevails. (Simon, 1981, pp. 23–4)

Understanding Change

What does this tell us about the propensity of primary schools to change? It certainly confirms the suggestion made earlier that schools are conservative places. It might also suggest that teachers are sensibly cautious about innova-tion, in that they are not prepared to sacrifice their children's learning at the expense of a current fad or whim. It also suggests that to change practice is considerably harder that might initially appear. This leads us to a discussion of the change process in educational contexts. Levin and Riffel (1997) suggest that school systems do not have adequate processes for learning about, under-standing and developing responses to change in the wider society. Instead schools tend to rely on extensions to existing practice rather than taking a long-term strategic approach in responding to new challenges and problems. To do this they need to understand the change process more clearly. Louise Stoll and Dean Fink (1996) draw upon the work of Fullan (1992) and others to produce a list of some of the central characteristics of the change process:

- There is never one and only one version of what the change should be. It is important for everyone involved to be able to share their experience and understanding and as a result to develop and change the initial proposals if experience suggests that this is appropriate.
- People need to understand the proposals and to work out their own meaning. Changes in teachers' behaviour are more likely to occur before changes in their beliefs.

- Change is a highly personal experience. This reinforces a point made by Drummond and McLaughlin (1994) that for adults as well as for children, learning is as much an emotional activity as it is a cognitive one.
- Change is approached differently in different contexts. Innovations need to be sufficiently flexible for schools to adapt them to their own circumstances and situations.
- Conflict and disagreement are inevitable. This is natural and if it isn't occurring, Huberman and Miles (1984) suggest it is likely that not much is happening.
- A combination of pressure and support is necessary. All of us need help and encouragement when learning something new and a little push on occasions to make sure that it happens.
- Change rarely involves singular acts. It is often the case that a number of different things will be happening at the same time. Sarason (1990) describes this as a 'rippling effect', changing something in one way leads to changes elsewhere.
- Effective change takes time, therefore persistence is essential. It has been argued that even small-scale change can take between three and five years, whilst more complex restructuring may take much longer.
- A school cannot always be developing otherwise it runs out of steam. This suggests an important role for school leaders. i.e. the change process has to be managed and controlling overload is essential.
- There are many valid reasons why change does not take place. It is not just resistance on the part of more recalcitrant colleagues.
- It is not realistic to expect everyone to change. There are often perfectly justifiable reasons why some teachers are unable to adopt to a proposal, often because of lack of knowledge or experience.

Gustavson (1955) recognizes, however, that most of us are,

> . . . afraid of drastic innovations, partly because (we) prefer the familiar, and partly because the vested interests of most people are normally bound up with the existing set up. Added to the weight against change is what might be called an institutional inertia, a proneness to keep the machinery running as in the past unless strong pressure for change materializes. (p. 72)

The extent to which these claims about change reflect reality as far as primary education is concerned was put to the test with the introduction of the National Curriculum from 1989. The requirement to introduce a National Curriculum and its associated assessment structure,

> . . . imposed changes which were in fundamental conflict with the values and deeply held beliefs held by many teachers . . . The Education Reform Act of 1988 and the processes of multiple change which followed it . . . highlighted

strongly the debate over the professional role of teachers with regard to the formulation and implementation of educational policy. (Osborn et al., 1997, p. 52)

The Ghost of Primary Present

The imposition of more central control in education is something that has been occurring in many countries in recent years. As Helsby and McCulloch (1997) comment,

> Faced with the restructuring of world economies, the growth of global markets and the accompanying political uncertainties, many of the advanced industrial nations have looked anew at the role of their educational systems in producing both the compliant citizenry and the skilled and flexible workforce deemed necessary to ensure social stability and economic success in the twenty-first century. (p. 1)

Whilst the governments of countries like Sweden, Denmark and the United States have elected to introduce change gradually, recognizing the importance of the characteristics of the change process described above, the British government adopted a much more aggressive stance,

> . . . involving minimum consultation, strong prescription and draconian systems of assessment and accountability. (ibid., p. 2)

This process has led many to suggest that teachers were being deskilled which was a major change in post-war government policy where there had been a strong tradition of teacher autonomy and limited governmental influence. A number of recent research projects have attempted to monitor the reaction of primary teachers to this imposed change, the most extensive of which has been the Primary Assessment, Curriculum and Experience (PACE) project. This project has studied the primary school experience of a national sample of the first group of children to have experienced the National Curriculum. The researchers involved in this project recognized that the decision to implement a National Curriculum,

> . . . imposed changes which were in fundamental conflict with the values and deeply held beliefs of many primary teachers . . . The Education Reform Act of 1988 and the processes of multiple change which followed it, . . . highlighted particularly strongly the debate over the professional role of teachers with regard to the formulation and implementation of educational policy. There were fears that the changes would deskill teachers and reduce them from being professionals exercising judgment to mere classroom technicians. (Osborn et al., 1997, p. 52)

The findings from projects such as the PACE project provides useful evidence of the ways in which primary teachers and primary schools respond to change and offers an indication of their propensity to cope with the changes required in the future.

A number of studies of National Curriculum implementation confirm that primary teachers have accepted and internalized the National Curriculum, but that they work in ways that relate to their beliefs about effective primary practice, that allows them to protect children and in some cases to be very creative. A good example of this creativity can be found in the study of a primary school in Cambridgeshire. In her case study of this school, Debbie Jack (1996) argues that the most common form of curriculum delivery in many primary schools has been through some form of thematic approach, the ubiquitous 'cross-curricular topic'. This she recognizes has been the subject of justifiable criticism, not least from the 'Three Wise Men' (1992), with their vehement condemnation of such primary practice,

> Over the last few decades the progress of primary pupils has been hampered by the influence of highly questionable dogmas which have led to excessively complex classroom practices and devalued the place of subjects in the classroom. The resistance to subjects is no longer tenable. (Alexander, Rose and Woodhead, 1992)

Jack describes the way in which the school that was the subject of her investigation attempted to create a curriculum framework which still retained the principles of primary practice that were agreed and accepted by the staff but at the same time fulfils the requirements of the National Curriculum. It was intended that the nature of individual subjects should be respected, the individual creativity of teachers should be permitted and above all the needs of the children should be met. The framework that was developed was called 'the modular curriculum'. The staff focused initially on science, geography and history and attempted to construct a set of themes that established appropriate links between the prescribed content. Where links were not possible the content would be taught separately or through focused 'experiences'. The headteacher at the school suggested the model as one way of 'regaining control'. Jack (1996) concludes,

> The modular curriculum is by no means the remedy of all curriculum-delivery ills. But for a school that believes the child is the centre of teaching and learning and that a teacher should be given the freedom to be creative and have ownership of the curriculum they deliver, the modular curriculum fulfils all these needs and any statutory requirements brought about by the new National Curriculum as well. (p. 43)

This example confirms the findings of the PACE project that many teachers have become skilled manipulators of the requirements of the National Curriculum such that their principles and beliefs are reinforced and sustained. Osborn et al. (1997) suggest that their findings indicate that teachers have adopted a range of 'coping strategies', from

> . . . compliance (complete acceptance), through incorporation (fitting the changes into existing means of working), mediation and retreatism (dropping out of teaching without any fundamental change in values) to resistance. (Osborn et al., 1997; Pollard et al., 1994)

The PACE team suggest that teachers have become what Osborn describes as 'creative mediators', filtering change through their own values. The project identified several different versions of 'creative mediation'. The 'protective mediators' are particularly concerned to protect children from external pressure such as assessment and the vastness of the National Curriculum. They emphasize the need to protect their relationships with children and maintain their ability to respond to the children's interests even if this does not comply with National Curriculum requirements. A second version of mediation is described as 'innovative mediation' and is illustrated by the case study described above. Creative and innovative ways of implementing the framework is central to this approach along with the facility to go outside the National Curriculum framework when it is felt necessary. This approach includes

> . . . the ability to make choices, to be adaptable and flexible, to see alternatives, although working within constraints and to have the confidence and motivation to put values into practice. These teachers were able to resist pressures to become technicians carrying out the dictates of others. They worked hard to create new ways of working with children which were exciting and lively and yet covered what were perceived as important parts of the National Curriculum. (Osborn et al., 1997, p. 60)

One of the benefits of the National Curriculum is the effect it has had on the ways teachers now work together. There is increased evidence of 'collaboration' and the PACE researchers describe this as another category of mediation. Osborn and Black (1994) found that classroom teachers began to make their own informal arrangements to mediate the effects of an overloaded curriculum. This involved teachers exchanging classes or the teaching of certain activities on the basis of their own confidence. As one junior teacher put it,

> If someone likes doing something or has a particular interest you should give them a chance. There is no place now for prima donnas. You must work with others. If you don't share ideas, planning and practice you will go under. The teacher who can't share is no longer a good teacher. (quoted in Osborn et al., 1997, p. 63)

In a small number of the PACE schools, collaboration has become somewhat more 'conspiratorial' where teachers see themselves as working together to implement the curriculum selectively and in a way they felt protects children by, for example, electing not to teach a particular part of the curriculum because it did not fit in with the school's plans.

There is other evidence, however, of the positive effects of the National Curriculum and its subject specific expectations. In a complementary but contrasting study of the effects of participation in a course to improve teachers' knowledge and confidence in teaching the geography component of the National Curriculum, Conner (1997) found that teachers learned new ways of doing things that extended their previous practice and by implication added to the expertise of the participating teachers. Continual reference to the importance of increased knowledge permeated the conversations with the teachers who participated on the course. As one participant commented,

> The course increased my knowledge of the subject and it has made me more confident as regards planning and evaluation. I am now, I feel, presenting the subject better and with more enthusiasm.

Other gains were emphasized by the teachers. For example a headteacher, who was also a course participant, talked of the effect of the course across the school as a whole. A central element of the course was a focus on geography as an 'enquiry based subject', a subject that can be organized around the questions that geographers ask. He argued that,

> . . . the most important development I think was the development of an enquiry based approach throughout the school, which we didn't do at all before. Geography tended to be very book-based and now all of our work involves geographical investigations, using the questions that geographers ask as the basis. Where is this place, why is it like it is, how is it changing, what might it be like to live here, how is it different to other places etc. It has led to a major change in the way that geography is taught and it has begun to influence our teaching in other areas of the curriculum.

The majority of the participants had a very limited background in geography, and even though a number did have some competence, there was a common suggestion that it changed their perception of the potential that geography brings to children's learning in the primary school. One of the teachers reinforced this when he said that geography is a subject that,

> . . . is accessible to all and that given a chance it can engage children's interests and passions. Most children of this age group feel passionately about the environment and geography gives them the facts and a focus. They care about the rights of people and issues like conservation and geography should be at the centre of such studies.

Another teacher suggested that geography has more relevance than she had previously realized and argued that it should have equal status to science,

Developing children's understanding, knowledge and appreciation of their own environment and that of others in the world beyond is relevant to children now and in their future to be able to live in harmony with others.

This stress on the importance of the future leads us to the next question which concerns the extent to which the strategies and practices which have been discussed here are appropriate for the demands of the future.

The Ghost of Primary Future

It was suggested earlier that it is not possible to predict the future with confidence, Neils Bohr, the famous physicist, once wrote that prediction is difficult, especially of the future and as Whitaker indicates,

> One of the characteristics of the modern world is that the predictions we were once urged to rely on, no longer work. It is increasingly difficult to tell our children what they can expect in their lifetimes. (Whitaker, 1997, p. 8)

This has not stopped a number of writers from attempting to offer possible proposals, however. For example Halpin (1996) suggests that schools can opt for one of two directions, 'they can imitate a particular version of the past' or 'they can engage with and anticipate change through innovation and risk-taking'. Robert Reich, writing in '*The Work of Nations*' in 1992, argued that in future there will be four main requirements of the educated individual. According to Reich, everyone will need to know how to conceptualize problems and solutions using at least four basic skills:

- **Abstraction:** the capacity to identify patterns and relationships and to construct meaning.
- **Systems Thinking:** the ability to see links between ideas and phenomena.
- **Experimentation:** the ability to go beyond the information given and construct new understandings, to try new and different ways of doing things.
- **Collaboration:** the ability to work with others as a member of a team, to learn with and from each other whether it be peers, a significant other or the teacher.

He suggests that formal education as it is currently conceived, 'entails just the opposite kind of learning'. Whitaker believes that primary teachers and primary schools are well placed to respond to Reich's suggestions and to opt for Halpin's risk-taking strategy.

Their work has always had a significant element of spontaneity and unpredictability about it and at their best they use their wits in a way that belies the complexity of the context in which they are managing. (Whitaker, 1997, p. 9)

Others, however, argue that it is the basics that need improving in primary schools not creativity, suggesting that, 'we had enough of that during the liberalism of the pre-National Curriculum era'. Evidence from comparisons with other countries suggest that we are falling behind our competitors in terms of educational achievement. In these arguments, the task of schools is seen as being to prepare children to fill an economic role. The future prosperity of our society is claimed to be critically dependent on how well schools fulfil this task. Does this matter? Is this the responsibility of primary schools? Alan Wells, Director of the Basic Skills Agency, certainly believes it does matter and that primary schools have an important role to play.

It should be fairly obvious to everyone why basic skills are important . . . Jobs that don't need good communication skills are few and far between and, even where they exist they're usually the most insecure jobs in the changing job market . . . Life's about more than work though and just as important is the impact on the individual . . . many individual adults in our country are unable to provide much help for their children when they come home from school . . . research indicates that adults who have poor basic skills are much more likely to have children who struggle with these same skills at school. Breaking this cycle is a major task for primary education in particular. (Wells, 1996, pp. 35–6)

There is of course much debate about what 'basic skills' actually means. It need not imply the basics of literacy and numeracy. Charles Desforges (1992), for example, argues for the development of skills that are transferable and applicable beyond schooling and into the real world of home as well as work. It is also the case that many industrialists argue for a broad range of competences from the education system. As Black (1995) points out,

Whilst industrialists stress the importance of literacy, numeracy and of science and technology they also add critical thinking, the need to be able to learn new skills, the ability to work in groups, decision making and willingness to take risks and exercise initiative, curiosity and a sense of service to the community.

Whilst the basic skills that Wells was referring to tend to focus on those of literacy and numeracy, Thompson (1996) has recently suggested, that we are at the threshold of a revolution which will effect the way we all learn. Information technology is widely seen as a change in society to which schools must respond and as a development that has tremendous implications.

> ... not since the invention of the 'modern' printing press over 500 years ago, has anything happened to rival the dramatic development in new communications technologies and their potential to influence positively the way we all learn both as individuals and as organizations. (p. 44)

The potential of information technology for improving learning, however, has, not yet been fulfilled. What Cohen (1987) described as 'extravagant hopes of easy revolution' has been followed by a 'steep drop into dreary disappointment.' David (1992) suggests that this is not surprising,

> The primary reason technology has failed to live up to its promise lies in the fact that it has been viewed as an answer to the wrong question. Decisions about technology purchases and uses are typically driven by the question of how to improve the effectiveness of what schools are already doing — not how to transform what schools do ... Moreover, as has been typical with innovations of the past, scant attention has been paid to preparing teachers and administrators to use new technology well and even less to their preferences about hardware and software.

The advice presented earlier about the change process appears to have been totally ignored. Levin and Riffel (1997) suggest that computers and information technology in general has considerable educational potential that we have hardly begun to tap. They argue that changes in school organization and classroom practice are essential if this is to be taken advantage of.

> In a situation of change, experimentation is the key. If we don't know what to do, we must try various possibilities, gather evidence about their impact and value and learn as we go ... In the area of technology, as in so many others, the key will be whether we can develop the capacities to allow us to learn enough so that we are not overwhelmed. (p. 114)

This implies that we need teachers for the new millennium who are not afraid of change, who are excited and enthused by it and who recognize the importance of gathering evidence in the process of introducing new ideas and practices In short, we need teachers who are researchers of their own and their colleagues practice.

Where there is some agreement about the future is in the importance of developing children as learners who have a 'lifetime commitment to learning'. This is not helped by a sterile inculcation into the knowledge of the past. Instead it focuses on the skills of learning itself, as Sir Richard Livingstone has suggested,

> The test of a successful education is not the amount of knowledge that a pupil takes away from school, it is the appetite to know and the capacity to learn. (cited in *For Life: A Vision for Learning in the 21st Century* published by the Royal Society of Arts. 1996, p. 19)

Whilst most of the debate about 'lifelong learning' has focused on adult education, there are those who believe that the key to successful life long learning lies in strengthening children's motivation in the early years of their education (Pascal and Bertram, 1997). As one might expect, however, there are contrasting views about learning and how it might most effectively be undertaken. For example, in his annual report of 1995, the Chief Inspector of Schools asked the question,

> Why is it that in too many primary schools 'learning by doing' is preferred to 'teaching by telling' to the point where sitting pupils down and telling them becomes almost a marginal strategy?

This is in direct contrast to what a great deal of recent research on learning would suggest. Caroline Gipps (1993) from the University of London Institute of Education argues that,

> The transmission model of teaching, in a traditional formal classroom, with strong subject and task boundaries and traditional narrow assessment, is the opposite of what we need to produce learners who can think critically, synthesise and transform, experiment and create. We need a flexible curriculum, active cooperative forms of learning, opportunities for pupils to talk through the knowledge which they are incorporating, open forms of assessment especially self-evaluation and reflection on learning: in short a thinking curriculum aimed at higher order performance and cognitive skills.

Saljo (1979) interviewed adults and asked them what they understood by the term *learning*. His analysis of their responses identified five qualitatively different conceptions of learning.

- **Learning as an increase in knowledge:** This view of learning is seen as a passive process, by which new facts and knowledge are added to the existing store of information. It is something that is done by teachers rather than learners and it is the teacher's responsibility to pass on their knowledge to their pupils and to create the disciplined classroom environment in which this is best done. Stevenson and Palmer (1994) liken it to the 'filling of a jug'.
- **Learning as memorizing:** This conception of learning is similar to the first in that what is learned are facts and information and there is no expectation that what is learned will be transformed in any way. However, there is more recognition that learners have an active role in this because they have to develop strategies such as rote repetition 'to get the information into their heads'. This view sees learning as the accumulation of unrelated facts because the learner does not recognize the need to relate them to pre-existing knowledge.
- **Learning as the acquisition of facts or procedures which can be used by the learner:** This kind of learning leads to the development

of skills which can be applied now and in future situations. The basic skills of literacy and numeracy fall into this category as do study skills and communication skills. As with the first two categories, there is no expectation that what is learned will be modified in any way by the learner. They will tend simply to be reproduced when circumstances demand. The emphasis in this approach is on practice so that skills become automatic.

- **Learning as making sense and abstracting meaning:** The learner who adopts this approach makes active attempts to understand the material to be learned by penetrating beneath the surface to update and modify existing beliefs and understanding. With this approach, learning is about trying to understand, to grasp underlying principles and concepts. In this view of learning, it leads to the ability to explain and apply things not just to remember them.
- **Learning as an interpretative process aimed at understanding reality:** This kind of learning extends the previous one. By actively relating new understandings to existing beliefs, this kind of learning has the potential to transform a learner's former perspectives and ways of doing things. As a result, they are able to think about things in new and different ways.

Each of the above has a place in a learner's repertoire and, by implication, should influence teaching. The ultimate test must be 'fitness for purpose'. When is it most appropriate for something to be learned by rote and when is it best to leave it to the learner to establish, extend, or modify his or her own understanding by their own active construction? To answer these questions requires the professional skills and knowledge of the teacher.

In order for the suggestions discussed in this chapter to be applied in the classroom, it is important to recognize the importance of the context in which learning takes place. Elsewhere (Conner, 1992), I have argued that context includes three main elements. First, there is the *physical* context: Is the learning environment a welcoming and comfortable one? Our physical comfort effects our predisposition to learn. The second element of context relates to the *affective* nature of learning. Can I expect to feel confident as I approach new learning? Am I likely to be supported in my learning and can I take risks and learn from my mistakes? Or am I likely to be placed in a potentially negative learning situation where I have a fear of failure? There is substantial evidence to suggest that one's self-concept as a learner is probably the most significant factor affecting learning (Dweck, 1986). The final feature of context recognizes that learning is a *social* experience as much as it is a cognitive one. Vygotsky (1962) emphasized the cooperative nature of learning when he suggested,

> . . . what the (learner) can do today in co-operation he (she) will be able to do tomorrow on his (her) own.

In order for the issues discussed here to effect thinking and practice, it is essential that the teacher also sees him or herself as a learner, prepared to engage in reflection on practice, to see whether appropriate opportunities have been provided and whether the most appropriate approach to learning has been made available to the children. As Lawrence Stenhouse (1975) once suggested, the most effective schools are those where the teacher as well as the children learns something new each day. It is in such schools that I believe we can face an uncertain future with confidence.

References

ABBOTT, J. (1994) *Learning Makes Sense; Recreating Education for a Changing Future,* Letchworth: Education 2000.

ALEXANDER, R. (1995) *Versions of Primary Education,* London: Routledge.

ALEXANDER, R., ROSE, J. and WOODHEAD, C. (1992) 'Curriculum organisation and practice in primary schools: A discussion paper', London: DES.

BEALING, D. (1972) 'The organisation of junior school classrooms', *Educational Research,* **14**, pp. 231–5.

BENNETT, N. and CARRE, C. (1996) 'Teachers' subject knowledge and the quality of teaching in primary science', Paper presented at the annual conference of the British Educational Research Association, Lancaster, September.

BLACK, P. (1995) 'Ideology, evidence and the raising of standards', Second Annual Education Lecture, Faculty of Education London, Kings College.

CENTRAL ADVISORY COUNCIL FOR EDUCATION (ENGLAND) (1967) *Children and their Primary Schools,* (The Plowden Report), London: HMSO.

CLEGG, A. (1971) *Revolution in the British Primary School,* Washington, DC: National Association of Elementary School Principals (NEA).

COHEN, D. (1987) 'Educational technology, policy and practice', *Educational Evaluation and Policy Analysis,* **9**, 2, summer, pp. 153–70.

CONNER, C. (1992) 'Is there still a place for learning in school?', *University of Cambridge Institute of Education Newsletter,* spring.

CONNER, C. (1997) 'Geography Is In Place. A study of the effects of participation in a course to support the teaching of geography in the primary school', in press.

DAVID, J. (1992) 'Realising the promise of technology: The need for systematic education reform', cited in LEVIN, B. and RIFFEL, J.A. (1997) *Schools and the Changing World: Struggling Toward the Future,* London: Falmer Press.

DESFORGES, C. (1992, September) 'Children's Learning: has it improved?' Paper presented to the Association for the Study of Primary Education (ASPE), Cheshire.

DRUMMOND, M.-J. and McLAUGHLIN, C. (1994) 'Teaching and learning-The fourth dimension', in BRADLEY, H., CONNER, C. and SOUTHWORTH, G. (eds) *Developing Teachers Developing Schools,* London: David Fulton.

DWECK, C. (1986) 'Motivational processes affecting learning', *American Psychologist,* **41**, pp. 1041–8.

FULLAN, M.G. (1992) *The New Meaning of Educational Change,* New York and London: Teachers College Press and Cassell.

GIPPS, C.V. (1993) 'Policy-making and the use and misuse of evidence', *British Educational Research Journal,* **19**, 1.

GUSTAVSON, C.G. (1955) *A Preface to History,* Toronto: McGraw-Hill.

HALPIN, D. (1996) 'Diversifying into the past or preparing for the millennium? Comprehensive schooling for a post traditional society', address to the Dept. of Educational Studies, University of Oxford.

HELSBY, G. and McCULLOCH, G. (eds) (1997) *Teachers and the National Curriculum*, London: Falmer Press.

HUBERMAN, M. and MILES, M.B. (1984) *Innovation up Close*, New York: Plenum.

JACK, D. (1996) 'Curriculum modularisation in the primary school: An effective tool for the delivery of the National Curriculum', in ANDREWS, R. (ed.), *Interpreting the New National Curriculum*, London: Middlesex University Press.

LEVIN, B. and RIFFEL, J.A. (1997) *Schools and the Changing World; Struggling Toward the Future*, London: Falmer Press.

OFSTED (1995) *The Annual Report of Her Majesty's Chief Inspector of Schools. Part 1: Standards and Quality in Education 1993/94*, London: HMSO.

OSBORN, M. and BLACK, E. (1994) *Developing the National Curriculum at Key Stage Two: The Changing Nature of Teachers' Work*, Birmingham: NASUWT.

OSBORN, M. with CROLL, P., BROADFOOT, P., POLLARD, A., McNESS, E. and TRIGGS, P. (1997) 'Policy into practice: Creative mediation in the primary classroom, in HELSBY, G. and McCULLOCH, G. (eds) *Teachers and the National Curriculum*, London: Falmer Press.

PASCAL, C. and BERTRAM, T. (1997) 'An emotional plea', *Times Educational Supplement, Part 2*, 30 May, p. 12.

POLLARD, A., BROADFOOT, P., CROLL, P., OSBORN, M. and ABBOT, D. (1984) *Changing English Primary Schools? The Impact of the Education Reform Act at Key Stage One*, London: Cassell.

REICH, R. (1992) *Work of Nations*, New York: Vintage Press.

ROYAL SOCIETY OF ARTS (1996) *For Life: A Vision for Learning in the 21st Century*, London: RSA.

SALJO, R. (1979) 'Learning about learning', *Higher Education*, **8**, pp. 443–51.

SARASON, S. (1990) *The Predictable Failure of Educational Reform*, San Francisco, CA: Jossey Bass.

SHULMAN, L. (1986) 'Those who understand; Knowledge growth in teaching', *Educational Researcher*, **15**, 2, pp. 4–14.

SHULMAN, L. (1987) 'Knowledge and teaching: Foundations of the new reforms', *Harvard Educational Review*, **57**, pp. 1–22.

SILBERMAN, C.F. (1970) *Crisis in the Classroom: The Remaking of American*, New York: Random House Education.

SIMON, B. (1981) 'The primary school revolution: Myth or reality?', in SIMON, B. and WILLCOCKS, J. (eds) *Research and Practice in the Primary School*, London: Routledge and Kegan Paul.

STENHOUSE, L. (1975) *An Introduction to Curriculum Research and Development*, London: Heinemann Educational Books.

STEVENSON, R.J. and PALMER, J.A. (1994) *Learning: Principles, Processes and Practices*, London: Cassell.

STOLL, L. and FINK, D. (1996) *Changing our Schools*, Buckingham: Open University Press.

THOMPSON, P. (1996) 'Hi, tech future', in RSA *For Life: A Vision for Learning in the 21st Century*, London: RSA.

TOFFLER, A. (1971) *Future Shock*, London: Pan Books.

VYGOTSKY, L.S. (1962) *Thought and Language*, Boston, MA: MIT Press.

WELLS, A. (1996) 'Forward to basics', in *For Life: A Vision for Learning in the 21st Century*, London, RSA.

WHITAKER, P. (1997) *Primary Schools and the Future*, Buckingham: Open University Press.

Part 3

Participants: Teachers, Children and Parents

6   Primary Teaching: Roles and Relationships

Jim Campbell

Our ideas of what teachers do when they are at work may be conditioned to a large extent by the memories of our own experiences of teachers when we were pupils. We think of teachers as having fairly short hours of work, roughly coterminous with their pupils' day, and rather long holidays by comparison with other workers in service industries. Moreover, teachers are thought to have it easy in another sense: the nature of the job itself is considered un-demanding, particularly when young children are involved, and only semi-professional in status. The image of teaching as a 9–3 job, and the adage that, 'Those who can, do; those who can't, teach', are deeply imprinted on the national, and perhaps the international, consciousness.

In England and Wales, the Teachers' Pay and Conditions Act 1987 did little to dispel this image. It specified that teachers could be required to work on not more than 195 days a year, of which 190 were days on which they could be required to teach pupils. They might be required to work at the direction of their headteacher for a maximum of 1265 hours a year. Colloqui-ally known as 'directed time', this is equivalent to about 33 hours per week, in an assumed 39-week working year. Any other time spent on work — 'non-directed time' — was discretionary in the sense that it was not directed by an employer or superior. It was specified loosely — 'such additional hours as may be needed to enable them to discharge effectively their professional duties' (School Teachers Pay and Conditions Document, 1989, para 36 (1)(f)) — with the consequence that how much time teachers spent on work beyond the directed 1265 hours would depend upon the strength of either their con-science or their fear of facing classes unprepared.

Most research studies have raised doubts about the accuracy of the pop-ular image of primary school teaching. The first, by Hilsum and Cane in 1971, cast doubt on the idea that teaching was a 9–3 job. The teachers worked a 44.5 hour week, 42 per cent of which was spent on work away from classrooms, out of contact with pupils. As Hilsum and Cane (1971) said:

> Teachers have often protested that their work outside the classroom goes
> unrecognized, and that the image of the teacher held by many outside the
> profession is far too narrow, in that he is thought of primarily as a practitioner
> in a classroom. Our figures show that less than three-fifths of the teacher's
> working day was spent in direct contact with classes; 15 per cent of the day

was spent in school but without class contact, and a quarter of the day was spent entirely outside school hours. These facts lend weight to the suggestion that an understanding and appreciation of the teachers' role as a professional person will not come from a study of the classroom alone: his work and interaction with pupils in the classroom setting may be an important, perhaps the most important, aspect of his professional life, but it must be seen in the wider context of the totality of his work. (p. 91)

More recent studies (Campbell and Neill, 1994; Office of Manpower Economics, 1994) conducted after the 1988 Education Reform Act, and therefore after the introduction of the National Curriculum and testing, showed primary teachers spending over 50 hours a week on work in term time. The difference since 1971 was pretty stark: whereas in 1971, 42 per cent of working time had been spent away from pupils, 20 years later the comparable figure was 55 per cent. This change is illustrated in the two pie charts at Figure 6.1.

The explanation for the difference is not that after the 1988 Education Reform Act teachers spent less time absolutely with pupils, but that their total working time had increased and most of the increase arose from their having to spend more time on planning, preparation and assessment, and on in-service training to help them implement the National Curriculum and its assessment. In the 1990s, primary school teachers typically spent about 18 hours actually teaching pupils, out of a 53 hour working week.

Two points need to be made here. Primary school teachers gain most job satisfaction from the intrinsic psychic rewards of working with young pupils (Nias, 1989; Evetts, 1990), and thus the restructuring of the balance of their work towards more activities away from children is likely to be comparatively unrewarding to most of them. The introduction of the National Curriculum and assessment led to increased amounts, not merely of private preparation and marking done at home, but to increased amounts of whole-school planning, staff meetings, school-based professional development, and professional development activities outside school. Involvement in these kinds of work requires teachers to work with other adults — with professional peers such as teachers, advisers, university staff and others — and the skills and sensitivities needed for it differ markedly from those needed to work with pupils when subject to the teacher's classroom authority.

In 1997 the Teacher Training Agency announced a raft of professional qualifications that teachers seeking promotion would need to gain, thereby reinforcing the restructuring of teachers' work outlined above towards more time on non-classroom activities (I explore this further below).

The second point is more banal, but it is worth making it explicit. We can think of teachers' work as having 'visible' and 'invisible' components: those that can be seen by lay people and pupils and those that cannot. Teaching pupils is visible; preparation and professional development are not. If we consider preparation and marking alone, the research shows that for every hour teachers spend teaching (visible work), they spend almost another hour

Figure 6.1: Total time on work

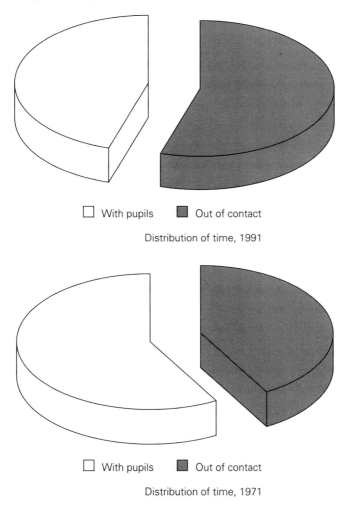

☐ With pupils   ■ Out of contact

Distribution of time, 1991

☐ With pupils   ■ Out of contact

Distribution of time, 1971

on preparation and marking (invisible work). Hardly any teachers can get by with less than one hour a day on preparation/marking, and most average between two and three hours per day across a seven day week.

A third point about the nature of teachers' work shown by research studies concerns it *intensiveness* rather than its *extensiveness*. Primary teachers' working time in schools is characterized by thousands of individual interactions with pupils; by routinely having to do two or three different things at once; by close encounters of an emotional kind with pupils and parents; by frequent interruptions to their teaching sessions; by 'snatching time' from breaks or lunchtimes to do work that needs quiet reflection; by juggling competing demands on time. This characteristic intensity leads to fatigue amongst even the most energetic young teachers, and to chronic occupational stress in some of the most experienced.

In almost all research studies of primary teaching in the post-1988 period, this felt intensity of the school day has surfaced in banal expressions by teachers who cite 'lack of time' as the major obstacle to doing all that is expected of them. However, some interview studies enabled teachers to talk in richer detail about what it meant. In one, most teachers referred to this intensity as a mental condition to be understood in the terms of personal symptoms, even though it was experienced in the routines of school. One of the teachers used a metaphor to describe the condition which I have called, taking up her phrase, the 'running commentary syndrome'. The teacher, who had a rich, if mixed, set of metaphors to illustrate her perceptions, had 32 children, year 1 and year 2 combined, in her class:

> Well, what is frightening now is that we are being blinkered now into the National Curriculum and so everything else is hanging on by its fingernails really. That's how I feel at the moment — the sheer amount of time required to cope with what you hope to achieve — but it just seems to be expanding to fill the day and I am constantly getting to the stage where, I am noticing it far more now, that I never complete what I hope to achieve. There is always, like, a carry-forward so that you never get the feeling at the end of a session or the end or a day, 'Great, I've done this that I hoped we would do' — there is always something else.

> Is that what you used to do, then?

> No, I didn't used to feel that, I didn't used to get to the end of the day and think, 'Oh gosh, I haven't done this', or 'I haven't done that' — I used to get to the end of the day and think, 'Oh great, we have done this' — so this has been a major change as far as I am concerned. So there is this running commentary really, in the background, saying that, 'You haven't done this', or 'You haven't done that', which I find very annoying, considering that you work so hard.

This syndrome, the enervating, subjective sense of working harder and feeling that they were achieving less, was seen by the teachers to be the product of expanding professional demands within the same timeframe. It was not necessarily created by the 1988 reforms, but was exacerbated by them.

Changing Roles and Relationships

Up to this point I have attempted to sketch a research-based picture of primary teaching. But teaching, like other occupations, is not static; it is subject to pressures for change in response to, among other things, reforms of the school system as a whole. There are three contemporary pressures, which I will briefly illustrate, both from the UK and from other educational systems, since these pressures are operating in teachers in most industrial societies.

Primary Teaching as Social Work

There is increasing pressure on primary teachers, to take on an ever-widening scope or range of activities, in addition to the task of teaching or instructing pupils. Increasingly in modern societies teachers are expected to be concerned with the social and moral dimensions of pupils' lives, with welfare matters, with health, and with the pupils' communities. We might characterize it as a shift from being expected to take responsibility only or mainly for instructing pupils to being expected to be a teacher, cum secretary, cum social worker, cum community liaison officer, cum paramedic, cum priest (though given the recent activities of some priests there may be reservations about this last aspect). One previous Secretary of State, John Patten, called for teachers to promote a fear of hell and damnation into their pupils, taking for granted that teachers could be expected to act for religious institutions. More recently teachers have been expected to become teacher trainers, expert spotters of child abuse, and advisers on safe sex.

It is not only the politicians who push this way: primary educationalists also promote the social work dimension. To take one example only, a recent book attempted to place responsibilities on primary teachers for (in addition to teaching the National Curriculum subjects) citizenship, racial and gender equality, awareness of economics and careers education, environmentalism, health and personal and social education. The main editors argue that:

> Social class domination and deference, racism, sexism, homophobia, the intolerance of disability, economic individualism and community and environmental recklessness are all recurring themes. Each negatively affects the self-image of some children in schools and perhaps ultimately and even more seriously, all children's images of 'others' are affected by these influences. The children of today will be the responsible and tolerant employers, employees, landlords, tenants and citizens of tomorrow, *or they may not.* The professional responsibility lies with us teachers, parents, and adult citizens ourselves, to create or recreate our society in the twenty-first century. (Siraj-Blatchford and Siraj-Blatchford, p. 3)

Such pressures are not restricted to the UK. A report in 1991 from the International Labour Office based on an analysis of teachers' work in more than 40 countries, argued that the nature of teachers' work was changing in response to a range of new expectations being placed on the schools. Not only were curriculum reform programmes being put in place but there was an accelerating trend for moral and social responsibilities, previously exercised by other agencies (for example, the home and family, the church, the welfare agencies, and local communities) to be transferred to schools. The reasons for this are obvious and banal; apart from the world created on TV screens, primary school is the only universally experienced institution in societies that are increasingly morally and socially fractured or fragmented. The schools thus become the prime site in which policies for the creation and reinforcement of a moral and social order can be implemented — the prime site, in which society attempts to create the identities it wishes. In some areas of these societies increasingly schools are the only site for such policies to be enacted, and teachers are compelled to take on the responsibility of implementing them. The most obvious locations are in the 'underclass' areas where, for some pupils, school is the main locus of moral and social stability. But it is, nonetheless, an expectation laid upon all teachers.

In Northern Ireland, for example, teachers are expected to 'educate for mutual understanding' pupils whose social world outside school — and sometimes inside it — has offered them little other than bigotry and stereotyped misunderstanding. In a more trivial, less dramatic form, I was in a classroom recently at registration time when a pupil came in with a note from her parent asking the teacher to punish the pupil because she had been kicking cars on the way home from school. In the same classroom a second parent came in and asked whether the teacher could clear up a squashed hedgehog, run over by a car, from the outside the school because some of the pupils had been jumping up and down on the corpse. The unspoken assumption of both parents was that the teachers should be responsible for pupil behaviour outside school, and that it was reasonable for teachers to take up time in school exercising such responsibility.

The Primary Teacher as Subject Specialist

The second pressure arises from the curriculum reform programmes being almost universally adopted across the post-industrial world in the drive for higher standards. This pressure, paradoxically in view of the social welfare pressure mentioned above, is pushing primary teachers into a more instrumental orientation, emphasizing pupil cognitive achievement above everything else. Often this achievement is the only, or the main, area that is publicly tested and is the source for teacher appraisal. Under this pressure the valuing of the work of the generalist class teacher is being replaced by a concentration upon the value of specialist subject expertise. In this country we have seen it emerge in two Select Committee reports (House of Commons Education, Arts and Science Committee, 1986; House of Commons, 1994) in the literature on primary education (Bennett and Carré, 1993; Campbell, 1985) in HMI and OFSTED reports on the system and its schools and in the continuous revision of primary teacher training priorities at both initial and in-service levels, where the significance of subject expertise and the deficiencies arising from its absence have been played up. The consequence is that subject expertise

— despite the serious problems of definition — has become a defining characteristic of the skills required by primary teachers to do their work effectively. As Philip Taylor has argued, 'primariness' itself is being redefined (Taylor, 1997).

Elsewhere similar pressures operate. In Italy for example, where curriculum reform programmes were defined in 1985 and introduced year-by-year from 1987, teachers who were previously generalists are now required to take responsibility for one of three specialist areas of learning (for example, linguistic-expressive, scientific–logical–mathematical, and historical–social–geographical) (OFSTED, 1994).

> Until very recently, most Italian primary teachers worked as generalists — teaching all subjects to their own classes. However, the new systems involving a shared curriculum and joint responsibility for classes . . . are forcing an element of semi-specialization in that teachers are expected to remain with their assigned 'areas of learning' for either two, three or five years. There is some debate within the system as to how effective these arrangements will prove. Teachers recognize the need to reduce their planning and assessment load, given the requirements of the national teaching programmes, but are unsure about narrowing their range of expertise for a prolonged period.

In general there remains in the UK substantial resistance to this pressure, at least where 'specialist teaching' in a secondary school style is involved. However, from the point of view of reducing the imbalance in the power relations between head and staff, (and increased 'professional' respect for the latter), the demonstrated possession of specialist subject expertise and its use in school planning may have considerable advantages. Primary heads may soon feel deskilled in relation to their specialist curriculum coordinators, who are up-to-date in their subject and exercise *de facto* leadership and authority in school decision-making on their specialist curriculum area.

The Primary Teacher as Team Player

By this pressure I mean the pressure to work collaboratively and to discuss educational practice by reference to theories, ideas and research. The pressure has been widely recognized both here and elsewhere. In this country Osborn and Black (1994), for example, reported that in their sample of Key Stage 2 teachers one significant change in work was 'an increase in collaborative planning and working. This mainly took the form of planning initially with colleagues, sharing the distribution of resource materials and working with others on a consultancy/advisory basis' (p. iv). Likewise, Webb's study of primary teachers' roles and responsibilities found them increasingly being expected to work in cooperation with colleagues, though her study revealed the constraints upon this happening effectively. (Webb, 1993). In Italian primary schools teachers are required to plan the work of year groups collectively at the beginning of the school year and to monitor progress collectively through regular staff group meetings. Research at the University of Warwick (Campbell and Neill, 1994) found primary teachers spending substantially more of their time with other teachers than had been the case some 25 years earlier.

> The teachers in our study spent 6.2 hours per week — 11 per cent of their working week — in contact with other adults, . . . This is a much larger time — whether absolutely or as a proportion of the working week — spent in the company of colleagues than was true for Hilsum and Cane's teachers in 1971. (p. 213)

Part of this shift in England is explained by the way the National Curriculum pushed teachers into collaborative planning, part by earmarked funding for professional development and part by the requirement on schools to create school development plans. The important thing about this pressure is its effect upon the classroom autonomy of primary teachers. Whereas in the period from about 1965 to 1985 primary teachers typically managed their classroom and curriculum without reference to other members of staff, or to a formally agreed curriculum policy, now the school's decision-making in these matters is collective. The earlier arrangement may have been attractive to teachers because of the independence it gave them in classroom and curricular matters, but it is now recognized that it was not in the interests of pupils, since it gave them no entitlement to a formally agreed curriculum. This pressure to become part of a team, which is sometimes called 'collegiality', now requires teachers to take responsibility for some part of the whole school's policies and practices, not just those in their own classrooms.

Changing Relationships with the State Towards the Nationalization of Primary Teaching

Over the next five years or so, primary teachers' work is highly likely to come under further state control, as the Government attempts to raise standards of literacy and numeracy in schools in the belief that economic competitiveness will be increased through doing so. I shall briefly outline three ways in which increased state control over primary teachers has been realized, though it is necessary to bear in mind that these are not new: they are extensions of trends emerging in the 1980s.

Increased Control Over Teaching Methods

The 1988 Education Reform Act prohibited the Secretary of State from specifying the methods that teachers should use. However, in the light of continuing evidence that the introduction of the National Curriculum and testing had not

Figure 6.2:   The literacy hour

		KEY STAGE 1	KEY STAGE 2
whole class	approx. 15 mins.	Shared text work (a balance of reading and writing)	Shared text work (a balance of reading and writing)
whole class	approx. 15 mins.	Focused word work	A balance, over the term of focused word work or sentence work
group work	approx. 20 mins.	1 Independent reading, writing or word work activities 2 Teacher works with each group twice in the week, focused on guided reading	1 Independent reading, writing word and sentence activities 2 Teacher works with each group for a sustained period (15 minutes) each week on guided reading or writing
whole class	approx. 10 mins.	Reviewing, reflecting upon and presenting work covered in the lesson	Reviewing, reflecting upon and presenting work covered in the lesson

Source: Literacy Task Force (1997) *The Implementation of the National Literacy Strategy*, London: DfEE.

been accompanied by raised standards of literacy and numeracy, in the mid-1990s the central Government agencies (under both Conservative and Labour administrations) attempted to intervene in primary school pedagogy. Experiments were established in Dagenham and Barking to import 'whole class interactive' teaching into primary classrooms — a teaching method involving substantial challenging question and answer sequences, and reduced time on individual or group tasks. The method was characteristic of primary teaching in the Pacific Rim countries, whose standards of numeracy outstripped those in the UK. National literacy and numeracy projects were established, which involved training primary teachers to adopt clearly specified teaching techniques as a condition of participation in the projects. When the Labour Government was elected on the slogan of 'education, education, education', it moved to require all primary schools to implement a literacy hour every day. Figure 6.2 shows the format of the literacy hour.

The literacy hour is in effect a national lesson plan for all teachers, and it is intended to adopt a similar model for a numeracy hour. What all these initiatives have done is to impose on primary teachers a required approach to teaching, and thereby removed from them the need or expectation that they should exercise their own professional judgment.

Increased Control Over Professional Development

The Conservative Government established in 1995 the Teacher Training Agency to fund the recruitment, training and development of the teaching profession, including the initial and continuing training of teachers. Amongst its other activities, it created a hierarchical framework of national professional qualifications for the profession: qualifications to achieve qualified teacher status; an advanced skills teacher; a subject leader; an aspiring headteacher; and even training for serving headteachers. Since the TTA had also laid down a National Curriculum and national standards for initial teacher training courses, and intended to inspect and accredit higher degree programmes being followed by teachers, it is difficult to avoid the sense that the TTA was attempting to lock the whole development of the profession in a suffocating embrace. Professional development was screwed down further because the TTA controls the funding for its own programmes and allocates it to those selected to participate in them, whereas teachers following alternative training programmes have to fund themselves. When it became clear that the intention was to make satisfactory participation in the training programmes a condition of promotion (and even of salary increases) the end of any serious professional autonomy for teachers was secured.

Increased Control Over Curriculum Innovation

Under the 1988 Education Reform Act, a possibility was envisaged whereby, in pursuit of curricular innovation and experiment, the curricular requirements in the Act might be disapplied to some schools, should they seek disapplication from the Secretary of State in order to develop experimental approaches to the curriculum at the level of the individual school. Although there are no published statistics, enquiries from the DfEE revealed that since 1988 only 'a handful' of schools had bid for disapplication, and no bid had been approved.

Nine years on from the introduction of what has been accepted as a flawed National Curriculum, no school has been permitted to develop a genuinely alternative curriculum, i.e. alternative to the basic curriculum of the 1988 Act, despite the immense variation in local and cultural interests, values, and needs of the 19,000+ primary schools in the system. Thus an infant school with a disproportionate number of pupils with poor reading achievement has not been allowed to teach history, geography, technology or RE in order to devote more time to the teaching of reading. With a set of Labour Government policies on education that is more, not less, interventionist, primary teaching over the next few years is likely to become less, not more experimental, and teachers will be required to strive to conform to the centrally defined curriculum specification on literacy and numeracy, rendered modern with a gloss of information and communication technology.

It is of course unwise to speculate too far into the future of a profession (and running counter to the three points made above is the embryonic creation of a General Teaching Council which might be able to reclaim some professional autonomy). However, two conclusions might be drawn from the speculation: primary teachers will have become *de facto* civil servants, under Government control but without the contractual and salary benefits associated with such status; and all the innovation in pedagogy and curriculum will have been driven out of the maintained, into the private sector. This may seem initially to lead to short-term improvements in the Government's sense of managing the primary teaching force more effectively, but in the long-term it will lead to an oppressed and moribund profession, lacking initiative and responsibility for its own development. This can not be good for teachers and probably will not be good for pupils, whose interests the profession is there to serve.

References

BENNETT, N. and CARRÉ, C. (1993) *Learning to Teach*, London: Routledge.

CAMPBELL, R.J. (1985) *Developing the Primary School Curriculum*, Eastbourne: Holt, Rinehart and Winston.

CAMPBELL, R.J. and NEILL, S.R.ST.J. (1994) *Primary Teachers at Work*, London: Routledge.

EVETTS, J. (1990) *Women in Primary Education*, London: Methuen.

HILSUM, S. and CANE, B.S. (1971) *The Teacher's Day*, Windsor: NFER.

HOUSE OF COMMONS (1994) *The Disparity of Funding Between Primary and Secondary Schools*, London: HMSO.

HOUSE OF COMMONS EDUCATION, SCIENCE AND ARTS COMMITTEE (1986) *Achievement in Primary Schools*, vol 1, London: HMSO.

INTERNATIONAL LABOUR OFFICE (1991) *Teachers: Challenges of the 1990s: Second Joint Meeting on Conditions of Work of Teachers*, Geneva: International Labour Office.

NIAS, J. (1989) *Primary Teachers Talking*, London: Routledge.

OFFICE OF MANPOWER ECONOMICS (1994) *Report on a Study of Teachers' Working Hours for the School Teachers Review Body*, London: Office of Manpower Economics.

OFSTED (1994) *Teaching and Learning in Italian Primary Schools*, London: HMSO.

OSBORN, M. and BLACK, E. (1994) *Roles and Responsibilities at Key Stage 3*, London: NAS/UWT.

SIRAJ-BLATCHFORD, J. and SIRAJ-BLATCHFORD, I. (eds) (1995) *Educating the Whole Child*, Milton Keynes: Open University Press.

TAYLOR, P. (1997) 'The "primariness" of primary education', *Education, 3–13*, **25**, 3, pp. 23–30.

WEBB, R. (1993) *After the Deluge*, London: Association of Teachers and Lecturers.

7 Primary Teacher Education and Development: Context, Assumptions and Issues

Chris Husbands

Transforming Schools and Teaching: Millenarianism and Fundamentalism

Few things betray the assumptions of their own time and place more clearly than predictions about the future; equally, few things inform planning for the future more than assumptions about the past. Debate about teacher education has, perhaps particularly, been bedevilled by the interposition into policy debates of questionable assumptions about the past and wild speculation about the future. Assumptions about the past come in a number of clearly defined categories: the myth of decline and the myth of progress are particularly potent. On some accounts, the present is a pale reflection of the past, since when standards have fallen, expectations declined and teachers become less professional, less effective and less marked out as scholarly experts than ever their pre-Plowden, pre-war or Victorian predecessors were. On other accounts, the educational present is the consequence of marked progress since the past: teachers are better trained in a more rigorously professional environment, schools provide more effective tailoring to the needs of individual pupils and there is a professional consensus about effective practice which ensures that quality is now maintained in a way which it never was. Many of the current debates about teacher education turn on the ways in which proponents of different arguments reflect these assumptions about the past: policy must either build on effective recent practice or address historical failures.

If these assumptions about the past are influential, they are crowded by assumptions about the future. As we embark on the twenty-first century, we are offered a series of portmanteau assumptions which can only be described as millenarial in character (Barber, 1996). Information technology is about to revolutionize learning (Barber, 1994). It will transform the school and the classroom to the point of extinction: liberated from the constraints of place (the classroom), of resources (books, chalkboards), the task of the teacher will be transformed alongside the development of quasi-intelligent learning resources: the information super highway will unleash models of learning, and therefore of teaching, in which learning is removed from the control and direction of the teacher and the school. This technological determinism will, by what 1960s radical commentators might regard as an ironic quirk, 'deschool' society (Illich, 1971; Hargreaves, 1995). Other models for the transformation of school are managerialist and industrial at root: learning, and teachers, must be 'managed' more professionally than before; headteachers must define for their schools 'missions' and 'professional direction', leading policy formulation and reviewing the quality of the processes and products which are the 'core purposes' of the school (TTA, 1996). Schools, rather like English cricket, it seems are always 'on the verge' of being transformed, so that it is always not a little depressing to turn from the exciting predictions of the millenarial prophets to the realities of the miscreant child, the leaking classroom and the dog-eared textbook.

The millenarialists, however, do not have it all their own way; David Halpin has described one set of responses to the anxieties and turbulence of rapid change as the birth of 'educational fundamentalism'. This 'fundamentalism' argues that the primary school will need, more intensively than heretofore, to ensure that pupils are schooled in 'key' or 'core' skills, to ensure that pupils can communicate effectively in writing, read clearly a variety of texts and master basic arithmetic. 'Fundamentalists' lay emphasis on the integrative and socializing role of the school at a time of perceived social breakdown, in transmitting 'core' moral and social values, and in 'producing' 'good citizens' (SCAA, 1996). In these versions, the transformation of work and society outside the school almost paradoxically redoubles the importance of the school's preparatory functions: pupils will need to have become adept readers, writers and arithmeticians, responsible and reflective proto-citizens *before* they can become flexible and adaptive learners (Letwin, 1988).

There are common threads running through these highly disparate assumptions and predictions. In the first place, there are, almost without exception, *monocausal.* They assume that professional and educational changes operate as a direct consequence of identified structural, technical or political developments. They connect assumptions of success or failure in unilinear ways to assumptions about future demands on the school system and teacher development. Schools will either be fundamentally different or they will be fundamentally the same. If they are to be different, then alternative models are needed for teacher development; if they are to be the same then pre-existent models need to be reestablished. Secondly, in spite of their attempts to project forward apparently already established historical tendencies, they are markedly *ahistorical:* their accounts of both future and past are partial and selective. One change or development is assumed to stand as a litmus test for more general policy development. Information technology 'will' therefore become a vehicle for the more general transformation of approaches to teaching and learning; managerialism will sharpen education's concern with accountability and performance indicators; moral and social concerns will provide a mechanism for the reinforcement of 'traditional' moral values and teaching methods. Again, however, the moments at which schools will be transformed are unspecified, and the circumstances under which different models translate into practice remain obscure. Finally, they appear to separate the school from the individuals who make it up, either pupils or teachers, and to lack any coherent understanding of the ways in which teachers adapt to *change*. The ways in which teachers' classroom and school practice absorbs, responds to or resists change are scarcely specified: the 'school' is generally seen as a social institution in which trends and attitudes can be read off from wider social and economic trends. Teachers themselves are regarded as operatives: they 'will' adopt new methods (in order to make the most effective use of information technology or to focus on literacy and numeracy), or they 'are', as a result of training deficiencies or their own intellectual weaknesses, responsible for poor performance.

The Context: Teacher Education and Primary Schooling

Most accounts of the relative performance of primary education in the UK over the last generation have concluded that its output performance in relation to other systems has been relatively mediocre, and that its ability to respond rapidly to structural or technical change is weak. On 'hard' measures of attainment in mathematics and to a lesser extent, literacy, the evidence suggests that other systems, most notably those of the Pacific Rim and some mid-European countries, have outperformed particularly English and Welsh schools fairly consistently over a long period (Reynolds and Farrell, 1996; Bierhoff and Prais, 1995; Foxman, 1992). This consistent pattern has been attributed to any number of policy and intrasystem features: primary schooling in England has been argued to have been overly influenced by child-centred and Plowdenesque models of learning at the expense of formalist and knowledge-led models of learning: Piaget rather than Vygotsky (Alexander, 1996; Woodhead, 1995). Primary teacher education in particular has been argued to be lacking in intellectual force and competency-based practice (Woodhead, 1995; Lawlor, 1990). Primary teachers themselves have been characterized as too intellectually mediocre for the task with which they have been charged (Lawlor, 1990). Finally, the system as a whole has been argued to have been too inward looking, and relatively insulated from the competitive, market-oriented and technologically led changes which have transformed industrial and commercial practices over the last 20 years (Barnett, 1986). In consequence, the transformation of primary schooling which is necessary to ensure that in an 'increasingly competitive and interdependent world' pupils have the 'key skills' to succeed will depend on transforming teaching methods, transforming teacher education and reshaping the teaching force.

In practice, these diagnoses and these prescriptions appear on closer examination to be partial at best. Whilst performance on numeracy indicators has generally been mediocre in relation to that of other countries, this performance is not simply a feature of the last 30 years. From the early years of the century, the output performance of schools in England and Wales in literacy and numeracy has been relatively weak (Foshay, 1962; Prais and Wagner,

1995). Moreover, there is little strong *empirical* evidence to suggest a secular decline in performance in literacy at least since the end of the Second World War. Brooks, Foxman and Gorman's review of research in these areas suggests that reading standards for 10/11 and 15/16-year-olds changed little between 1945 and 1994, though there may have been a slight fall in the standards achieved by 6–8-year-olds in the later 1980s. There was a slight fall in number skills between 1982 and 1987, but a rise in attainment in geometry, statistics and measurement at the same time, so that by the end of the 1980s standards in Britain were relatively high in geometry and statistics but relatively low in number (Brooks, Foxman and Gorman, 1993; Campbell, 1996). This is a particularly persistent feature of the English education system, and its causes *may* lie outside schools in wider social and cultural assumptions (Barnett, 1986; Weiner, 1985): in particular, school-by-school variation was more marked in England and Wales than elsewhere, and poor performances on output indicators were chiefly the result of a 'long tail' of low attainers (Reynolds and Farrell, 1996; Brooks, Foxman and Gorman, 1995; Brooks Pugh and Schagen, 1996). In addition, there are other measures of educational outputs which suggest the relative strength and vitality of the English primary system. Alexander's review of the difficulties of international comparison ends by suggesting that primary schools have been successful in their moral, social and pastoral roles (Alexander, 1996). Recent research suggests that schools in the later 1980s were largely successful in raising science attainments for primary pupils (Reynolds and Farrell, 1996). If the general performance indicators of the system are more complex than either millenarialists or fundamentalists might claim, so too are those elements which are adduced to celebrate strength or explain relatively poor performance. For good or ill, there is little evidence from HMI reports to suggest that English primary classroom practice in the 1970s and 1980s was swept by a Plowdenesque commitment to child-centred liberalism (HMI, 1978). Summarizing the research and inspection findings, Campbell (1993) suggests that:

> The curriculum (before the 1988 Act) was narrow, emphasizing literacy and numeracy through repetitive exercises; despite encouragement, work in science was patchy and haphazard; standards in social subjects were lower than might be expected; pedagogy was often characterized by undifferentiated focus on pupils in the middle levels of attainment within a class, and expectations of the able children were undemanding. (p. 89)

Evidence on the entry qualification of teacher trainees is similarly mixed. Whilst the academic attainments of entrants to teacher training have historically been and have remained lower than those to other more generously remunerated professions, there is no evidence to suggest a relative or absolute decline in the quality of recruits over the last generation. It is, furthermore, a teaching force which has shown itself to be flexible and adaptive in the face of complex and externally imposed change (ibid., Campbell and Neill, 1994). The

National Curriculum, somewhat to the surprise of policy-makers, was generally welcomed by primary teachers, and circumstantial and inspection evidence suggests some important pockets of success in the implementation of a generally flawed reform: teachers protected teaching time for English and mathematics, gave priority to science and were generally imaginative in their response to other less familiar features of the new curriculum such as history and geography (ibid., OFSTED 1996). There *is* considerable evidence of both systemic weakness and poor practice in the deployment of information technology in classrooms over the last 15 years, but even here, there is substantial evidence that an inadequately trained and inappropriately supported teaching force has *attempted* to respond to a rapidly changing and complex area which combines challenges to teachers' technical competence with challenges to their pedagogic practice (OFSTED 1996; Fullan, 1993).

Policy Development in the Face of Complexity

Taken together then, the evidence on primary education and the primary teaching force is relatively complex; there have been marked successes and long-standing weaknesses in provision and practice. Faced with complex and sometimes competing demands, primary teachers have made choices about priorities which reflect both central policy direction and their own assumptions and training (Campbell and Neill, 1994). Primary education has neither been an outstanding success nor a historical failure. As with any complex system, there are successes and failures. System-wide generalizations are complex, but a managerial view might suggest that there has been insufficient clarity in defining system objectives, insufficient policy clarity in pursuing these objectives and, in consequence, a lack of consensus on either the appropriate performance indicators for primary education as a whole or the training of teachers to staff it. In articulating policy for primary teacher education, these complexities need to be confronted and accommodated. Rather than construct policy formulation on the basis of prediction and prejudice, it seems more sensible to indicate the starting points for teacher education policy which recent research evidence and practical experience suggest.

The first is that the long-standing, highly persistent and structural weakness in outcome performance indicators in numeracy must be confronted both inside schools and more generally. In terms of teacher education, this suggests that policy must be informed both by a focus on effective pedagogy in literacy and numeracy and, given the experiences as pupils of most primary teachers, pedagogic content knowledge in these areas (Shulman, 1987). Over the last century, one of the most enduring features of English primary education has been the deployment of the generalist class teacher, teaching a class of perhaps 30 or 35 pupils for their entire curriculum experience. The demands which this places on classroom teachers, both in terms of their curriculum and pedagogic expertise and their sheer stamina are considerable. During the later

1980s and 1990s, the prevalence of this model in the face of extensive curriculum prescription was probably one of the chief causes of widespread teacher stress (Cockburn, 1995). In a more complex educational environment it is almost certain that retention of the class-teacher model will prevent the development of teacher education programmes which prepare teachers effectively. Subject specialism, particularly in literacy and numeracy, must become far more widely established. There is a wider degree of consensus amongst policy-makers and researchers on this issue than perhaps on any other (Millett, 1997; Aubrey, 1994; Campbell, 1992; Reynolds and Farrell, 1995), though the organizational and management constraints on medium-sized and especially, small primary schools are considerable. More effectively subject-grounded primary teacher education programmes would enable the development of appropriate subject-specific pedagogies in primary schools and go a considerable way to breaking down the frequently undifferentiated conceptions of 'effective primary practice' which bedevil much of the literature and assumptions about work in classrooms (Alexander, 1995).

If the first policy prescription is to do with the long-standing problems of subject-knowledge, the second is to do with the consequences of more recent change. Early work on the impact of information technology on teaching and learning suggests that it will produce educational practices which fall short of the expectations of either the millenarialists or the fundamentalists. Information technology both narrows pedagogy — in the scope which some programmes and packages provide for the development of drill — and expands its range immeasurably — in the scope which generic programmes provide for the learner to assume control of and responsibility for their own learning. The balance between these extremes — the ways in which teachers choose to make use of rapidly developing technology — will remain pedagogic decisions. IT will neither deskill teachers nor make their presence redundant. Instead, IT will *offer* teachers teaching and learning technologies the deployment of which will create a variety of classroom possibilities. Put differently, IT will demand of a teacher *more* sophistication in the choice of pedagogic styles. Its development should take debates about classroom learning beyond some of their narrower manifestations on the whole-class/individual teaching divide, but it will place a high premium on teachers' ability to engage critically with the pedagogic demands of new technology. It may well be sensible to ensure that all schools are connected to the Internet, but if the pedagogic base of the teacher education which follows is not secure, then the money and the technology will be wasted. Information technology will, then, demand of teachers a commitment to *continuous* learning, and *continuous* adaptation and change of classroom organization and structures. It is difficult to see in either current teacher education provision, or most of the prevalent policy nostrums a serious attempt to grapple with the implications of this.

The third policy prescription follows from the first two; it is to do with preparing schools and teachers for teaching and learning in a changing and competitive environment. The first two policy prescriptions — a clear focus on subject-knowledge and a clear commitment to reviewing pedagogy — place demands on initial and continuing teacher education. Andy Hargreaves has described the circumstances in which most teachers work as an 'egg-box culture' in which teachers are isolated each from the other, in which the conditions of work militate against the genuinely collegial culture which might support professionalism at a time of rapid change (Hargreaves, 1992; cp. Nias, 1992). Michael Fullan has argued that this collegiality need be neither soft-edged nor unaccountable, and that some measure of such a culture is an essential prerequisite for effective school development (Fullan, 1993). In spite of the difficulties, some researchers have described examples of schools and staffroom cultures which support open-ended professional development which is focused on classroom improvement (Nias, 1992). My point here is that the sorts of professional discourse which will support improvement, and a climate which engenders change are a prerequisite for real teacher development. Edwards and Collison (1995) offer some examples of the ways in which involving primary teachers more closely in the professional learning of beginning and new teachers can support real improvements in classroom practice; the danger under current policy preoccupations — for example, the development of a lengthy set of standards for the award of QTS (TTA, 1997) — is that we will focus on the development of the individual teacher rather than on the teacher in the context of the school, yet it is this sort of open, professional, hard-edged and collegial climate in schools which is essential to longer-run change.

The fourth policy prescription is less clear cut, than the other three, but it is to do with the nature of the teacher force. We have already seen that the quality of intake into teacher education is variable at best. Current policy initiatives, or exhortations, to raise the academic requirements for primary teacher education are, in this narrow sense at least, impossible to dispute, though they come at a time of buoyant recruitment and after a decade and a half of rising output performance indicators in schools. There are some difficulties. The first is related to the gender and ethnic structure of the primary teaching force. For over a century, elementary and primary teaching has had little real difficulty in recruiting from particular segments of society: essentially the primary teaching force has remained white, female and drawn from the lower middle class; it has, given the economic and social assumptions which then underpin women's work, partially become a *part-time* workforce after qualification. The second is to do with the expectations and assumptions which underpin teachers' work. Inspection and research evidence continues to suggest that much teacher time and energy is dissipated in largely low-level organizational and administrative tasks: it is difficult to see that the collection of dinner money, or the supervision of pupils at break, demands a university degree. We need to consider carefully what are our expectations of our teachers, how they might be selected and what commitments they, and their employers have, to their continued development.

Debates about teacher education are never, at root, debates about what schools *are* like, but about what they might become: teachers who qualify in the year in which this book is published will still be teaching towards the middle of the twenty-first century. There is a considerable range of research evidence which suggests that classroom and pedagogic practice established early in teachers' careers, often during their training, are immensely influential throughout their careers. We may not know what the future holds — to what extent the millenarialists or the fundamentalists will prevail — but we can at least agree that teacher education and development need to equip teachers for their part in the debate about how we should educate our children.

References

ALEXANDER, R.J. (1995) *Versions of Primary Education*, London: Routledge.

ALEXANDER, R.J. (1996) *Other Primary Schools and Ours: Perils and Pitfalls of International Comparison*, University of Warwick: CREPE.

AUBREY, C. (ed.) (1994) *The Role of Subject Knowledge in the Early Years of Schooling*, London: Falmer Press.

BARBER, M. (1994) 'Power and control in education, 1994–2004', *British Journal of Educational Studies*, **10**, xli, 1, pp. 1–11.

BARBER, M. (1996) *The Learning Game: Arguments for an Education Revolution*, London: Gollancz.

BARNETT, C. (1986) *The Audit of War: The Illusion and Reality of Britain as a Great Nation*, London: Macmillan.

BIERHOFF, H.J. and PRAIS, S.J. (1995) *Schooling as Preparation for Life and Work in Switzerland and Britain*, London: National Institute for Economic and Social Research.

BROOKS, G., FOXMAN, D. and GORMAN, T. (1993) *Standards in Literacy and Numeracy 1948–1994*, London: National Commission on Education.

BROOKS, G., PUGH, A.K. and SCHAGEN, I. (1996) *Reading Performance at Age Nine*, Slough: NFER.

CAMPBELL, R.J. (1992) *Managing Teachers' Time in Primary Schools: Concepts, Evidence and Policy Issues*, Stoke-on-Trent, ASPE, Trentham Books.

CAMPBELL, R.J. (1993) 'The national curriculum in primary schools: A dream at conception, a nightmare at delivery', in CHITTY, C. and SIMON, B. (eds) *Education Answers Back: Critical Responses to Government Policy*, London: Lawrence and Wishart.

CAMPBELL, R.J. (1996) *Standards of Literacy and Numeracy in English Primary Schools: A Real or Manufactured Crisis?*, University of Warwick: CREPE.

CAMPBELL, R.J. and NEILL, S.R.ST.J. (1994) *Primary Teachers at Work*, London: Routledge.

COCKBURN, A. (1995) *Teaching Under Pressure*, London: Falmer Press.

EDWARDS, A. and COLLISON, J. (1996) *Mentoring and Developing Practice in the Primary School*, Milton Keynes: Open University Press.

FOSHAY, A.W. (1962) *Educational Achievement of Thirteen Year Olds in Twelve Countries*, Hamburg: UNSECO.

FOXMAN, D. (1992) *Learning Mathematics and Science (Second International Assessment of Educational Progress in England)* Slough: NFER.

FULLAN, M. (1993) *Change Forces: Probing the Depths of Educational Reform*, London: Falmer Press.

HARGREAVES, A. (1992) 'Cultures of teaching: A focus for change', in HARGREAVES, A. and FULLAN, M. (eds) *Understanding Teacher Development*, London: Cassell, pp. 216–40.

HARGREAVES, D. (1995) *The Mosaic of Learning: Schools and Teachers for the Next Century*, London: DEMOS.

HMI (1978) *Primary Education in England: A Survey*, London: HMSO.

ILLICH, I. (1971) *Deschooling Society*, London: Calder and Boyars.

LAWLOR, S. (1990) *Teachers Mistaught?*, London: Centre for Policy Studies.

LETWIN, O. (1988) 'Grounding comes first', *Times Educational Supplement*, 11 March, p. 18.

MILLETT, A. (1997) lecture given at King's College.

NIAS, J. (1992) *Whole School Curriculum Development in the Primary School*, London: Falmer Press.

OFSTED (1996) *The Annual Report of Her Majesty Chief Inspector of Schools*, London: HMSO.

PRAIS, S.J. and WAGNER, K. (1995) 'Schooling standards in England and Germany: Some summary conclusions based on economic performance', *Compare*, **16**, pp. 5–36.

REYNOLDS, D. and FARRELL, S. (1996) *Worlds Apart?: A Review of International Surveys of Educational Achievement Involving England*, London: HMSO.

SCAA (1996) Values, Education and the National Curriculum: a discussion paper, London: HMSO.

SHULMAN, L.S. (1987) 'Knowledge and Teaching: Foundations of the New Reform', *Harvard Educational Review*, **57**, 1, pp. 1–21.

TTA (1996) *National Standards for Headship*, London: TTA.

TTA (1997) *Standards for the Award of Qualified Teacher Status*, London: TTA.

WEINER, M.J. (1985) *English Culture and the Decline of the Industrial Spirit*, London: Routledge.

WOODHEAD, C. (1995) *A Question of Standards: Finding the Balance*, London: Politeia.

8   Children Yesterday, Today and Tomorrow

Mary Jane Drummond

In this chapter I will explore the proposition that the most important considerations in the debate about how primary education should be reformed for the twenty-first century are not questions of power politics, nor of whose definitions of curriculum should prevail. The core of the debate must focus on the children who will be living and learning in the next century; we need to consider the characteristics of these children, before we can shape a curriculum that is fit for them. As a starting point, here are the first few lines from a book I sometimes use on in-service courses, in my work with teachers and other educators.

> Once upon a time there was a little girl.
>
> She had a Father, and a Mother, and a Grandpa, and a Grandma, and an Uncle, and an Aunty; and they all lived together in a nice white cottage with a thatched roof.
>
> This little girl had short hair, and short legs, and short frocks (pink-and-white striped cotton in summer, and red serge in winter). But her name wasn't short at all. It was Millicent Margaret Amanda. But Father and Mother and Grandpa and Grandma and Uncle and Aunty couldn't very well call out 'Millicent Margaret!' every time they wanted her, so they shortened it to 'Milly-Molly-Mandy,' which is quite easy to say.
>
> Now everybody in the nice white cottage with the thatched roof had some particular job to do — even Milly-Molly-Mandy . . .
>
> And what did she do? Well, Milly-Molly-Mandy's legs were short, as I've told you, but they were very lively, just right for running errands. So Milly-Molly-Mandy was quite busy, fetching and carrying things, and taking messages.
> (from *Milly Molly Mandy Stories*, Joyce Lankester Brisley)

First published in 1928, the Milly-Molly-Mandy stories were reprinted in paperback right through the 1970s, 1980s and 1990s. They are still in print, still being asked for in bookshops, still being read by children today.[1]

When I ask early years educators on in-service courses to read a chapter or two of Milly-Molly-Mandy's adventures, many of them admit to having loved her dearly during their own childhoods. Those educators who meet Milly-Molly-Mandy for the first time are divided: some cannot get excited by this relic of a bygone age, but others are disgusted by her vacant expression and little beady eyes. With encouragement, the educators list her other characteristics: her obedience, her immature speech, her dependence (it takes six mature adults to protect and provide for her) her politeness, her sweet tooth, her thrift, her innocence of pain and grief (and mud). We go on to note how quiet, clean, safe and snug is her thatched cottage, how enclosed and self-contained her well-kept village, how the adults in her life rarely talk to one another, and never, ever say anything the slightest bit disagreeable.

What's the point of this discussion? To trigger an investigation into the taken-for-granted concepts *childhood* and *children*; to stimulate questions about the nature of children, especially 'child-like children'. This is a concept that the Japanese have a word for;[2] I have found it useful in the process of examining my own values and beliefs about children and childhood. What about this child, for example?

We lit fires. We were always lighting fires.

I preferred magnifying glasses to matches. We spent afternoons burning little piles of cut grass. I loved watching the grass change colour. I loved it when the flame began to race through the grass. You had more control with a magnifying glass. It was easier but it took more skill. . . . We'd have a race; burn, blow it out, burn, blow it out. Last to burn the paper completely in half had to let the other fella burn his hand. We'd draw a man on the paper and burn holes in him; in his hands and his feet, like Jesus. We drew long hair on him. We left his mickey till last.

We cut roads through the nettles. My ma wanted to know what I was doing going out wearing my duffle coat and mittens on a lovely nice day.

— We're doing the nettles, I told her.

The nettles were huge; giant ones. The hives from their stings were colossal, and they itched for ages after they'd stopped stinging. They took up a big corner of the field behind the shops. Nothing else grew there, just the nettles. After we hacked them over with a sideways swing of our sticks and hurleys we had to mash them down. (Doyle, 1993)

I use this extract like the first, to raise questions that may not get asked very often among those who live and work with children, questions that are, however, still worth thinking about. Is Paddy Clarke a child-like child? If Milly-Molly-Mandy misses out on noise and danger and rough words, what's absent in Paddy Clarke's life? Is he more or less of a child than she is? If an intelligent

Martian, with a working command of English but no conception of children or of childhood, were to be confronted with these two extracts, what sense could he, she, or it, make of them?

Where these questions lead is towards other, and more serious ones: whose definitions of children and childhood do we, parents and educators, subscribe to, probably without even knowing it? Whose images of the child-like child do we carry, deep in our mind's eye, as we care for and educate children in the late twentieth century? Do we know enough about the effect these images, definitions, expectations might have on the children in our families and our primary schools? It is not difficult to accept the proposition that the way we (you, I, society at large) see children in general affects the ways in which we treat them as a whole; it is harder to disentangle cause and effect in particular adult interactions with children, in individual adult/child relationships. And yet I believe this is an area well worth exploring, since our practices in educating children must be inextricably tangled up with our aspirations about what kind of people we think they are, and what kind of people we want them to become.

As such an exploration gets under way, as it now is, in numerous research studies and seminars, in books and journals,[3] it is necessary to be aware that it can only proceed on the basis of our rejection of a different way of understanding children, a mind-set that James and Prout (1990) diagnose as the 'old paradigm' of childhood. In this version, children are seen in stark contrast to the adults whom they will one day become. James and Prout list the characteristics of adults and children, in this 'old paradigm', as if they were two different instances of the same human species.

Children	Adults
immature	mature
irrational	rational
incompetent	competent
asocial	social
acultural	cultural

(adapted from James and Prout, 1990, p. 13)

The passage from one state of being to another is achieved, according to socialization theory, by the natural process of development (from the simple to the complex, from the irrational to the rational) and by the equally natural process of parenting. The adults direct, the children respond; the adults trigger learning and cooperation by operating reward and punishment systems; the social order is perpetuated, as the irrational, passive infant becomes the competent, active adult. In this model, the universal child, natural and culturally naked, as it were, is transformed into the adult at home and at ease in a particular, ordered, taken-for-granted, social world.

James and Prout reject this way of seeing, forcefully arguing that although the physical, biological facts of infancy and childhood are fixed, their cultural manifestations can and do vary dramatically. The facts get taken over by the ways in which society, (which includes parents and teachers), apprehend, interpret and give shape to the facts. In the 'new paradigm', James and Prout claim, it is recognized, first, that childhood is always socially constructed, and, secondly, that children are also social-constructivists, that they make meanings for themselves, as they contribute to the shaping of the world of childhood they inhabit.

Tobin, Wu and Davidson (1989), provide vivid, chapter-long illustrations of the social construction of childhood in three very different worlds, in China, Japan and the US. English early years educators with whom I have used this challenging book are often especially excited by the description of Hiroki, a 4-year-old boy in a Buddhist pre-school in Kyoto.

> On the day we videotaped at Komatsudani, Hiroki started things off with a flourish by pulling his penis out from under the leg of his shorts and waving it at the class during the morning welcome song. During the workbook session that followed, Hiroki called out answers to every question the teacher asked and to many she did not ask. When not volunteering answers, Hiroki gave a loud running commentary on his workbook progress ('now I'm coloring the badger, now the pig . . .') as he worked rapidly and deftly on his assignment. He alternated his play-by-play announcing with occasional songs, entertaining the class with loud, accurate renditions of their favourite cartoon themes, complete with accompanying dancing, gestures, and occasional instrumental flourishes. Despite the demands of his singing and announcing schedule, Hiroki managed to complete his workbook pages before most of the older children (of course, those sitting near him might have finished their work faster had they a less distracting tablemate) . . .

> Lunch over and the room cleaned up, Fukui-sensei (the teacher) returned to the balcony where, faced with the sight of Hiroki and another boy involved in a fight (which consisted mostly of the other boy's being pushed down and climbed on by Hiroki), she said neutrally, 'Are you still fighting?' Then she added, a minute later, in the same neutral tone, 'Why are you fighting anyway?' and told everyone still on the balcony, 'Hurry up and clean up (the flash cards). Lunchtime is over. Hurry, hurry.' Hiroki was by now disrupting the card clean-up by rolling on the cards and putting them in his mouth, but when he tried to enter the classroom Fukui-sensei put her hand firmly on his back and ushered him outside again. Fukui-sensei, who by now was doing the greatest share of the card picking-up, several times blocked Hiroki from leaving the scene of his crime, and she playfully spanked him on the behind when he continued to roll on the cards.

There is plenty more to read about Hiroki's exciting day, and typically the discussion becomes quite heated, especially when we turn to comments made by other participants in Tobin's study — the educators representing the 'three cultures' being investigated.

Comments Arising from the Observation of Hiroki

- Staff team at Hiroki's school:
  'We think Fukui-sensei (Hiroki's teacher) dealt with Hiroki in a sat-isfactory way. We think it is right to ignore the most provocative, aggressive and exhibitionist actions. This is a strategy we have agreed on.'
- Higashino: Assistant Principal of Hiroki's school:
  'We should not punish Hiroki. He has pride and he will be hurt if we yell at him or make him sit alone. We must avoid confronting or censuring Hiroki'.
- American early years specialist:
  'Hiroki is bored, he finishes his work quickly, his behaviour is an attempt to make things more exciting, better matched to the pace and level of stimulation he needs. He is gifted, talented, intelligent.'
- Fukui-sensei — Hiroki's teacher:
  'Hiroki is not especially intelligent; if he is so clever, why doesn't he understand better? If he understood better, he would behave better'.
- Yoshizawa: Principal of Hiroki's school:
  'Misbehaving, including fighting, is a lost art for today's sheltered nuclear-family raised children.'
- Fukui-sensei — Hiroki's teacher:
  'I let the boys fight because it is natural for boys of that age to fight, and it is good for them to have the experience while they are young of what it feels like to fight.'

When the heat of the discussion has died down, it is time to think about what Hiroki can teach us about our own observations and perceptions of children. What internal categories, invisible to ourselves but glaringly obvious, we must assume, to Hiroki's educators, govern our understanding and our practices? And are these categories compatible with our most cherished aspirations for our children?

As the discussion continues, the participants begin to disentangle the strands that make up *our* version of *Tobin's* account of *Hiroki's* story. It becomes easier to see which bits of children, and of a particular child, are necessarily part of being a child; these can then be set apart from those parts that are the outcomes of firm expectations, however unself-consciously en-forced, those parts that are a projection of our most optimistic aspirations, and those parts that children construct for themselves. For if Hiroki teaches us nothing else, he certainly reminds us that children have voices and important things to say, just as much as their educators.

We need not, of course, travel to Japan to find differences in the ways we construct children and childhood. Here in England, in January 1996, the School Curriculum and Assessment Authority (SCAA) published a slim document called *Desirable Outcomes for Children's Learning on Entering Compulsory Educa-tion*. Reactions from the early years professional community were, on the whole, hostile.[4] But in one quarter, the early years educators were more than hostile: they were implacably opposed, on principle, to the desirability of some of the 'desirable outcomes' set out in the document. These educators were speaking on behalf of the Steiner-Waldorf kindergarten movement, an international group who draw their inspiration from the philosophical writings of Rudolf Steiner (1861–1925), and whose kindergartens number more than 1000 worldwide. Their work is dedicated to a particular view of childhood, and the ways in which children under 7 (or, in their own terms, before the second dentition) grow, develop and learn. Their account of the essential features of early childhood parts company with SCAA's desirable outcomes approach in several important particulars. The chief of these is the way in which the SCAA document sets out key expectations for early achievement in literacy.

> Children enjoy books and handle them carefully, understanding how they are organized. They know that words and pictures carry meaning and that, in English, print is read from left to right and from top to bottom. They begin to associate sounds with patterns in rhymes, with syllables, and with words and letters. They recognise their own names and some familiar words. They recognize letters of the alphabet by shape and sound. In their writing they use pictures, symbols, familiar words and letters, to communicate meaning, showing awareness of some of the different purposes of writing. They write their names with appropriate use of upper and lower case letters. (ibid.)

These capacities — outcomes or achievements — whatever we might choose to call them, have no place in the Steiner kindergarten. There the educators use no picture books or printed material of any kind. They do not require their children to learn either the names or the sounds of the letters of the alphabet.

The rationale for their approach is to be found in Steiner's teaching about certain key stages in the development of children. Drawing on a three-fold model of adult humanity, comprising the powers of the head, the heart and the will (thinking, feeling and doing), Steiner educators maintain that young children are essentially in 'doing' mode, exercising their whole bodies, under the control of their will, in sustained, creative, imaginative exploration of their world. In the Steiner kindergarten, there is no place for the abstraction of the printed page or the letters of the alphabet. But their 3 to 7-year-olds are not deprived of stories, folk tales, myths, poetry and song. Their lives are daily enriched by the most entrancing stories and songs, as I know from my own observations in the Rosebridge Kindergarten in Cambridge.[5]

The programme for these young children is built on very different foundations from the 'areas of experience' familiar to mainstream nursery educators.[6] The Steiner programme is based on rhythm, routine, reverence, ritual, creativity, stories and song. At the centre of this programme are the children, who, like children anywhere, are by turns boisterous, dreamy, fretful, absorbed, noisy, joyful, wondering, inventive and energetic. During the morning session they move from a period of spontaneous imaginative play to gather round the big table for painting, baking or craft activities. There is a time for ring-games and songs, and for outdoor play in a wonderful garden. There are times to come together to eat the bread they have baked, to celebrate festivals, to listen to their teacher tell them stories. These stories are selected not just for their rich language and literary worth, but for their moral meanings; they are stories that will act as a grounding for the children's moral life. All knowledge, claims one Steiner educator, starts with a state of wonder; the kindergarten seeks to support and foster this sense of wonder. The adults in the kindergarten are the guides who protect the children absorbed in exploring their world, and who feed their energies with nourishing activities.

Several times now, I have invited Steiner educators to contribute to my in-service courses for early years practitioners. They are listened to in a profound silence, which is half born of incredulity (that a system so different could exist on one's very doorstep), and half born of respect for the reverence and intensity with which these people speak of their work with children. Once, however, I remember, a nursery teacher from a huge inner-city primary school, serving an economically disadvantaged estate, with all its associated problems, was moved to object to what she was hearing. The essence of her strenuous objection was that the Steiner kindergarten and its trappings — muslin, candles, wooden blocks, flowers, shells, logs, brown bread and freshly made jam — could not be said to constitute a preparation for the *real* world, where the children she knew best were living and learning. The Steiner educator paused for a moment and gently replied: 'Surrounded by the beautiful, being shown what is good . . . I don't think that makes you *un*prepared for the world.' Needless to say, the discussion did not end there.

But the point the speaker was making[7] has a wider relevance than a discussion about the advantages — or disadvantages — of the Steiner approach. At the heart of her proposition is the simple principle that the prime responsibility of educators, of whatever philosophical or political conviction, is to give their children the intellectual and emotional nourishment that will match their growing and developing powers. Difficulties and differences only arise when educators disagree about what these powers are, and which are the most important. Where Steiner educators prioritize the good and the beautiful, the authors of SCAA's *Desirable Outcomes* prioritize (among other things) capital letters, word recognition and numbers up to 10. At stake here are different constructions of childhood, different conceptualizations of what it is that young children should do and feel, know and understand, represent and express.

Where do we go from here? Recognizing differences, and accepting the inevitability of such differences is only a first step. But it is an important step, because it reminds us that we — parents, teachers, society at large — do have real choices to make. In early years provisions in nurseries, infant, first and primary schools, it is possible for people, parents and educators, to come together to do some thinking work around these issues, returning perhaps, as a starting point, to the Japanese concept of the child-like child. What *do* we understand by 'child-like children', of 3, of 5, of 7 or 11?

Any attempt to come to terms with these difficult questions will be im-measurably enriched by close attention to the work of the early years edu-cators in the region of Emilia Romagna in Italy. Here the services to young children, from birth to 3, and from 3 to 6, are justly world famous. Their work has been celebrated in a staggeringly impressive travelling exhibition *The Hun-dred Languages of Children*, which was seen in England for the first time in the summer of 1997, in two venues, under the auspices of the *British Associa-tion for Early Childhood Education*.[8] The title of the exhibit refers to the principle at the heart of the Reggio-Emilia approach, (as it has come to be known) — the principle that children have at their disposal 100 languages, of which the school steals 99. In Italy children start elementary school at the age of 6; in the full day childcare available from birth to 6 in the pre-schools, nurseries and toddler centres of Reggio-Emilia, the educators are committed to restoring the full 'one hundred languages of children'.

Their approach

> fosters children's intellectual development through a systematic focus on symbolic representation. Young children are encouraged to explore their environment and express themselves through all of their natural 'languages' or modes of expression, including words, movement, drawing, painting, build-ing, sculpture, shadow play, collage, dramatic play and music.[9]

These are not empty words, or wishful thinking; this description of the educators' aspirations is followed through into practice.

In every provision for young children there is a richly equipped workshop -cum-studio — the *atelier* — staffed by a professionally trained artist/educator, the *atelierista*. In the *atelier*, children's powers to represent their experiences, their questions, their problems, and their dreams, are given the richest oppor-tunities for growth. Using the multitude of materials available, children are daily engaged in complex representations of their pressing emotional and cognitive concerns. Child-like children, in Reggio-Emilia, are honoured for character-istics that make 'the appropriate use of upper and lower case letters' look like very small beer. Carla Rinaldi, a pedagogical coordinator who works to support curriculum development and in-service work in a group of pre-schools, sums up their principled position:

> The cornerstone of our experience, based on practice, theory and research, is the image of children as rich, strong and powerful . . . They have the desire to grow, curiosity, the ability to be amazed and the desire to relate to other people . . . (They) are open to exchanges and reciprocity as deeds and acts of love, which they not only want to receive but also want to offer.

In describing the Reggio-Emilia approach so enthusiastically I am not trying to suggest that it could simply be transplanted, root, branches and flowers, into primary education in this country. But I do believe that British teachers and other educators would do well to assimilate the understanding that Rinaldi refers to as their 'corner-stone', their confident belief in children's powers.

In the years since 1988, and the passing of the Education Reform Act, untold time and energy (and forests of paper) have been expended in the project of devising and revising curriculum structures (programmes of study, attainment targets, end of keystage descriptions, desirable outcomes), through which a whole generation of primary and pre-school children have passed. These structures have been elaborated in terms of knowledge, concepts and skills; their reference points are to the external world, as we apprehend it through the subject studies of the National Curriculum, themselves derived from the academic disciplines of the grammar schools of earlier centuries. The curriculum review now under way, which will take us into the twenty-first century, is an opportunity to start again with a different set of conceptions in mind, the conceptions that are the theme of this chapter. If we decided to design a primary curriculum for the future by *starting with children*, we would be well on the way to constructing a curriculum fit for children. This would be a more truly educational enterprise than perseverating in our attempts to fit children into a curriculum imposed from without.

Starting with children would entail, as the Italian educators do, recognizing their powers. It would mean abandoning our tendency to focus on children's weaknesses and incapacities, as evidenced in hundreds of items in baseline assessment schedules that record what children cannot do, or do not seem to know. It would mean recognizing that all children learn, that learning is what they do best, and that they have been doing it from birth. It would mean that child-like children, right through the primary school, would have their powers acknowledged, exercised and strengthened. Their power to speak at least two languages, for example, grossly neglected in many present-day schools, could be recognized. Their powers to imagine, 'to see into the life of things', in Mary Warnock's expressive phase (Warnock, 1978), could be more effectively nourished if we accepted that the absolutely logical consistency required of the flight controller or income tax inspector is not a characteristic of children's thinking. As the celebrated American kindergarten teacher, Vivian Gussin Paley (1981), puts it:

> (The 5 or 6-year-old child) is at a singular period. He is not a captive of his illusions and fantasies, but can choose them for support or stimulation without self-consciousness. He has become aware of the thinking required by the adult world, but is not committed to its burden of rigid consistency. (pp. 29–30)

Magical and imaginative thinking, in Paley's version of the child-like child, is not a weakness, but young children's way of deploying their power to see things as they might be, not simply as they are. And this power brings insight and understanding.

> The child is the ultimate magician. He credits God and lesser powers, but it is the child who confirms the probability of events. If he can imagine something, it exists . . . As soon as he learns a language well enough, and *before* he is told he cannot invent the world, he will explain everything. (ibid., p. 81)

Warnock (1978) pushes home the point in terms of what educators must do if these powers are to survive in school:

> I have come very strongly to believe that it is the cultivation of imagination which should be the chief aim of education, and in which our present systems of education most conspicuously fail, where they do fail . . . in education we have a duty to educate the imagination above all else.

When Diderot and his associates, a group of radical French philosophers, drew up the syllabus for the great Encyclopaedia, published in 35 volumes between 1751 and 1776, they used the simplest of frameworks. All of humanity's great achievements, all of society's accumulated knowledge and wisdom, all was subsumed under just three heads: Memory, Reason and Imagination (see Furbank, 1992). Such bold simplicity, with its emphasis on the powers of the human intellect, encourages me to argue that acknowledging what we know about young children's intellectual and emotional powers is a promising starting point for their education. The Italian educators in Reggio-Emilia choose to start here, and they have convincingly documented the exceptional quality of children's lives in their nurseries and pre-schools.

But not every society chooses to start from the same premise. In the US, the *Quality 2000 Project* has announced that the first national educational goal for the twenty-first century is to be: 'All children will start school ready to learn'. This is an absurd inversion of the priority for the future as I see it; the first step must be to ensure that all schools are ready for children who have been learning since birth, who are already, when they cross the threshold of formal education, dedicated learners, adventurous explorers, committed scientists, expressive artists and compassionate friends.[10] It is up to schools to make sure they stay that way, while they lead them on to greater things.

Not all educationalists are convinced that schools are capable of meeting this responsibility. Mary Willes' challenging study of what happens to young children when they become pupils, stands as an awful warning of what does happen in some schools, where she carried out her observations, and what could happen in many more, if teachers and other educators ignore or neglect the essential characteristics of the children in their classrooms.

> The minimal inescapable requirement that a child must meet if he is to function as a participating pupil is not very extensive. It is necessary to accept adult direction, to know that you say nothing at all unless the teacher indicates that you may, to know that when your turn is indicated you must use whatever clues you can find, and make the best guess you can. (Willes, 1983, p. 83)

The pupils evoked in this chilling passage have had their powers stripped from them. Even more pessimistic is Willes' scathing summary of what it is to be a pupil.

> . . . Finding out what the teacher wants, and doing it constitutes the primary duty of a pupil . . . (ibid., p. 138)

Even allowing for exaggeration, which can be attributed to the author's passionate desire for a better deal for children, there is an uncomfortable grain of truth in Willes' observation. Everyone who has ever worked with young children in large numbers, knows that, for at least part of the time, harmony in the classroom depends on compliance. Many aspects of life in the primary school routine are predicated on obedience. What would happen, I sometimes wonder, if one day, when the teachers of England rang the bell for the end of morning playtime, the children simply refused to respond?

This fantasy of country-wide school refusal has been strengthened by reading Iona Opie's painstaking observations of *The People in the Playground* (Opie, 1993). Opie made weekly visits to observe in a junior school playground from January 1970 until November 1983. Her prime purpose was a continuation of her and her husband's earlier researches into schoolchild lore, games, songs, riddles and jokes; she found in the playground an astonishingly rich vein to mine. The main interest for the primary educator is in what Opie saw that the teachers on playground duty rarely see (because they are busy looking for trouble): the energy and enthusiasm that the children (or *people* as they always refer to themselves) invest in their imaginative and physical play. One image stick in my mind: two girls plunging down the steps into the playground; one calls to the other 'going on with witches and fairies, right?' The fractions and the apostrophes on the blackboard are left far away as the children fly back to their shared imaginative worlds. In schools of the future, my fantasy continues, this energy, and this power to live through the imagination, will be characteristic of classrooms as well as of playgrounds.

It is interesting to note that for Kieran Egan (1988), this possibility is no fantasy, but an educational necessity. Egan's work starts by considering the traditional opposition between the powers of logical reason and those of fantasy. Education as we know it, so far, has been constructed around the primacy of rationality; fantasy, 'which ignores the boundaries of reality, is seen as the enemy' (p. 11). He goes on to call for a redistribution of emphasis; drawing attention to young children's mental lives, of which a prominent part is fantasy, he argues that the education of young children must take account of this way of thinking, which is, he claims, energetic, wholesome and important for intellectual growth. In *Primary Understanding* he sets about the project of devising a whole primary curriculum, and a range of teaching methods, that would enable teachers to get in tune with children's robust imaginative powers.

Kieran Egan's version of the childlike child is a person who may, on the one hand, 'be unable to conserve liquid quantity, (but who) may, on the other, lead a vivid intellectual life, brimming with knights, dragons, witches and star warriors' (p. 23). The children of today — and tomorrow — argues Egan, deserve a curriculum 'made up of *important* content, rich in meaning . . . our curriculum concern will be to get at what is of human importance to our social and cultural lives' (p. 199). And so, once again, we see there are choices to be made; the choices we make in constructing our own versions of child-like children will in turn affect the decisions we make in selecting important educational content, which makes human sense to them.

Conclusion

In this chapter, I have argued that the children of tomorrow, who will live and learn in the primary schools of the twenty-first century, deserve an education that fosters and strengthens their powers to do, to feel and to think: an education for the domains of the will, the heart and the head, as the Steiner educators would put it. To be able to provide such an education, parents and educators, the whole community of those concerned for children's lives, will need to recognize that there is work to be done, together, in thinking through what these words entail. The quality of this thinking is crucial. The task is a challenging one: to debate what sorts of children we want to become the citizens of the future, to consider what sort of lives we want them to lead, in childhood and in adulthood, to investigate the conception of the 'good life' for children, and for the society in which they learn. The rigour and creativity of the thinking we engage in, the openness with which we explore difference and dissent, the energy with which we collaborate in the task — all these will affect the quality of the primary education of the future.

Notes

1 See, for example, 'Mary's story' in Andrew Pollard's fascinating case studies of children at home and at primary school (Pollard, 1996).

2 Kodomorashii Kodomo: translated as a 'child-like child', this concept is fully discussed in Tobin, Wu and Davidson (1989). The authors cite a survey of Japanese teachers on the characteristics of a 'child-like child' and found the traits most highly valued were empathy, gentleness, social consciousness, kindness and cooperativeness.

3 There is an ever-increasing number of publications devoted to problematizing the issues discussed briefly in this chapter. See, for example, Holland (1992); Kessel and Siegel (1983); Mayall (1994); Pilcher and Wragg (1996); and Walkerdine (1997).

4 See, for example, my own reaction, based largely on a review of professional responses to the consultation version of the document, published in *Forum*, **38**, 2, pp. 56–8 with the title 'An undesirable document'.

5 I am deeply grateful to Janni Nicol and Stephanie Grögelein for allowing me to observe from a corner of their kindergarten, and for giving so much time to help me understand what I saw.

6 The areas of experience that form the basis for the *Desirable Outcomes* are personal and social development, language and literacy, mathematics, knowledge and understanding of the world, physical development, creative development. These were adapted from a document by HMI (1985).

7 My profound thanks to Ute Towriss of the Cambridge Steiner Project for the contribution she has made to my thinking over the last five years.

8 A useful collection of papers written in honour of this exhibition is *Reflections on Early Education and Care*, edited by Pat Gura, published by the British Association for Early Childhood Education.

9 From the opening paragraph of a valuable book describing the Reggio-Emilia approach (Edwards, Gandini and Forman, 1994).

10 For children as artists, see, for example, Matthews (1994); for children's friendships see, for example, Dunn (1988) and Selleck (1996).

References

DOYLE, R. (1993) *Paddy Clarke Ha Ha Ha*, London: Secker and Warburg.

DUNN, J. (1988) *The Beginnings of Social Understanding*, Oxford: Blackwells.

EDWARDS, C., GANDINI, L. and FORMAN, G. (1994) *The Hundred Languages of Children*, NJ, Norwood: Ablex.

EGAN, K. (1988) *Primary Understanding*, London: Routledge.

FURBANK, P.N. (1992) *Diderot: A Critical Biography*, London: Minerva.

GURA, P. (ed.) (1997) *Reflections on Early Education and Care*, London: British Association for Early Childhood Education.

HMI (1985) *Aspects of Primary Education: The Education of Children Under Five*, London: HMSO.

HOLLAND, P. (1992) *What is a Child?*, London: Virago.

JAMES, A. and PROUT, A. (eds) (1990) *Constructing and Reconstructing Childhood: Contemporary Issues in the Sociological Study of Childhood*, London: Falmer Press.

KESSEL, F. and SIEGEL, A. (eds) (1983) *The Child and other Cultural Inventions*, New York: Praeger.

MATTHEWS, J. (1994) *Helping Children to Draw and Paint in Early Childhood: Children and Visual Representation*, London: Hodder and Stoughton.

MAYALL, B. (ed.) (1994) *Children's Childhoods Observed and Experienced*, London: Falmer Press.

OPIE, I. (1993) *The People in the Playground*, Oxford: Oxford University Press.

PALEY, V.G. (1981) *Wally's Stories*, Cambridge, MA: Harvard University Press.

PILCHER, J. and WRAGG, S. (eds) (1996) *Thatcher's Children? Politics, Childhood and Society in the 1980s and 1990s*, London: Falmer Press.

POLLARD, A. (1996) *The Social World of Children's Learning*, London: Cassell.

SELLECK, D. (1996) *Communication Between Babies in their First Year*, London: National Children's Bureau.

TOBIN, J.J., WU, D. and DAVIDSON, D. (1989) *Pre-school in Three Cultures*, Princeton, NJ: Yale University Press.

WALKERDINE, V. (1997) *Daddy's Girl Young Girls and Popular Culture*, London: Macmillan.

WARNOCK, M. (1978) *Imagination*, London: Faber.

WILLES, M. (1983) *Children into Pupils*, London: Routledge and Kegan Paul.

9 Pupil Experience and a Curriculum for Life-Long Learning[1]

Pat Triggs and Andrew Pollard

Introduction

We want to argue in this chapter that the educational 'reforms' of the 1980s and 1990s largely ignored pupil experience, the issue of motivation and even learning itself. We would suggest that the period was dominated by a mind-set which prioritized curriculum specification, its delivery through instructional teaching, and the measurement of results. Whilst this may seem to represent the gradual achievement of a more 'efficient' system, we fear that it could actually undermine children's dispositions to learn and thus have unintended consequences in terms of 'lifelong learning'.

We begin by reviewing the research from which these concerns are derived. Four major conclusions are then identified, together with their educational implications. These lead to a proposal for a revised primary school curriculum based on a new conception of the 'core' and 'foundation' curriculum.

Identity, Self-confidence and Learning

The *Identity and Learning Project* (ILP)[2] began in 1987 and is a very detailed, longitudinal study of social influences on the learning of 16 children as they progress through 12 years of schooling (from age 4 to 16). Analysis of classroom teaching/learning episodes is complemented by study of the influences of the parents and siblings, schools and successive teachers, and of friendships, peers, youth, media and technocultures. Narrative case studies of pupils learning over time show the enormous complexity of intellectual, affective, pedagogic, social, cultural and linguistic factors involved in pupil learning.

In two books (*The Social World of the Children's Learning* and *The Social World of Pupil Careers*) Andrew Pollard and Ann Filer have told the stories of these children, growing up through successive cycles of experience which spiral on and on through life. They have represented the factors which affect children as shown in figure 9.1.

This model highlights the way in which identity and self-confidence affect each child's engagement with learning. Classroom performance is, in

Figure 9.1: *A model of learning, identity and social setting*

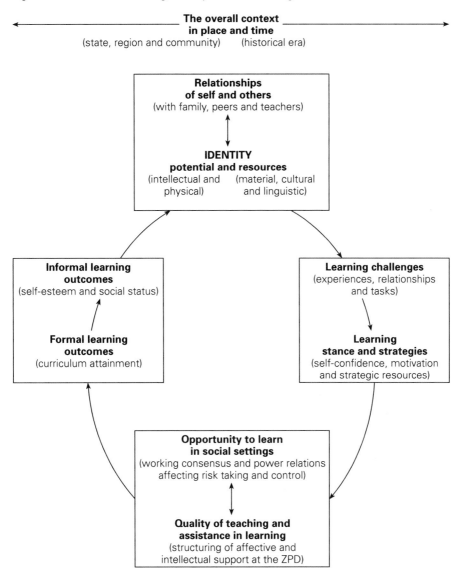

these terms, as much a product of the child's learning disposition and of social factors, as it is the result of effective instruction. Indeed, it is argued that the two sets of factors go together: the child and the teacher; the learner and the curriculum; the social context and the instructional context. Consider, for instance, the sort of factors which this mother refers to when talking about the development and achievements of her 6-year-old daughter, Mary.

Mary has grown increasingly self-confident over the year. She has grown physically so is able to do more, i.e. she is taller, stronger, can cope without getting so tired. Also her mental development has meant that she can also do a lot more as she is able to understand things, communicate, read and express herself better. She has gained pleasure from these developments.

Mary likes to do things well and she has never really attempted to do things before she is ready — in contrast to her brothers. Therefore with these new physical and mental developments she is able to do a lot more things — and do them well. She can express herself much better so is able to hold her own in an argument. She can reason and see others' point of view more clearly. She can work out and calculate things like money and tell the time which both give her more freedom: i.e. she can go out and spend her pocket money, or go out and play and be back at a specific time. She can now brush her hair and bath herself and choose what she wants to wear which obviously makes her more independent. In fact she is quite keen to take more control of her life — she likes to get her own breakfast, prepare all her clothes for school and ballet and often it is Mary who reminds me about things for example, she is going out to tea or must not forget something for school etc. etc.

Mary's sense of humour and fun has developed in the last years. She is quite cheeky and mischievous and something of a mimic. She is quite confident about 'holding court' and making everyone laugh — (with her and at her)! She loves performing on stage, at school and at ballet. This year her ballet school put on a show which involved three live performances. Mary had one solo and two other dances to perform which she really enjoyed. The show was at St George's Hall and she loved getting dressed up and made up and the behind stage atmosphere. She thoroughly enjoyed performing and the applause, and the sheer 'theatre' of it all. After it finished on the final night Mary went home in floods of tears because it had all ended. I am sure ballet has helped her self-confidence as she is so successful at it and has always been highly commended in all her exams. It is also an area personal to her i.e. her brothers have nothing to do with it so cannot encroach or steal her thunder.

Mary's main areas of frustration are when she is tired and she is not allowed to do something which she wants to, i.e. stay up late to watch something on television or have a friend round. Her stock phrases in this situation are 'I hate you mummy' or 'I am leaving home to find a nicer mummy', though she is beginning to argue more rationally and question my decisions and try to compromise in a much more mature way. In fact she is trying much harder to rationalize and understand things in all spheres of life. (Mrs Inman, parent diary, July 1989, year 2)

The ILP's detailed study of children's lives demonstrates conclusively that *what is taught is not necessarily learned*, and that there are major intervening variables concerned with pupils' personal self-confidence as learners. This affirms the opinion of many teachers and parents that school education should be based on a balanced consideration of teaching and curriculum *and* of learning and learners. A simple way of expressing the key educational process is shown in figure 9.2.

Figure 9.2: *Complementary factors in pupil learning and educational standards*

TEACHERS   **CHILDREN**

Curriculum   >>>>>>>>>>   PUPIL   <<<<<<<<<<   Learning skills
and teaching   LEARNING   and self-confidence

EDUCATIONAL STANDARDS

This research also draws attention to the crucial mediating role of parents in learning, the considerable influence of relationships with siblings and peers, and the need for skilful, sensitive and socially-aware management of pupil motivation by teachers. *The Social World of Pupil Careers* provides narrative stories of children negotiating their paths through successive teachers at school. They adapt their strategies actively as they encounter new classrooms and practices. For many, their friendships are the more stable part of school life and for most, their parents provide a source of care, advice and affection as the children struggle, progressively, to make sense of their new experiences and to cope effectively with new circumstances and challenges.

Taken as a whole, this analysis suggests that an emphasis on curriculum and teaching, whilst necessary, is educationally imbalanced unless it is complemented by a parallel focus on learners and learning. It suggests that standards can only be maximized if the learning skills and self-confidence of pupils get attention in the education system to complement present concerns with curriculum and teaching methods — a far cry from the present position.

Primary School Assessment, Curriculum and Experience

The *Primary Assessment, Curriculum and Experience* project (PACE)[3] focused on the primary school experience of a national sample of the first full cohort of pupils to have been taught through the National Curriculum. Their responses and behaviour in relation to curriculum, pedagogy and assessment were documented annually.

In the first phase of the study (1991–93) the PACE team found that children were to a large extent being 'protected' from the effects of a reformed curriculum which their teachers saw as inappropriate and potentially damaging to centrally important teacher–pupil relationships. Teachers, the study reported, were 'mediating change' and, in particular, moderating the impact of the revised assessment procedures on their pupils. Much of what was reported then reflected the constants of classroom life, characterized by Jackson as 'crowds, praise, power'. As the children moved on into Key Stage 2 pupils seemed to be becoming progressively instrumental and concerned to satisfy the requirements of their teachers. Whilst the children were younger, they had placed high priority on being active in their classrooms; now they were concerned with being successful. This, as was acknowledged, is not a new story.

In following the children through the remaining two years of their primary experience and reviewing the longitudinal data the PACE team were able to look for the issues emerging within the continuity. One of the themes to emerge from the project was how the children were constructing their view of what it is to be a learner. What the children said in the interviews, conducted annually throughout the project, suggests that their classroom experiences were not leading them to develop the skills and attitudes associated with being the kind of 'lifelong learners' that we are told will be characteristic of the next century. We can illustrate that here by looking at an analysis of their responses as they experienced a continued tightening of the frame in the three dimensions of pedagogy, assessment and curriculum.

Pedagogy

In each year of the study the 54 children in our longitudinal cohort were asked, 'Do you like it best when you choose what to do or when your teacher chooses?' Almost two-thirds of the pupils in years 1 and 2 recorded that they preferred to control their own activities. In year 5, only 44 per cent of the children said they would prefer to choose, 37 per cent liked their teacher to choose, with an interesting 13 per cent who preferred the choosing to be shared. The reasons the children gave for preferring to choose for themselves involved having more fun, being able to avoid things they didn't like or found hard, being able to choose what they liked best. However, in addition, there was a clearly identifiable strand of responses that was to do with wanting to choose in order to have more control over how they learned,

> Cos sometimes miss says do your maths when you want to finish your topic — and the other way around. (year 5)

> Cos say, like, you have English and you are really up-to-date — you feel like going on with your topic because you might be behind. (year 6)

> Because if you have stuff to catch up on you can do it when you want. Sometimes you have loads of pieces of topic work to do and you get 15 minutes — and then you go straight to maths for about an hour. (year 6)

These comments introduce a theme that runs though this analysis: the children have a sense of time as a scarce resource. They were aware of the pressure to 'get things done'; felt there was not enough time to do things properly, not enough time for them to learn as they would like, often not as much time as their teachers might like to give them. They were being urged to hurry up and learn because it was necessary to 'get on'.

By year 6 almost half the children had given up any preference for controlling their own learning and said they preferred their teachers to choose.

The reasons they gave for this give us another perspective on the argument we are developing.

Analysis of responses from the first four years of the PACE study produced signs of the children, as they got older, adopting more instrumental strategies to accommodate the progressive challenges they faced in school. This was confirmed by the later data. The categories 'because it's easier', 'because it's better for me/teacher knows best' became, in the last two years of Key Stage 2, as important as (and in year 6 more important than) having activities that were 'interesting'. A sample of the reasons they gave for why 'teacher knows best' gives an indication of their thinking.

> I just like it when miss decides because you really know what to do, cos she explains it. (year 5)

> You get a clear idea of what to do to get house points for good work. If you choose the work yourself you might not understand the right thing in the book, but if sir explains it is easier. (year 5)

> Cos he picks all the right things, and we don't. (year 5)

> If she chooses she tells you how to do it. If you choose you might take it to the teacher and she says it's all wrong. (year 6)

> If we choose we might not be learning what our teacher makes us work for. (year 6)

> If the teacher chooses you get to learn more than when you're choosing. (year 6)

> If we choose it might be something we've already done or are good at or like. (year 6)

> Because if she lets us do whatever we want we will just play games and not learn anything because we won't do any work. But the teacher will give us maths and English and a good selection and then we can learn a lot. (year 6)

If the teacher chose it was 'better for me' because it offered the security of knowing what to do and what was required. Increasingly, also, as children moved into years 5 and 6, their answers indicated a perception of learning as something possessed by the teacher — teachers know what you have to learn so it's better to let them decide what you should do. Greater prescription of the curriculum and the emphasis on categoric assessment in year 6 appeared to produce a strategic teacher-dependence in the pupils in the sample. As seen by the children, teachers made sure they didn't 'do the wrong thing' and saved them from a natural tendency to avoid work, go off-task and be over or underambitious. Where time is short it is important not to waste it by doing things you are good at or like and to avoid 'doing something we've already done'. Learning, the children were telling us is linear, not spiral; and it has little to do with enjoyment or what you already know, understand or can do.

In giving reasons why it was 'easier' when the teacher chose the activities the children also touched on aspects of classroom management, resourcing and learning processes. Pupils, they explained, had problems with choosing so it was better if they didn't as it wasted time. If they did choose there would be problems with access to resources, with finding people to work with, with having to do what someone else had chosen, and with all the attendant noise and movement.

It was more efficient to be teacher-dependent.

We don't have to waste time asking her if we can't think what to do. (year 3)

If she says to everybody 'You can choose' you find someone else is doing what you wanted. Sometimes I can't think of what to do. (year 3)

Then there aren't a lot of people rushing to different places. We are all in one place doing the same thing. (year 5)

Most of the time if we wanted to do something that's our own idea we wouldn't have the stuff. (year 5)

When the teacher decides there is not a big noise, everything goes quietly — no-one is saying 'What shall we do? What shall we do?' (year 6)

I can never make up my mind if I have to decide. (year 6)

When you choose you have got to think what to do and most people do something different, but when she chooses you can all work together. (year 6)

He can make a decision. I'll take forever. (year 6)

Because I don't have to sit and decide and take ages thinking — I like to have set work so that I can get on and do it and not hum and ha about it. (year 6)

Curriculum

One indication of children's view of learning is the expression of their preferences in different curriculum areas. In each year of the study the children in our longitudinal sample were asked to identify curriculum activities they 'liked best' and those they 'liked least'. The PACE team produced 'league tables' based on the rank order of the net score when the percentage 'best liked' was set against the percentage 'least liked' for each subject or activity in each year. In year 1 the most liked were PE, painting, the home corner and sand. Three of these held their place in year 2 but maths appeared in second place and sand was less popular. The first two years of Key Stage 2 saw the core curriculum subjects — maths, reading and writing — figuring in the top four with singing and drawing, In fact maths was at the top of the table in both years. However in years 5 and 6 there was a startling change. In each year only five curriculum activity areas ended up with a positive ranking. Art and PE were well ahead at the top of the league, followed by technology, TV, teacher reading stories and topic.

In years 5 and 6, it seems, most children found little enjoyment in the core curriculum with its increasingly categoric assessment. Art was preferred because it was fun and interesting, because it was an activity where it was possible to exercise some autonomy over what you did and where it was easy to succeed. PE was liked because it provided an opportunity to be active and have fun and where evaluation was not an issue.

A small selection of what the children in years 5 and 6 told researchers gives an indication of their perspective.

> Art is fun and you can draw different things and shade things in and draw real-life pictures. You sometimes have choice. With maths we have to do set papers and I don't find it easy to do.

Schools were beginning to respond to the pressure created by the publication of SATs results in league tables. For teachers the core curriculum subjects took on a 'high stakes' status and the children appeared to sense their teachers' priorities. Thus these pupils contrasted the atmosphere in maths with the more relaxed approach to other curriculum areas:

> In maths the teacher always tells you not to talk, they prefer you to get on with your maths but with art it's not so bad. It's fun to do and not hard, people can always help me with it.

> I like making things and I feel proud of what I've made. In maths I get muddled and I might have to stay in at play so maths is more worrying.

For two years maths was the most liked subject for this girl:

> I normally do lots (of maths) at home and so do my brothers. My mum gives me some too. (year 3)

> In maths you can work really hard. You don't have to tell anybody and just get on with it. (year 4)

But this changed in year 5 when it became her least-liked activity.

> I don't get on with it. I normally can't do it that well. I don't like working out sums — I might get them wrong.

Already we are involved with the highly significant area of assessment.

Assessment

Throughout the PACE study data has been gathered on children's response to situations in which various forms of assessment or evaluation were involved. In particular the team has reported children's feelings in this situation and considered how their responses reflect their attitude to learning. In each year children have been asked 'Do you like it when your teacher asks to look at your work?'. Their responses were placed in one of four categories: positive, negative, mixed and neutral. Across the six years, not unexpectedly, we saw a fall in positive feelings. However in year 4 over 40 per cent of children were still feeling positive about this situation. In year 5 this fell dramatically to 20 per cent and in year 6 to 13 per cent. There was a marked increase in children having mixed feelings about evaluation and assessment.

The comments made by the children enabled exploration of what lay behind this development. In years 5 and 6 when children felt positive about the process they talked of 'seeing if I get it right', 'seeing what mark I get'. They hoped for reward in the form of house points or certificates or (less often) the pleasure and approval of their teachers or family. Neutral comments were characterized by expressions that teachers were just 'doing their job' and 'helping me to learn'. The large proportions of mixed and negative feelings stemmed from two sources. First was the children's own assessment of their work — they applied criteria of quantity, neatness and correctness that they assumed would be applied by their teachers. In addition their feelings varied with their own assessment of the 'effort' they had put into the work. The second source of negative or mixed feelings was a strong sense of uncertainty — about whether they had done what was required, about how their teachers would react, about whether they had 'understood'. The most negative responses revealed considerable fear and apprehension about the consequences of 'getting it wrong'. At best this would mean the disappointment of the teacher that they had failed to meet expectations. At worst this would involve teacher censure, public humiliation and embarrassment or 'telling parents', or having to do the work again (probably in break or dinner time).

In each year of the study, data was also gathered on the children's own assessment of their attainment. They were asked to evaluate their work in reading, writing, maths and science using the labels 'good', 'OK' or 'not so good'. The data showed that the children's confidence in their abilities fell sharply as Key Stage 2 progressed.

The Whole Picture

What do we find when we bring all these strands of pupil experience together? Where we saw children experiencing a tightening of the curriculum frame and a more restrictive and teacher-controlled pedagogy in a climate heavily influenced by high-risk categoric and overt assessment, what was the impact on their attitudes and learning behaviour? What kinds of learners did they tell us they were?. At the end of Key Stage 2 the children in the study were very aware of the importance of 'good marks', 'getting things right'. In a climate of explicit and categoric assessment, however, many of them avoided challenge and had a low tolerance of ambiguity.

> In science we just find things out and do experiments and you don't know if you're right or not. (year 6)

> In maths I find it easy and I've just got onto the highest level. In science I don't always understand what I have to do. (year 6)

For those who found it easy, maths offered the security of success. For others the risk of failure left them vulnerable.

> In maths they give you hard sums and sometimes you get so worried you don't know what you are doing. (year 6)

They expressed a preference for easy tasks and had low persistence when they found things hard, escaping into 'thinking of other things'. They provided defensive explanations for poor attainment and increasingly referred to their performance as a reflection of their innate ability.

> I like watching TV because I don't have to write. With writing I get mixed up with everything and my pen leaks all the time. (year 6)

> I don't know much about it because I haven't been taught much. I hold my pen funny that's why writing is a problem. (year 6)

> I'm no good at geography because me dad didn't tell me nothing about it. (year 5)

> I'm not as intelligent as some of the other pupils. (year 6)

> I'm no good at maths I just can't work it out. (year 6)

Few of the reasons the children gave for their curriculum preferences were categorized as 'educational' — that is associated with learning, challenge or progression.

As we have already mentioned, one feature of the tightening frame which ran as a continuous thread through the children's responses was their sense of time as a scarce commodity. They felt the tension between what has to be done and the amount of time to do it. They also felt the impact of this on the learning experiences they were offered or felt inclined to take.

> I don't like topic. We have to go in groups and people mess around and we don't have enough time. (year 6)

The dilemmas created as curriculum, pedagogy and time come together were captured by one child who could not decide whether he preferred to choose or to let his teacher do it.

> When my teacher decides sometimes it's good but sometimes it's not. When I decide sometimes I can't decide . . . That's the reason I didn't choose a card in art because they all looked really hard; because they were all done by proper artists and they were all done in like a year or something; but when we do it we have to do it in a term or less and we have less time to do it because we're in school and we have only an hour a week.

Sean's perception of the task his teacher had set as unrealistic and unachievable in any terms to which he might aspire raise questions about motivation and the nature of the learning experiences available where the curriculum is crowded and time is at a premium. Was Sean learning to be an intrinsically motivated, confident, lifelong learner? Could he realistically aspire to engage in 'deep' learning, below the surface level? In the climate that produced his reflection, could his teachers realistically hope to create the conditions in which he and others could learn differently?

Four Major Arguments

From the brief review of research provided above we can identify some of the issues related to children as learners that need to be addressed as we move towards the next century. We can generate some arguments which are of vital significance for the title of this book: 'How shall we school our children?'.

The Fundamental Educational Argument

Primary education is concerned with the development of young children during a formative period of their lives. They progressively acquire the skills, knowledge and understandings which are part of the formal curriculum, and they also begin to develop unique identities, attitudes and values which will underpin their future development and lifelong learning. Additionally, their school experiences have intrinsic worth. The National Curriculum and its associated assessment procedures should be designed to complement and extend developmental processes. There is evidence that it may remain constraining and overspecified.

A Strategic Argument

The rapidity of social, economic, cultural and technological change is likely to continue in the twenty-first century. A strategic emphasis on basic, transferable skills, conceptual knowledge and self-confidence in learning could be of particular importance for our future citizens and for national competitiveness. The very crowded, subject-based National Curriculum of the early 1990s is traditional in structure, conservative in content and may unwittingly undermine forms and processes of education which are necessary preparations for the future.

An Instrumental Argument

Policies of the 1980s and 1990s have been underpinned by a conception of education which focuses on subject knowledge and its effective delivery in classrooms. Systemic professional development based on this conception should increase the quality and consistency of teaching across schools. However, it reflects a partial and ultimately invalid model of learning. To maximize standards of learning attainment, teachers must complement appropriate subject knowledge with knowledge and skill concerning pupil motivation, and awareness of the physical, intellectual, emotional, social, cultural, linguistic and economic factors which affect all learners.

A Contextual Argument

We also need to remember that poverty, insecurity and social exclusion is a reality for many families in the UK. Social differentiation has increased in recent decades. Despite considerable knowledge of inequalities associated with social class, ethnicity, gender and disability, the education system has not been designed responsively. The fundamental challenge is to extend the extent and security of employment, and to strengthen communities, but the education system also has an important role in increasing social cohesion and enabling children to fulfil their potential.

How Then, Should We 'Reform' Primary Education?

The Purposes of Education

There are strong arguments for reconceptualizing the meaning of 'broad and balanced' in terms of the curricular aims which are set out in the Education Reform Act of 1988. Whilst maintaining existing commitments to literacy and numeracy, this could be addressed in relation to: transferable skills, knowledge and conceptual understanding; personal, social and moral education; and maximizing educational opportunities for all.

Lifelong Learning and the World of Work

Lifelong learning requires the development of positive self-confidence as a learner, judgment and skill in deploying learning strategies appropriately and the capacity to reflect on learning in open-minded and self-critical ways. These capabilities and attributes could certainly be taught and nurtured in schools through processes such as planning, review, self-assessment and conferencing. There is a danger that narrow, categoric forms of assessment could actually undermine learning disposition.

Flexibility

The research on pupil perspectives and motivation suggests that the curriculum of the 1990s has been overloaded and overconstrained, so that teachers are insufficiently able to respond to local circumstances and pupil needs. Children need time to learn if their knowledge and understanding is to me more than superficial. They need time and appropriate experiences to develop mastery of concepts and skills. Outside the core curriculum, teachers need more scope to exercise professional judgment.

The Structure of the National Curriculum

There is a strong case for establishing a more focused, responsive and flexible National Curriculum framework than has existed through the 1990s. This framework would need to take account of two key factors. The first is the transition in the learning needs of pupils at different ages — from the needs of nursery education to the Key Stage 3 secondary school curriculum. Second, we have to recognize that a new national focus on literacy and numeracy inevitably means that other curriculum content would have to be lightened, particularly for younger children. Our initial suggestions are as follows:

> 'Core subjects' and 'core permeations' could be thought of as delineating an essential, statutory content which is necessary for national development, individual entitlement and lifelong learning. These could be the main focus for minimum national standards, assessment, reporting and inspection systems.
>
> 'Foundation subjects' could be thought of as areas of curriculum which developed from modest specification in years 1 and 2, through greater detailing in years 3 and 4, and on to the greater subject specification in years 5 and 6 as a precursor to Key Stage 3.

	KEY STAGE 1, Years 1 and 2	KEY STAGE 2, Years 3 and 4	KEY STAGE 2, Years 5 and 6
CORE SUBJECTS AND CORE PERMEATIONS	English	English	English
	Maths	Maths	Maths
	Learning skills, understanding and IT capability	Learning skills, understanding and IT capability	Learning skills, understanding and IT capability
	Personal, social and moral education	Personal, social and moral education	Personal, social and moral education
FOUNDATION SUBJECTS	Science and technology	Science and technology	Science
			Technology
	Humanities	Humanities	Geography [depending on KS3 developments]
			History
	Physical education	Physical education	Physical education
	Expressive arts	Expressive arts	Music
			Art
			Modern foreign language
OTHER REQUIREMENTS	Religious education	Religious education	Religious education

Compared with present National Curriculum structures, a curriculum of this type would be more focused on key capabilities, more responsive to the learning needs of young children and, subject to clarification at years 5 and 6, more flexible to implement in schools and classrooms.

Conclusion

The curricular innovations of the 1990s have achieved a great deal. However, as we have suggested, they also seem to have had some unintended consequences which could easily undermine positive dispositions to lifelong learning. An agenda for the twenty-first century must therefore include revisions to the structure of the National Curriculum and to associated assessment systems. In so doing, the curriculum should both be conceptualized as a whole and be underpinned by a sound understanding of learners and learning to complement the dominant view of teaching and curriculum. However, despite the title of this book, such a suggestion is not actually 'radical'. It is merely sensible — and overdue.

Notes

1 This chapter is an expanded version of a paper prepared by Andrew Pollard for a SCAA conference held in June, 1997. We would like to acknowledge the work of Patricia Broadfoot, Ann Filer, Elizabeth McNess and Marilyn Osborn, our collaborators in the two research projects on which we have drawn for this paper.

2 The *Identity and Learning Project* is codirected by Andrew Pollard and Ann Filer. Now in its fifth phase, target pupils are being tracked through secondary schools. The most relevant book on the work is Pollard, A. with Filer, A. (1996) *The Social World of Children's Learning*, London: Cassell. The next book will be Pollard, A. and Filer, A. (1998) *The Social World of Pupil Career*, London: Cassell.

3 The *Primary Assessment, Curriculum and Experience* project is codirected by Andrew Pollard and Patricia Broadfoot. Published work includes: Pollard, A. et al. (1994) *Changing English Primary Schools*, London: Cassell; and Croll, P. (ed.) (1996) *Teachers, Pupils and Primary Schooling*, London: Cassell. For a synoptic analysis of all the data on pupil experiences, see Pollard, A. and Triggs, P. (forthcoming) *Policy, Practice and Pupil Experiences: Changing Primary Education*, London: Cassell.

10   Transforming Primary Education in Partnership with Parents

Titus Alexander

Introduction

We are at the start of a revolution in primary education based on the growing recognition that parents are a child's first educator and families provide the foundation phase for learning. As in any unplanned transition, the circumstances are confusing, the goal unclear and the process often painful. This chapter aims to sketch a vision of where we are going and a path of how to get there. When we do, primary education could be utterly transformed.

The previous Government emphasized the role of parents as consumers of education. It strengthened parents' rights to information, to choose a school and to complain. Many of these rights are important, but some were unrealizable and some undermined the essence of education as a human process in which people participate. This chapter emphasizes education as a shared activity concerned with citizenship, learning and the capacity of each individual to create their own future in a global society.

The world is changing fast. The Internet, multichannel television, computers and mobile phones revolutionize the potential for human development, while the dangers of climate change, cars, drugs and economic change increase our fears. A decade from now the world will be even more different. How can we ensure that primary education will serve people throughout an ever changing future? In my view we can only do this by transforming primary schools into local learning resource centres for children and families.

Three central features of this transformation grow out of the growing recognition that parents are a child's first and most enduring educators.

First, as parents and home circumstances are acknowledged as the largest influence on children's attainment at school, families will be seen as the foundation phase of education, on which primary schools must build in partnership with parents. Second, primary schools will see work with parents as equally important as work with children. All schools will develop a whole school approach to work with parents, weaving it into every aspect of policy, practice and training. Third, primary schools could become a central focus for family learning within the community, owned and controlled by local people as a cornerstone of our constitution as a nation.

In an information economy where knowledge, design and the ability to use information are increasingly important, the primary school becomes a local gateway to learning. For many parents and children, it opens the door to the potential of public libraries, television, the Internet and other agencies for learning. Local management of schools has also started an irreversible process that could transform every school into a democratic learning community, funded through a variety of sources in addition to taxation.

This chapter attempts to sketch each of these transformations in order to paint a picture of the potential of primary schools as the forefront of a new learning revolution in partnership with parents. It is deliberately visionary, building on fragments of existing practice to project an ideal for the future. Given the new Government's commitment to family learning and its bold steps in relation to funding higher education, there is perhaps more room for imagination than before.

The argument is largely based on my experience in three overlapping areas of work. First, of talking with parents and staff when visiting schools in many different parts of the country as an adviser; second, of supporting parenting education programmes, and third, of helping to implement local management of schools.

Families as the Foundation Phase of Education

Demands and expectations of family life have changed enormously over the past 30 years. Contraception, feminism, new technologies, advertising, television, the social security system, immigration and changing employment patterns have produced profound changes in culture and attitudes among men, women and families. The divorce rate has doubled. Over a quarter of children under 16 experience their parents' splitting up. The number of single parents and stepparents has grown significantly. More families live further away from grandparents and other relatives. Families are also polarized between the work rich but time poor, where both parents work, and families which are time rich but money poor, where both parents are unemployed. All of these changes have increased pressures on parents in every social class. The responsibilities of bringing up children demand a great deal of time, money and above all personal capacity for which many feel unprepared. It is not easy being a parent, and for many there are few sources of advice and support.

The difficulties of parenthood are dramatically highlighted by evidence of family failure. While horrific cases of child abuse occasionally hit the headlines, about one in 10 people suffer sexual abuse in childhood and many more suffer physical or emotional abuse. More than six million people, about one in seven, suffer from mental disorders at any one time (OPCS, 1994; see also Mihill, 1994). In many cases these can be traced back to distressing experiences in childhood or a failure to develop the inner resilience on which positive mental health depends.

These and other concerns have contributed to a growth of parenting education and life skills courses (Pugh et al., 1994). Although at present less than 4 per cent of parents participate in any form of parenting education during their lives (Smith, 1996), relationship skills and preparation for parenthood programmes are rapidly spreading in many areas. Some schools are introducing parenting programmes for pupils, parents or both.

At the same time, there is a growing recognition of the importance of families as a place of learning. Children learn to talk, walk and develop their core behaviour and beliefs at home. About half of a person's learning abilities develop by the age of 4, and 80 per cent by the age of 8 (Bloom, 1964). Between birth and school leaving age children spend less than 15 per cent of waking time in school. Of this, about a quarter is spent in the playground. Each child in a group of about 30 gets little individual attention from a teacher. Parents and other carers, by contrast, are responsible for 85 per cent of a child's waking time. They can, if they choose, give children undivided attention for longer than any teacher.

Inequality between home backgrounds is still the greatest source of inequality in educational attainment. A wide range of research shows that home influences are more important for educational achievement than school (CACE, 1967). For almost all measures of scholastic attainment, differences between schools account for far less than features of the family or home (Rutter and Madge, 1976). A consistent aspect of successful schools is parental support for children's learning (Rutter et al., 1979; Rutter and Madge, 1976; Henderson, 1987). One of the most rigorous accounts of school effectiveness states that all studies which have compared the relative importance of home and schools 'have clearly shown that for almost all measures of scholastic attainment, the differences between schools accounted for far less of the variance than did features of the family or home' (Mortimore et al., 1995, p. 289). In the mid-1980s Gordon Wells showed 'the very strong relationship between knowledge of literacy at age 5 and all later assessments of school achievement' (Wells, 1986, p. 147). Similar evidence convinced American educator Earl Shaefer to switch his attention from classrooms to living rooms, declaring that 'parents should be recognized as the most influential educators of their own children' (Shaefer, 1970, 1972).

Social class often appears to be a significant factor in differences in school attainment, with children from professional and white collar backgrounds making significantly greater progress at school than other groups (Mortimore et al., 1995, pp. 132–3). While 80 per cent of young people from professional backgrounds go to university, the proportion from unskilled lower-income families is only 10 per cent. But studies of successful young professionals from poor families show that enthusiastic parental involvement in their education was the common characteristic, regardless of social class (Bloom, 1985). A longitudinal study of almost 7000 people born in 1958 suggested that there was scarcely any correlation between private education and occupational attainment. 'What matters, it seems, is good parenting, irrespective of the class or education level of the parents, and good parenting can be found in all social classes.'[1]

Thus family culture and ethos are more important for attainment than social class in itself. Children who participate in mealtime discussions, for example, develop the highest aptitude for reading and vocabulary. One large-scale study showed that mealtime conversations use about 10 times more sophisticated words than other situations, including school and playtimes.[2]

The implications of this evidence is that parents alone cannot cope with the demands of bringing up children. In the words of an African proverb made famous by Hillary Clinton, 'It takes a village to raise a child'. Intermediate agencies are needed to provide advice, support and social sanctions. In the past, church, faith community and extended family performed many of these tasks. Today television, schools and public services have taken on many intermediate functions. But in their present form these agencies cannot provide the intimate support adults and children need. Supporting parents as primary educators provides a powerful and positive way to raise educational achievement, increase well-being and improve social cohesion. Primary schools in particular could play a leading role in supporting parents.

Transforming Schools

The transformation of our schools is probably the single most important task in securing the long-term prosperity and stability of this country. Most attention and resources have gone into the organization, content and process of schooling, but school improvement is not enough.

Unless *all* parents are actively involved in their children's education, schools will continue to be polarized. Some parents are able to choose high performing schools which build on the active learning at home. These schools use their popularity to select children, overtly or covertly, thus creating a virtuous cycle of school improvement and supportive families. Less popular schools inevitably have to look after children with greater needs and often less support at home. In these schools a growing proportion of staff time is remedial. As teachers cope with the consequences of family stress, other children get less attention and a negative cycle sets in.

Blaming parents, or trying to discipline parents through home–school contracts, will only displace the problem onto other agencies, most of which are more expensive. This increases pressure on public spending and stokes the vicious cycle of families under stress, struggling schools and overstretched public services.

Changing the relationships between school and home could be the most constructive starting point from which to transform schools themselves. It could also help to create a new relationship between schools and local communities which enables families and other agencies to cope better, perhaps even to flourish. Schools cannot solve parents' problems, but in recognizing their primary role as educators in the home, they would contribute to a wider regeneration of family and community life.

The unprecedented changes in curriculum, structure, funding, inspection and testing over the past decade have been enormously expensive in terms of morale as well as money. Yet more is needed to improve premises, technology, training and staffing. But none of these reforms have taken account of the fundamental importance of home as a place of learning. It is as if we rewired and redecorated the house as the foundations crumbled. The foundations are learning within families.

Supporting Parents as a Child's First Educators

In many British schools today there is relatively little constructive communication between teachers and parents. Primary schools are much better than secondary, and infant schools better than junior, but most communications between home and school are instructions *from* school *to* parents, mainly about administrative matters. Parents are often treated as instruments for the delivery, discipline and domestication of children, rather than the *primary* partner in education. Parents are often told what they can do to help the school. Few schools ask what they can do for parents. Active involvement in their child's learning is often limited to a book going home. Communication about educational matters is almost entirely about how the school sees their child, rarely about parents' views of the child or the child's experience of school. Apart from annual parents' evenings, many parents are only invited to meet the teacher when things have gone wrong.

Teachers cannot be blamed for the low level of relationships between home and school. Work with parents usually has to be done in a teacher's own time on top of a full teaching load and growing administrative burdens. Most teacher training courses do not cover parental involvement. School funding takes no account of the need for home–school links. Government policies and guidelines for schools do not include partnerships with parents, apart from an inadequate section in the OFSTED *Framework for Inspection*. The recent requirement for schools to draw up a home–school contract appears to be designed to exclude 'difficult' parents rather than support all parents and is likely to prove counter-productive in practice. A growing number of schools recognize the importance of working with parents, but often as a desirable extra rather than an essential task. Few schools see the partnership with parents as a central responsibility which requires as much effort, preparation and skill as teaching itself.

Work with parents must be embedded in every aspect of every school, from its overall development plan to daily lesson plans. Parents' knowledge of their child must be recognized as 'equivalent expertise,'[3] with equal status as a teacher's training. To be truly effective, primary schools need to recognize that they can only build on and extend the learning that takes place at home. If that foundation is shaky, then the school needs to find a way of enabling parents to become more effective as educators.

In my experience, most parents want to be more involved in their children's education. Parents' attitude to education is often influenced by their own schooling and their experience of taking their children to school for the first time. The way in which the school treats parents when they first join has a profound influence on their relationship with the school system for the rest of their lives. Some schools have a culture of involvement, so that parents arrive expecting to be active participants in their child's education. In most schools, parents are uncertain of their role. They are often given an implicit message that teaching is the school's job and all parents have to do is to bring their children on time. Many parents tell me that they would like more information on what their children are being taught and more detailed advice on how to help them at home. Many parents buy educational books from WH Smith or Boots in order to help their children. They do not tell teachers in case they are told off or because they don't want teachers to think that they are critical of school. Very few parents want nothing to do with their children's education.

Whole-school Policies for Working With Parents

Every school needs to develop a proactive whole-school policy for partnership with parents. Varying circumstances mean that each school would need to draw up its own policy to meet the particular needs of its staff, parents and children, but there are a number of benchmarks which every school could be expected to work towards. These are:

- a welcome and induction programme for new parents, starting well before their child begins school;
- baseline assessment of each child involving parents and teacher together, to develop an individual learning plan for each child;
- regular information on what children are being taught and how parents can help;
- regular home learning activities, backed by advice or training on helping children learn at home;
- termly meetings for parents, teachers and children to discuss progress;
- recognition of the diversity of languages, cultures and abilities in any school community;
- regular meetings of all parents in a class;
- a parent partnership post with non-contact time to develop work with parents.

Home–school contracts, required under recent legislation, must become a support for parents rather than a stick to select or exclude them. Schools should also aim to set up a parents' forum with two representatives from each class, for each year, Key Stage or the whole school depending on school size.

Developing whole-school partnerships with parents on this scale needs to be supported by national guidelines and training materials[4] with funding for training and support. Work with parents should also become a central focus of teacher training, school inspections and the National Curriculum as it is revised. Eventually every school or cluster of schools should have a trained family education worker. This could make a striking contribution to the standards and quality of education among children and adults, especially in areas where educational achievement is low. Areas like Devon and Liverpool already have well-developed parent support programmes from which the rest of the country can learn.

Schools as Community Centres for Lifelong Learning

Parental involvement is a key feature of effective schools, together with positive leadership, shared goals, an attractive and stimulating environment, high expectations and good teaching (National Commission on Education, 1993; see also Sandy, 1990; Mortimore et al., 1995; Rutter et al., 1979; National Commission on Education, 1995). *School Matters* demonstrated that 'disadvantaged children in the most effective schools can end up with higher achievements than their advantaged peers in the less effective schools' (Mortimore et al., 1995, p. 217). But the creation of a learning society in which families are seen as the foundation phase of education means that we need a new vision of how schools might develop as community education centres. The following paragraphs describe some existing initiatives which could be generalized, where appropriate, by every local education authority.

Having a child, particularly the first, can be very lonely and difficult. The local primary school, in partnership with health centres and voluntary organizations, could form a network of support for parents as educators from before the birth. In Birmingham, health visitors give every family with young children an introductory pack with a book, poster and information on local services through the Bookstart project.[5] Elsewhere, voluntary schemes such as community mothers, parent mentors and Homestart offer valuable support in the early years. Parental involvement in support groups, mother and toddler clubs, pre-schools and nurseries can develop confidence and competence within families. Newpin, Homestart, Family Caring Trust and Parent Network offer families both support from trained volunteers and opportunities for parents to become trained helpers themselves.

Home visits by a teacher or educational visitor in the year before school starts can also provide active encouragement for learning as well as building the partnership between home and school. Class teachers could act as a learning consultant to a group of 8 or 10 families from birth or 3 years old and continue with the same group until the age of 10 or 12, as they do in some continental schools.

To achieve this, *average* pupil–adult ratios in Key Stage 1 must be improved from 27:1 to 15:1 or even 10:1, which is the average pupil-teacher ratio in private primary schools. The ratio of children to a teacher/family learning consultant should start at about 8:1 in the early years, rising to about 20:1 at junior school age and 30 or even 40:1 in secondary. More intensive support in the early years should lead to more scope for independent learning, peer tutoring and more variety in group sizes for different activities and specialist subjects as children get older. For example, the school day might include whole class instruction for groups of 40, 60 or more, followed by paired exercises, small group work with an older pupil or class teacher, with one-to-one coaching for those who need it. The average pupil-teacher ratio across the school system might be similar to now, but there would be many more teachers in early years and more self-directed study groups, resource-based learning and projects at secondary level.

Children would start at school when they were ready and able to learn as part of a group. The parent and child would meet with their teacher/learning consultant to make a joint assessment of what the child can do and what he or she could best learn next. This 'baseline assessment' would be used to draw up a personal learning plan, which would be kept by the parents and used as a reference point for future meetings with the teacher. This joint assessment could be by appointment in the family home, unless parents preferred to meet elsewhere. It would be repeated every term.

Teachers and parents of each child would meet as a class group at least once every half-term to discuss the curriculum, progress and anything affecting the class as a whole, as currently happens in most continental schools. All parents would also meet the teacher individually for an in-depth discussion at least once every term. The communications revolution means that a growing number of parents and teachers will also communicate through the Internet or voice mail. School could become also a vitally important resource base for the many families who cannot afford Internet access, but it is conceivable that an Internet terminal in every family home would be an education policy objective early in the next century.

Many parents, family members and other adults would spend more time in school, sharing their experience and knowledge, helping out and learning themselves. Continuity of experience between home and school would flow both ways, with school fostering the intimate, interactive meaningful personal learning that takes place in most homes, while the range of knowledge, skills and issues developed at home would deepen. Lessons would draw on children's experience and activities outside school, including multimedia, television, film, hobbies and excursions. There would be less emphasis on the transmission of information, as in the present National Curriculum, and much more on the development of understanding and skills through dialogue, experience and application. Young people would take tasks home to apply, practise and extend what they have been taught in school.

The functions of home and school would still be distinct. With a clear partnership between home and school, skilled and knowledgeable teachers could be confident that children would expect to learn and enjoy hard work on something they had chosen. Whole-class teaching might even become more widespread, because lessons would be focused on what children were ready and willing to learn. But there would also be a lot more small group learning beyond the classroom, including voluntary activities such as community projects, drama groups or adventure clubs, as well as study centres in schools and public libraries.

The logical step from parental choice of schools is the right of parents and learners to choose where, how and what they want to learn. This might include making portage available to parents who for one reason or other want to educate their children away from school (portage schemes provide materials for children to learn at home or in hospital due to illness or other special needs). Schools should also be allowed to admit pupils (and adults) on a part-time basis, so that children learning at home can attend school for certain subjects, such as languages, science or sport.

Community Ownership of Education

Schooling is more than a consumer good. Like choosing a partner, following a faith, joining a profession or acquiring citizenship, attending school demands commitment. It means joining a community which requires certain attitudes, ways of behaving and values. Information can be transmitted more effectively by electronic media, but understanding, values and behaviour can only be developed through relationships with others. Schools are the second most important means through which common values are developed after families.

As a community centre for lifelong learning, every school should have a democratic structure in which the community, parents, staff and students have a say in how the school is run. This would increase the sense of ownership and provide practical lessons in citizenship. School democracy might include a variety of forums, such as class meetings and a council for students and for parents, a staff group, and a community council, with the governing body as executive. Schools would have much more scope to experiment with different structures, such as collegiate management or an elected head, as in many continental schools, or even a federal system of smaller learning units with no overall hierarchy. Developing democracy in schools would make them a focus for citizenship within our evolving constitution.

Going to school is an apprenticeship in citizenship. Just as families and states seek to balance freedom and responsibility within their boundaries, so school communities regulate their own affairs within a local area as a microcosm of society. Many schools today bring together people from different faiths, denominations and, in some areas, different social backgrounds and ethnic origins. This makes schools natural successors to places of worship as a focus for community life, in which community values, experience and knowledge are shared and developed. Schools are often the only institutions in which a substantial part of the community is linked in any meaningful way. In many areas schools have played a significant role in confronting racism and improving relationships between people of different faiths, cultures and ethnic origins. Thus a community school which serves everyone within a neighbourhood has considerable potential to increase social cohesion at a time when so many other forces separate people from each other. As building blocks of the local community, schools can link families together in a common endeavour. Democratic reform of schools must become a crucial branch of constitutional reform, as important as devolution, the European Union or the United Nations.

Good schools enable people to transform their lives. Young people can discover and develop themselves by learning together with experienced adults. Parents often become more interested in learning themselves when their children start school. Some parents become active in the local community through school, organizing after-school clubs, helping at school events or campaigning. A local school that becomes a centre of attraction with a high standard of provision can transform the fortunes of an area. Involving parents as educational partners, as outlined above, is probably the most important step in transforming schools and the local community.

Investing in Education

The biggest and most important inequality in education spending is between those families who give their children time, books, educational toys, computers, visits to museums or other encouragement for learning, and those who do not. This difference outweighs all other inequalities in the education system. Funding for schooling in Britain is grossly unequal, both between public and private provision and within the state sector. The most obvious inequality is the ability of some parents to pay more, in fees or through fund-raising.

Once we recognize families as the most important 'sector' of education, then the argument that all education should be free of charge becomes untenable. State spending could never equalize the educational resources available in the most affluent homes. But the *way* in which state spending is allocated could make a huge difference to parental commitment to education.

Control over finance is a crucial test for community ownership, local democracy and public participation. It is an area where radical thinking is also needed if all parents are to have real power over local provision and to address inequalities within each area. To increase the potential of schools as significant social units, families need real ownership and control over their local community school. Local management of schools and devolution of responsibility to governing bodies have already produced a significant shift in power since the days when most spending decisions were made at county hall. There are still teething problems as school governors and staff learn new skills, local authorities and the Government attempt to establish fair funding formulae, and education support services become more customer-orientated, but devolved powers will not be removed. If anything, there needs to be further devolution of powers to parents at a class level. Many schools also want more responsibility for maintenance and even capital spending. Participation in running local schools has considerable potential as the first step towards greater local democracy and a more pluralistic system of public services. New forms of community ownership could give local people direct control over individual schools, with powers to raise loans for capital spending, improve premises and transform provision in response to local needs. There will still be a role for elected local or regional Government to take strategic decisions over the allocation of public funds. But most decisions over the management and content of education could be made by families and their all-purpose local community education centre.

Although increased state funding is desirable, it is not necessarily the best or sole solution to increasing resources for education. Education is not a 'good' or even a service, but a process in which people participate. Ultimately what people learn is what they make their own. Many people already choose to pay for courses in keep fit, the arts, computing, complementary medicine, sports, personal growth or leisure. Public libraries charge for videos, computer games and CDs but lend books free of charge. Giving people a direct stake in local provision for education would encourage a more active interest in the nature, costs and quality of what is provided. We should therefore at least consider the possibility is that in future the state might fund educational premises and essential running costs, leaving local people to pay by subscription or local education rates, assessed on a sliding scale by income. In the United States school boards campaign for public agreement to borrow money or raise local taxes through local referenda, so that major education spending decisions are taken by the whole community. Inequality between geographical areas must be addressed through the school funding formula and local Government Standard Spending Assessments. As a society we need to spend much more money on education to improve school premises, reduce class sizes, keep pace with technology and raise achievement. Allowing for greater flexibility in how we pay for schooling could release more public funds to ensure that every child gets the support they need to achieve their potential. The present system of roughly equal funding for every child, regardless of home circumstances, perpetuates underlying social inequalities.

Schools with a common educational philosophy have a much greater degree of parental involvement and commitment from staff. Holland and Denmark both have a system of education funding which enables groups of parents to get state funding for schools. As a result both countries have a greater variety of schools following many different curriculum models. In Britain, the Third Sector Alliance[6] is campaigning for a similar system of diversity within the state system.[7] This issue is inevitably clouded by our class-based private school system, which is both educationally and socially divisive. However, we should consider the possibility that greater variety and community control within the state system could erode the economic base of privileged private education by creating a better alternative within a more diverse state sector. Recent research suggests that even sending children to fee-paying private schools makes less difference than support and encouragement from parents.[8] Thus the most significant difference for educational outcomes may not be between state and private schooling, which has more to do with status than attainment, but between home and school. These grounds alone would justify a significant increase in spending on family centres, parenting education and support for learning at home, particularly in areas where educational achievement are low.

Creating Learning Communities

Primary schools are only one of many agencies which work with children and parents, particularly in the early years. Community health services, leisure centres, pre-schools and other agencies all have an educational function, whether they are aware of it or not. They need to work more closely together and increase support for parents as educators and partners in education.

Opportunities for parenting education and family learning should be available to all who want them. Parents should be able to develop their skills and seek support without fear of being stigmatized as unable to cope. Families also need a wide choice of affordable activities, courses and provision to support and extend learning in the home. Television, multimedia, cable and the Internet are bringing new resources for learning into many homes, although their potential is largely untapped and many families cannot afford access. Many of these facilities come under the heading of arts, leisure and recreation. They are often seen as less important than education, but in practice they are just as likely as school to stimulate enthusiasm for learning and encourage parents and children to learn together. Opportunities for informal learning all year round should be developed and sustained with as much commitment as formal education. Trained staff in small neighbourhood play areas, local branch libraries and parks can make a big difference in encouraging children to use their energy creatively and involving adults in running activities with children. The scope for family learning facilities has scarcely been scratched. We need local learning action plans that embrace all facilities for informal learning, setting standards for access, provision, staff training and variety of opportunities, as well as promoting participation by the public. It could be part of the learning cities initiatives in many parts of the country.

In this context the school system has a choice. Schools could become hubs for family support networks as centres for lifelong learning and neighbourhood democracy, or they could become competing fragments in a patchwork of specialist provision serving a divided society. The first model suggests a new form of comprehensive education, in which primary schools have a pivotal role within a diverse range of opportunities for family learning open to all. The second model is a logical development of our present system, in which schools segregate people by covert or open selection. Each model reflects a different decision about the role of parents. The first sees parents and children as citizens, with a right to education and equal participation in society, while the second sees parents as consumers, with a right to choose the education they want and can afford. In practice, there will always be a mixture of both, but the principle of whether parents are treated primarily as citizens or as consumers has a profound influence on the future of schools and society.

Conclusion: Families as the Foundation of a Learning Society

Families provide the foundation course for every single profession or occupation. Once we fully appreciate that family life is the foundation of learning, we will devote more effort, time and resources to making it more fulfilling, secure and joyful for all. Primary schools could become a community focus for family learning and citizenship in the emerging knowledge-based society. As new communication technologies open extraordinary possibilities within a global society, we also need to pay more attention to the local, where families connect in a neighbourhood. People need to be able to understand issues that affect their lives as well as increasing opportunities to have a say in them. Education has a vital role in democracy as well as the economy. Schools are a seedbed of citizenship as well as learning and prosperity.

Wealth and well-being depend more and more on the application of skills and knowledge in a fast moving complex world. Global competition is deepening the gap between those who succeed and those who are excluded. While homes with multimedia and the Internet now have more access to information than most universities 40 years ago, many families still lack books and basic information. Persistent underachievement among a significant proportion of British young people means that our society is increasingly polarized and relatively poorer, both culturally and economically.

We cannot avoid living in a world of global competition, but we can strive to ensure that every family is able to participate in the emerging world on equal terms. Developing equal partnerships with parents as a child's first and most enduring educators could be the start of a far-reaching transformation of the schools into community education centres within a holistic support system for lifelong learning.

Notes

1 Peter Saunders, National Child Development Study, cited in ESRC Annual Report 1994/95, London: ESRC.
2 Catherine Snow, Harvard University Graduate School of Education, reported in the *Times Educational Supplement*, 2 February 1996.
3 To quote Professor Sheila Wolfendale.
4 Titus Alexander, John Bastiani and Emma Beresford, Home School Policies: a Practical Guide, JET Publications, 67 Musters Road, Ruddington, NG11 6JB, £14.95.

5 Bookstart, c/o CORE Skills Development Partnership, 100 Broad Street, Birmingham, B15 1AE, 0121 248 8083.
6 Third Sector Alliance, c/o Human Scale Education, 96 Carlingcott, nr Bath, BA2 8AW.
7 CARNIE, F., LANGE, M. and TASKER, M. (eds) (1996) *Freeing Education: Steps Towards Real Choice and Diversity in Schools*, Hawthorn Press, 1 Lansdown Lane, Stroud, GL5 1BJ, £9.95.
8 Peter Saunders, National Child Development Study, cited in ESRC Annual Report 1994/95, London: ESRC.

References

BLOOM, B.S. (1964) *Stability and Change in Human Characteristics*, New York: John Wiley.

BLOOM, B.S. (1985) *Developing Talent in Young People*, New York: Ballantine.

CENTRAL ADVISORY COUNCIL FOR EDUCATION (ENGLAND) (1967) *Children and their Primary Schools* (The Plowden Report), London: HMSO.

HENDERSON, A. (1987) *The Evidence Continues to Grow: Parental Involvement Improves Student Achievement*, Columbia, NY: National Committee for Citizen's Education.

MIHILL, C. (1992) 'Mental ill health hits 1 in 7', *The Guardian*, 15 December.

MORTIMORE, P. et al. (1995) *School Matters: The Junior Years*, London: Paul Chapman Publishing.

NATIONAL COMMISSION ON EDUCATION (1993) *Learning to Succeed*, London: Heinemann.

NATIONAL COMMISSION ON EDUCATION (1995) *Success Against the Odds*, London: Routledge.

OPCS (1994) *Surveys of Psychiatric Morbidity in Great Britain, Bulletin No 1: The Prevalence of Psychiatric Morbidity Among Adults Aged 16–64 Living in Private Households in Great Britain*, December.

PUGH, G. et al. (1994) *Confident Parents Confident Children: Policy and Practice in Parent Education and Support*, London: National Children's Bureau.

RUTTER, M. and MADGE, N. (1976) *Cycles of Disadvantage*, London: Heinemann.

RUTTER, M. et al. (1979) *Fifteen Thousand Hours*, London: Open Books.

SANDY, A. (1990) *Making Schools More Effective*, Coventry: CEDAR, University of Warwick.

SHAEFER, E. (1970) 'Need for early and continuing education', *Education of the Infant and Young Child*, New York

SHAEFER, E. (1972) 'Parents as educators: Evidence from the research', *Young Children*, New York.

SMITH, C. (1996) *Developing Parenting Programmes*, London: National Children's Bureau.

WELLS, G. (1986) *The Meaning Makers*, London: Hodder and Stoughton.

Part 4

Procedures and Outcomes:
Ways, Means and Results

11 The Primary School Curriculum: Changes, Challenges, Questions

Colin Richards

Introduction

'Curricula are artificial. Though to many pupils and teachers alike they have an aura of permanence and inevitability, curricula are man-made and liable to change, distortion or elaboration by those who design them and those who receive them' (Taylor and Richards, 1985). Published at a time when top-level civil servants and HMI were urgently considering a way to define the school curriculum leading in late 1986 to the first public announcement of moves towards establishing a National Curriculum, that statement was needed to alert teachers and others in the education service to contest the taken-for-granted nature of the school curriculum, to consider the interests the curriculum embodies and serves and to consider the possibility not just of modifications but of major changes in the light of 'social changes, political revolutions, economic transformations, advances in knowledge and reevaluations of the past'.

That reminder is even more pressing at present after a decade in which the National Curriculum has dominated the curricular policy and practice of English (and Welsh) primary education and in which, though subject to a multitude of internal readjustments, it has seemed to teachers, parents and politicians to be a taken-for-granted, inevitable feature of the educational landscape, one that in its fundamental structures is permanent and inevitable.

This internalization by teachers, especially newly-qualified teachers, of *a* particular national curriculum as *the* National Curriculum and the conception of their role as essentially that of technical 'delivery' rather than one of reflective engagement with the curriculum and its consequences have been further entrenched by the promulgation of the National Curriculum for Initial Teacher Training by the Teacher Training Agency focusing exclusively on the core subjects and ICT (DfEE, 1997a) and by the Government White Paper, *Excellence in Schools* (DfEE, 1997b) which though promising 'a thorough review of the National Curriculum', may have already pre-empted that review by demanding that 'the priority for the curriculum must be to give more emphasis to literacy and numeracy in primary education' (p. 22).

In an attempt to characterize the current primary curriculum this chapter provides a brief analysis in terms of the nature and extent of legal prescription; the rationale for the curriculum; the dominant metaphors informing it; its contents in broad terms; its assessment; and its effects. Such an analysis can also form the framework for comparing past, present and future curricula (Richards, 1998).

The National Curriculum 1988–1998

The legal basis of the current National Curriculum is an Act of Parliament (the Education Reform Act [ERA] of 1988) and associated regulations. None of the requirements of the Act as they apply to the curriculum have been repealed during the decade following its enactment; there is no evidence that the new Government elected in 1997 has any plans to do so. The ERA has remained a 'given' in the curricular landscape. The detailed regulations, however, have been subject to many modifications, especially in respect of assessment arrangements but also in terms of content following the Dearing Review of 1993 (SCAA, 1993). *De jure* the ERA does not prescribe the totality of the school curriculum; schools have discretion to go beyond the National Curriculum if they so wish. Initially there was some 'official' encouragement for schools to make explicit provision for a range of cross-curricular issues and themes but this support was soon withdrawn and *de facto* such issues remain minority provision and only in a minority of schools. Yet many would argue for the increased significance of such issues (for example, citizenship and environmental education) in any future responsible and responsive primary curriculum.

In 1988 the Conservative Government of the day did not provide, either within or without the ERA, a developed rationale for the curriculum. The only semblance of a rationale was given in what civil servants disparingly referred to as the 'motherhood and apple pie' clauses of section 1 which, in a throw back to the 1944 Education Act, entitled every pupil in a state school to a balanced and broadly based curriculum which '(a) promotes the spiritual, moral, cultural, mental and physical development of the pupils at the school and of society; and (b) prepares such pupils for the opportunities, responsibilities and experiences of adult life'. Neither of the QUANGOs set up to advise on the school curriculum have attempted a worked up rationale. Arguably, in a fast-changing world one is needed for any future legally prescribed National Curriculum.

The metaphors underlying current curricular arrangements are largely drawn from business and in particular from accountancy. For example, '"*work*" is what schools do, children do and teachers do' (Taylor, 1997). Objectives and targets need to be 'smart': specific, *measurable*, achievable, relevant and time-scaled (Tabberer, Hine and Gallacher, 1996). Progress needs to be '*checked*' and schools made *accountable* (DES, 1987). Teachers need to be equipped 'with the *toolbox* of skills they need to be effective' (Millett, 1997). '*Investment* in learning in the twenty-first century is the equivalent of *investment* in the machinery and technical innovation that was essential to the first great *industrial* revolution' (DfEE, 1997b, my emphasis). Many more such metaphors have been, and could be cited. Are such metaphors adequate, or even apposite, to a reformed primary curriculum?

The current contents of the National Curriculum for primary education consist of the three core subjects (with science being relegated in practice to 'second-rate' core) and six or seven other foundation subjects depending on whether information technology and design technology are treated separately or together as the twin components of the legally prescribed 'subject', technology. In addition religious education has to be taught but part of what the ERA describes as the 'basic', not National Curriculum. For the core and other foundation subjects the content is spelt out for each Key Stage in detailed statutory orders, less detailed than they were, consequent on the Dearing Review, but still 118 closely written pages. Current legal requirements do not as yet prescribe teaching texts or materials, the way the curriculum is to be organized or the teaching methods to be used, but Conservative politicians have attempted to influence primary teachers' pedagogic practices (for example, see Alexander, Rose and Woodhead, 1992) and the new Labour Government is putting pressure on teachers to adopt particular forms of curriculum organization (literacy and numeracy 'hours') and particular teaching methods, pretentiously and inaccurately described as 'in line with *proven* best practice' (DfEE, 1997b, my emphasis). The extent of future prescription of both process and content is likely to be a key issue in the future politics of primary education.

Integral to the current National Curriculum are legally prescribed assessment arrangements related to children's performance and progress, particularly in the core subjects. Grandiosely and unrealistically these arrangements were originally intended to serve a variety of purposes simultaneously — formative, summative, evaluative and informative. In reality, Government policy based on the recommendations of the TGAT report (DES, 1988) proved too far ahead of the assessment 'technology' available to deliver it. Partly in consequence the summative aspects of individual assessment are now pre-eminent along with the use of national test data to compare the performance and effectiveness of individual schools. Despite the claims of *Excellence in Schools* (DfEE, 1997b) it is *far* from certain that 'We now have sound, consistent, national measures of pupil achievement for each school at each Key Stage of the National Curriculum'. Consideration of the reliability, validity and utility of current assessment arrangements needs to feature prominently in any reformulation of National Curriculum policy for primary education.

The effects of National Curriculum policy have been mixed: reality has not matched political rhetoric; practice has not matched policy — but whenever have they? Evidence from research and from inspection tally in certain respects. It is clear that from both sources that schools have made determined efforts to implement National Curriculum requirements; deliberate noncompliance has been rare; full compliance, particularly before the Dearing Review, has proved problematic because of content overload; only a minority of schools have felt able to go beyond legal requirements; those provisions of the ERA enabling schools to opt out aspects of the National Curriculum in order to carry out educational experiments have remained a 'dead letter'.

Research, inspection and monitoring by national agencies have also demonstrated clear weaknesses in policy formulation and implementation: content overload, especially in the period 1989–93; impossibly complex assessment requirements in the initial stages; a badly flawed assessment system which promised much but failed to deliver; considerable incoherence and lack of clarity in many of the initial statutory orders; and lack of encouragement for local experimentation and discretion.

Beyond that, the research evidence is equivocal. Some research provides evidence of change while other studies suggest general continuity with previous practice rather than substantial change (see Pollard et al., 1994; Alexander, Willcock and Nelson, 1995; Campbell and Neill, 1994a, 1994b; Campbell, 1997; Plewis and Veltman, 1996). Inspection evidence is far less equivocal. Based on comparison with inspection findings prior to 1988 the National Curriculum appears to have brought about real, though unspectacular, improvement as least as judged in terms of the values held by inspectors. Overall, compared with the curriculum 'lottery' (Richards, 1997a) which operated prior to 1988 there is a more consistent curriculum in operation across English primary schools. Both whole school and individual teacher planning have improved. Collaboration amongst teachers has increased. Expertise in teacher assessment has been enhanced. Established curricular and pedagogic practices have been questioned and, in some cases, reconstituted. In general primary aged children have a broader curriculum than hitherto, broader both in terms of the subjects learnt and the range of content within each subject; there is greater continuity and progression in their learning; their progress is assessed rather more accurately; their standards of work in subjects such as science and history have improved; there is *no* evidence that overall pupils' achievements in reading and number have fallen, though there is *no* evidence that they have improved either.

Judging from inspection evidence, monitoring by the School Curriculum and Assessment Authority (SCAA) and from other work English primary schools are currently providing one of three alternative curricula:

(i)   Many, probably the majority, are 'playing safe' and providing a *legal entitlement curriculum* (Richards, 1997b) — teaching their pupils what the law demands (the National Curriculum and locally determined religious education) but nothing beyond that, i.e. *not* attempting to create a distinctive curriculum of their own by adding other elements. To use a sartorial analogy such schools are offering an 'off-the-peg curriculum'.

(ii)   Some are providing an *enriched legal entitlement curriculum* — giving their pupils their legal entitlement in terms of National Curriculum subjects and religious education but going beyond these to offer new elements to enrich the basic curriculum 'fare' in line with their particular interests, expertise or environment. Some schools, for example, are teaching 'new' subjects such as a modern foreign language, classical (or Cornish!) studies or philosophy to one or more year groups. Some are developing 'specialist' emphases to their curricula by offering a subject or more than one subject to a much greater depth and/or range than the current National Curriculum requires. Some are devoting time to teaching cross-curricular issues such as environmental education, citizenship or, less often European studies. Some have developed programmes of personal and social education throughout the school. Some are undertaking a combination of these. To use the sartorial analogy, such schools are attempting to provide a 'tailor-made curriculum'.

(iii) In the light of accountability demands, intensified, not mitigated, by *Excellence in Schools* (DfEE, 1997b), myths of declining standards in 'the basics', unfavourable comparisons with other countries and an OFSTED-inspired curriculum focusing ever more tightly on the core subjects, a growing number of primary schools are providing a *neo-elementary school curriculum*: devoting more time than ever before to literacy and numeracy (especially those aspects appearing in national tests) and providing a rudimentary, superficial coverage of other National Curriculum subjects and religious education. This is a curriculum similar in its broad emphases, time allocations and pedagogy to the practice in many English elementary schools prior to the 1944 Education Act. This find of provision could well be dubbed a 'hand-me-down curriculum'.

The Future of the Primary Curriculum

In the spirit of the opening section of this chapter there needs to be a review of the current primary curriculum but realistically a review carried out on two different timescales and with different agendas. Almost 10 years on from the beginning of its implementation there are inevitably modifications which need to be considered and applied pragmatically to the structure and content of the current National Curriculum in primary schools. Such modifications can be considered, and implemented, in the short-term — perhaps over a period of two or three years. However, there is also the need for a fundamental rethink, all the more necessary given that the necessary fundamental debate did not happen 'the first time around' in 1987–8. This can, and should, take longer and involve philosophical and ethical as well as pragmatic considerations.

Short-term

In the short-term, and accepting for the time being the basic structure of the current arrangements, a number of key questions need to be posed and answered. Each person interested in curriculum matters will have their own list and their own tentative answers for the Qualifications and Curriculum Authority to answer. Listed below are my suggested questions and answers:

- What age range should any revised National Curriculum embody? (3–14)
- Should the notion of key stages be retained and if so covering which age groups? (a pragmatically useful device which should be retained but 'recalibrated' — Key Stage 1: ages 3–6; Key Stage 2: ages 6–8; Key Stage 3: ages 8–12; Key Stage 4: ages 12–14)
- In what ways should a revised National Curriculum be described? (areas of learning for under-6s, broad areas of learning for the 6–8 age group; subjects for pupils aged 8–14)
- Should the range of the curriculum be broader or narrower than currently? (no narrower at any Key Stage but with all schools required at each Key Stage to provide selective enrichment in one or more areas or subjects)
- Should the balance of the curriculum (in terms of time allocations) be prescribed legally? (a compulsory minimum and maximum for each National Curriculum subject or area but with groups of schools determining their own time allocations within those limits)
- Are the expectations embodied in the current National Curriculum both realistic and challenging? (challenging in all subjects; but not always realistic for example, in information technology and design technology)
- Are current assessment arrangements valid, reliable and useful? (current system to be scrapped; the notion of 'attainment levels' dispensed with; major development into teacher assessment of a range of core elements [not core subjects] commissioned; a series of short, basic national standardized tests introduced at ages 7 and 11 to meet inevitable accountability demands)
- Should there be a national recording format giving teachers a clear and realistic expectation of what, minimally and statutorily, should be recorded about achievement? (a small number of nationally approved recording formats, one of which is to adopted by all schools in an LEA)
- What aspects should a revised National Curriculum legally prescribe? (content perhaps in more detail than currently, but no legal prescription of curriculum organization or teaching methodology)
- Should there be centrally prescribed texts? (centrally *approved* texts and teaching/learning materials including computer programs and packages)
- Should schools be allowed a measure of discretion to address locally identified needs or capitalize on particular strengths? (a key requirement of any revised curriculum)

The answers provided by the Qualifications and Curriculum Authority and the Labour Government to such questions will reinforce as the modal curriculum one or other of the three alternative primary curricula outlined above. Thus, suggestions advocating, for example, the restriction of children's entitlement at Key Stage 1 to the core subjects, cutting back on the programmes of study of the other foundation subjects at Key Stage 2 and introducing a new round of national tests at age 9 to complement those at ages 7 and 11 would reinforce the modality of a *neo-elementary school curriculum*. Suggestions which focus on making very minor adjustments to the current statutory orders, which retain the current assessment regime, which fail to build on some of the more innovative post-Dearing practice and which do not require, or even encourage, local initiative or interpretation would reinforce an adherence to a *legal entitlement curriculum*. On the other hand retaining breadth and balance as two key principles at all key stages, recommending maximum and minimum time allocations to prevent imbalances of a neo-elementary kind, replacing the current assessment regime with enhanced teacher assessment complemented by a minimal degree of national standardized testing, recommending the abandonment of performance tables and the vain attempts to arrive at educationally valid measures of genuine 'value-added', and releasing the creativity and imagination found in many primary schools to provide their own distinctive curricula embodying but going beyond National Curriculum requirements would reinforce the modality of an *enriched legal entitlement curriculum* (Richards, 1997a). Which of these three alternative curricula would provide the most appropriate seedbed for the radical, longer term rethink required to provide a curriculum, responsive to the early twenty-first century?

Longer Term

In the longer term, perhaps over a 10-year period, there needs to be a genuine national (i.e. UK-wide) debate about what the young should be taught, or should experience, in our society: a debate involving not just those in the education service but also parents, governors, politicians (even!), the wider community and particularly the young themselves. That debate needs to involve a number of very fundamental issues: the nature of the society we are trying to create; the principles and values underpinning its governance and operation; the personal qualities and understandings required to realize that society and cope with an ever-changing, interdependent world; the nature of personhood and citizenship. There would be questions relating to education and, in particular, to the curriculum including the primary curriculum.

Adopting the analytical framework used earlier in this chapter, these might include

The nature and extent of legal prescription
- Should primary education, whether provided by schools or by other means, be legally compulsory?

- Should a primary curriculum be legally prescribed?
- If so at what level — local? regional? country? UK? European Union? United Nations?
- Should different components be legally prescribed at different levels?
- Should a comprehensive primary curriculum be prescribed or should there be elements of discretion — at school, local, regional etc. levels?
- What should be legally prescribed? — aims and purposes? content? assessment? organization? teaching methodology?

The rationale for the curriculum

- What should be the core aims and values a primary curriculum is attempting to promote?
- What kind of personal qualities, skills, intelligences, understandings and knowledge should primary age children develop as a result of engagement with such a curriculum?
- How far should a primary curriculum attend to issues such as
  - economic and workplace needs in the context of change, globalization and uncertainty;
  - individual development, freedom and fulfilment;
  - personal and collective morality;
  - social justice and social cohesion;
  - culture, broadly and pluralistically conceived;
  - the needs and obligations of the citizen in a democratic society.

Dominant metaphors

- From where might metaphors be drawn to help characterize a future primary curriculum? — information processing? quantum mechanics? ecology? neurological science? aesthetics? psychotherapy? moral philosophy?

Contents

- Should a primary curriculum provide more or less than the current range of core and other foundation subjects and religious education?
- If less which should be omitted and at what stage?
- If more which should be included and at what stage? — a modern foreign language? philosophy? psychology? ecology? sociology etc.?
- Should a primary curriculum make provision for cross-curricular themes and if so which and when? Should new 'candidates' be considered for example, European studies, legal studies, moral education, media studies?
- Should it involve explicit attention to teaching children transferable metacognitive skills, understanding and capability?
- Should a curriculum be organized in terms of subjects, areas of learning, broad areas, modules, topics etc and at what stages?

Assessment
- Should all elements of a primary curriculum, or only a 'core', be assessed? If a 'core', of what should it comprise?
- Who should be involved in that assessment? — teachers? parents? children themselves?
- What form should that assessment take?
- What purposes should assessment (or different forms of assessment) serve? — formative? summative/evaluative? informative?

There are doubtless many more questions and issues that might be raised.

Unfinished Business

In *Excellence in Schools* (DfEE, 1997b) the Government promises 'to conduct a thorough review of the National Curriculum in due course. We will set a sensible timetable for consultation and comment so that we will have a genuinely collaborative exercise in which all our partners in education will have the chance to participate. The curriculum for the next century — and its associated assessment — will be guided by:

- our vision of a curriculum reflecting a common framework and a common entitlement;
- the needs of children at different ages and different stages in their development; and
- the needs, character and ethos of the individual school. (p. 22)

The Government has to redeem its promises and not just for ethical or political reasons. Broad, deep and fundamental thinking about the primary school curriculum *is* needed in *both* the short and longer term to meet the challenges of the early twenty-first century in *both* personal and national terms. More than ever, professional questioning and judgment on primary curriculum matters leading on to intelligent action and purposeful engagement by both teachers and children are required . . . But after a long period of demoralization, disillusionment and loss of collective self-confidence can the teaching profession trust the Government (and itself) enough to contribute wholeheartedly and wholemindedly?

References

ALEXANDER, P. (1997) 'The new primary curriculum: Basics, core or margins?', paper presented at the SCAA conference, *Developing the Primary School Curriculum: The Next Steps*, June.

ALEXANDER, R., ROSE, J. and WOODHEAD, C. (1992) *Curriculum Organisation and Classroom Practice in Primary Schools*, London: DES.

ALEXANDER, R., WILLCOCK, J. and NELSON, N. (1995) 'Change and continuity', in ALEXANDER, R. (ed.) *Versions of Primary Education*, London: Routledge.

CAMPBELL, R. (1997) *Standards of Literacy and Numeracy in Primary School: A Real or Manufactured Crisis?*, CREPE occasional paper, University of Warwick.

CAMPBELL, R. and NEIL, S. (1994a) *Primary Teachers at Work*, London: Routledge.

CAMPBELL, R. and NEIL, S. (1994b) *Curriculum Reform at Key Stage 1: Teacher Commitment and Policy Failure*, London: Longman.

DEPARTMENT FOR EDUCATION AND EMPLOYMENT (DfEE) (1997a) *New Requirements for All Courses of Initial Teacher Training*, Teacher Training Circular Letter 1/97, London: HMSO.

DEPARTMENT FOR EDUCATION AND EMPLOYMENT (DfEE) (1997b) *Excellence in Schools*, London: HMSO.

DEPARTMENT OF EDUCATION AND SCIENCE (DES) (1987) *The National Curriculum 5–16: A Consultation Document*, London: DES.

DEPARTMENT OF EDUCATION AND SCIENCE (1988) *National Curriculum Task Group on Assessment and Testing A Report*, London: DES.

MILLETT, A. (1997) 'Bringing a new professionalism into teaching', *Education Journal*, **10**.

PLEWIS, I. and VELTMAN, M. (1996) 'Where does all the time go: Changes in pupils' experience in year 2 classrooms', in HUGHES, M. (ed.) *Teaching and Learning in Changing Times*, Oxford: Blackwells.

POLLARD, A. et al. (1994) *Changing English Primary Schools?*, London: Cassell.

RICHARDS, C. (1997a) 'Enrichment as entitlement', Paper presented at the SCAA conference, *Developing the Primary School Curriculum: The Next Steps*, June.

RICHARDS, C. (1997b) 'The primary curriculum 1988–2008', *British Journal of Curriculum and Assessment*, **7**, 3.

RICHARDS, C. (1998) 'The elementary/primary curriculum: The English experience 1862–2012', in MOYLES, I. and HARGREAVES, L. (eds) *The Primary Curriculum: Learning from International Perspectives*, London: Routledge.

SCHOOL CURRICULUM AND ASSESSMENT AUTHORITY (SCAA) (1993) *The National Curriculum and Assessment: Final Report*, London: SCAA.

TABBERER, R., HINE, T. and GALLACHER, S. (1996) 'Seven obstacles to effective target-setting', *Education Journal*, **7**.

TAYLOR, P. (1997) 'The' 'primariness' of primary education: Past, present and future', *Education 3–13*, **25**, 3.

TAYLOR, P. and RICHARDS, C. (1985) *An Introduction to Curriculum Studies*, 2nd ed, Slaigh: NFER.

Further Reading

ASSOCIATION OF TEACHERS AND LECTURERS (1998) *Take Care, Mr. Blunkett*, London: ATL.

MOYLES, J. and HARGREAVES, L. (eds) (1998) *The Primary Curriculum: Learning from International Perspectives*, London: Routledge.

SCHOOL CURRICULUM AND ASSESSMENT AUTHORITY (SCAA) (1997) *Developing the Primary School Curriculum: The Next Steps*, London: SCAA.

12   Change and Progress in Primary Teaching

Nigel Hastings

Introduction

A visit to the doctor's surgery is a fairly routine, if infrequent, event in most Western lives, and so it has been for most of the twentieth century. Some aspects of what takes place there have not altered through those years while others have changed: patients still wait in waiting rooms until it is their turn to be seen, doctors still ask them questions and conduct examinations, issue prescriptions and offer advice. This much would be recognizable to anyone who had not visited a doctor's surgery since, say, 1930. What has changed is the expertise employed. In the intervening years, medical knowledge has moved on. Diagnostic procedures have been refined, medical technology has developed and new treatments have been identified and evaluated. Medical practice may not be expected to deal with all conditions, but the general belief of those who sit in the waiting rooms, held with some justification, is that the chances of correct diagnosis and effective treatment have improved over the years.

Ask about the source of these improvements and research will soon be mentioned. Within fields like medicine and engineering, research is considered central to developments in practice. Indeed, the whole rationale for research in these areas is its potential to yield enhanced understanding and refinements in strategy which improve the effectiveness of practice. This does not mean that research is the sole spur for change — politics, fashion and economics also play their parts. Nor does it imply that research is invariably sound or fluently feeds into practice. The point is simply that, in these fields, research plays a significant role in the development of professional practice and in determining the standards by which practitioners' practice will be judged. If robust research evidence indicates that treatment X has a better success rate than treatments Y and Z, then prescribing treatment X will be regarded as better practice than its alternatives, other things being equal.

But this chapter is not about medicine or engineering, it is about teaching. More specifically, it is about teaching in primary schools over the next 10 or 15 years, a period which lopsidedly straddles the milestone between millennia that compels both retrospection and an uneasy mixture of prediction and aspiration. If our predictions and aspirations about the future of primary teaching converge, we'll fell pretty good about tomorrow.

My purpose in beginning with some lay observations about the nature of progress in other professions is to begin to argue that teaching needs to become more like them in the ways in which its practices develop. This is not a new proposition. I am conscious that others have previously argued not only that this kind of development should take place but, wrongly as it happened, that the time was then ripe for it to occur. Nevertheless, the turn of a century is a time for boldness so I too will suggest that there is a need for a change of this sort and also that it stands a good chance of becoming established in the next decade.

Progress in Primary Teaching

There have, of course, been changes in primary education just as there have been changes in medical practice, even though, as with the doctor's surgery, the primary (elementary) classroom of the 1930s and its contemporary equivalent have many similarities. The organizational unit typically remains as one teacher and a class of children; more time is still spent on maths and English than any other curriculum areas; activities involving writing are prominent and teachers continue to reprimand children more often for talking than for anything else. But there are differences as well, in resources, in organization and operation, as well as in the breadth of the curriculum. Children no longer sit in rows but generally work in groups of four to eight; drill and recitation are less evident; work is more differentiated; resources are more plentiful and varied and written materials are more lively in presentation. We may feel no concern about any of these developments, but investigation of their genesis and development quickly reveals that research evidence of their benefits for learning played no part.

Change is not the same as progress. Progress entails the notion of improvement. If we approve of a particular change we will call it an improvement and deem practice to have progressed. However, this is not the same as having evidence of increased effectiveness and it is difficult to find any change in general primary teaching which has taken place on the basis of evidence of effectiveness. They tend to have arisen in much the same manner as changes in the curriculum — through argument, persuasion and the generally well-intentioned influence of those with responsibilities and power. Evidence, as contrasted with assertions, of improvements in educational outcomes has barely featured in debate and decisions. But, in the absence of a robust body of such evidence, nor could it.

The idea of teaching needing evidence to inform decisions and progress has been argued for well over a century, but to little effect. Asking 'Why no pedagogy in England?' Brian Simon noted in 1981 that the word *pedagogy* is rarely used in England, whereas in other European countries, in which there are 'pedagogical institutes', the idea of a 'science of teaching' is not at all unfamiliar (Simon, 1981). He reminds his readers of the Scottish philosopher

Alexander Bain's book, published in 1879 and entitled *Education as a Science*, in which Bain made a case for education as a discipline which would develop its own theories, concepts and methods of investigation to yield understanding and knowledge which would inform practice. David Ausubel argued similarly in 1953, suggesting that the teaching profession had failed '. . . to make the progress it could reasonably have been expected to make in providing a scientific basis for pedagogy' and criticized research in education as rarely addressing those questions which are most significant for teaching (Ausubel, 1953).

Now, at the end of the century, precisely the same claims, criticisms and ambitions have been expressed by David Hargreaves in launching the Teacher Training Agency's drive to establish teaching as a 'research-based profession' (Hargreaves, 1996). Perhaps a little more cautiously, the National Committee of Inquiry into Higher Education, which commented that 'teaching is, or should be, a "research-based" profession', has also endorsed the case (NCIHE, 1997). It is not without significance that two national bodies have lent their support to an evidence-based conception of teaching in a context where a new Government, elected on a manifesto which placed education at the centre of its agenda, is pressing for improvements in the standards children achieve in schools, particularly in literacy and numeracy.

This need for evidence about teaching in order to assess and improve its effectiveness, argued by Bain, Ausubel, Simon, Hargreaves and plenty more, over a period of 120 years, now seems barely contestable. Yet, as we noted earlier, the idea has never taken root in the profession as a whole. However, the circumstances have never been quite as promising as they are now, not least because, for the first time in history, we have a body of research evidence which is sufficiently robust to begin to inform policy and teaching decisions.

Evidence of Effective Teaching

In the last 25 years, a series of investigations[1] undertaken in British primary classrooms has begun to yield information about the nature of teachers' and pupils' activities, about the relationships between the two and about the links between teaching methods and important educational outcomes, such as academic progress and behaviour. Although individually interesting, and also deficient in various ways, these studies have consistencies and resonances between their findings which render them particularly important and useful. For when similar patterns of relationship between aspects of classroom life appear in studies conducted at different times, in different places and using differing research methods, confidence in the findings grows.

This is not the appropriate place, or space, in which to attempt to review the main findings emerging from this body of work;[2] its significance in this discussion arises from its existence rather than its detailed nature. Having this evidence places today's primary teachers in a position that is different from every previous generation, and also from their secondary colleagues, for whom no comparably robust body of research evidence exists. However, this is not sufficient for it to be used or useful. If evidence is to become integral to the development of primary teaching, a number of other conditions need to be right. These conditions include beliefs about teaching by teachers, parents and policy-makers and also the organization and conduct of educational research. I will consider each of these in turn.

Beliefs About Teaching

Beliefs about teaching and learning vary a good deal, both within the profession and without. Because teaching is fundamentally a moral activity — we do it because we believe it improves youngsters — teachers and others concerned with education often hold beliefs about their teaching with great conviction. In general, this is an admirable quality in a public service, but some beliefs are not compatible with the idea of teaching as a research-based profession. Acceptance of four superficially non-contentious propositions seems particularly important if research is to be able to play any part in the development of primary teaching as a whole.

'The Purpose of Teaching Is Learning'

This apparently self-evident idea requires emphasis, for learning has not been central to debates about education. Indeed, Simon argues persuasively that the lack of attention paid to pedagogy and its development in England is historically rooted in the public schools' prime function being seen as the socialization and character formation of the young, rather than their education. Socialization and character are not taught, as they are not consciously learned, and therefore learning was not, in practice, the most important aspect of a school teacher's work.

A second, and not unrelated, reason for the somewhat marginal position of learning in educational discussions has been the widely held view, nowadays generally an implicit assumption, that each child has a limited potential which places a ceiling on their possible achievements. If intelligence and potential are deemed to be fixed, and judged in particular cases to be fixed at a low level, teachers' expectations will be modest, as will their efforts to support pupils' learning. After all, there is little point in pushing an immovable object. It is interesting that the assumption of fixed potential is more prevalent in British culture than in many others where effort and learning are assumed to be the more significant components of achievement. One can readily speculate about the consequences of these differences in belief about learning.

Whatever psychology might ultimately reveal about such matters, beliefs about learning matter, especially in the minds of teachers and parents. We need to invigorate the understanding that the purpose of teaching is learning and the belief that *all* children can learn and make progress. The currently popular 'zero tolerance of failure' slogan emphasizes the belief that all children can learn and that it is schools' and teachers' responsibility to support learning and achievement.

Primary teachers have long been expected to work with and for the 'whole child' and that will properly remain their responsibility, but the focus of their work on learning and achievement is currently being sharpened through a series of Government and professional initiatives. With learning highlighted as the central purpose of teaching and an attitude of 'zero tolerance of under-achievement', a concern for ways of improving teaching, supported by evidence, follows.

Teaching is a Skilful Activity

Discussions of teaching, lay and professional, often employ the concept of 'teaching style'. Indeed, one of the most protracted and fruitless of educational debates concerns the relative merits of 'traditional' and 'progressive' teaching. In some of the research literature too, there have been attempts to make sense of life in classrooms by identifying 'styles' of teaching and to determine their contributions to learning and progress. Conceptualizing teaching in terms of 'types of teacher' has not been helpful for the development of the profession. It invites identification with one type, solidarity with fellow members of that type and a defensive reaction to any criticism or evidence which indicates that another approach is, in any way, better. Moreover, when teaching is described and considered in terms of 'styles of teaching', or 'types of teacher', improvement would seem to involve teachers of a less favoured type abandoning all that they currently do and engaging in a metamorphic transformation into the better type of teacher or enthusiastic practitioner of the better style. Few volunteer.

If research is to inform the development of teachers' performance, in initial training and subsequently, a more disaggregated conception of teaching is needed than the notion of style or type. Recent developments in the way in which training requirements for teachers have been specified, first as *competencies* and now *standards*, may be helpful here as they have contributed to a move away from holistic, 'package deal' descriptions of teaching towards a model of teaching as a skilful activity. To those who consider a skill to be nothing more than a set of coordinated physical actions, considering teaching as a skill underestimates and undervalues the activity. However, this is to misunderstand the nature of a skill, and skill. A skill entails both performance and, crucially, well informed judgment. A surgeon who is a dab hand with a scalpel but regularly uses it in inappropriate situations, performing neat and tidy appendectomies when they are not needed, for instance, would not be described as skilful. Skilful activity requires mastery of relevant techniques and knowledge and understanding to support judgments about which techniques, if any, should be employed in a particular situation. In this sense, teaching is a skilful activity, *par excellence*. Teachers have at their disposal a range of strategies, some having more than others, but it is not just fluent proficiency in the use of these strategies that constitutes skilful teaching; it is also informed judgment about when, where and how to deploy them that makes the difference.

The development and improvement of teaching is not a threatening idea if teaching is conceptualized as a skill as it is in the nature of a skill that it can continually be developed and refined. Moreover, improving a skill does not involve abandoning all current practice in favour of a whole new approach. Rather it entails elaborating the knowledge base which currently informs judgments and/or improving aspects of performance through review and practice. If teaching comes to be more widely viewed as a research-based skill, we may shed the habit of taking an advance in pedagogic knowledge to require identification of someone to blame for not having previously known it and as an attack on certain 'types of teacher'.

'Each Child is Not Unique'

The third aspect of teaching which requires some rethinking within primary education if research evidence is to be seen as potentially relevant to teachers' work is the idea that every child is unique. In several important senses, every child *is* unique. Each is a unique combination of biology and biography, as well as having a morally or spiritually unique status. However, recognition of this unique quality of individuals does *not* mean that each of us is completely unlike anyone else. Believing that 'every child is unique' can sit quite comfortably with the idea that every child is like most others in some respects and like different sets of others, again possibly most others, in other respects. Identifying similarities does not deny or challenge individuality any more than the fact that an aspirin helps my headache as well as yours is an affront to your, or my, status as an individual. In primary education, however, there has been a tendency to celebrate individuality and to interpret the proposition that 'each child is unique' as meaning not only that each has a proper status as an individual but also that, because each is a unique case they each have 'their own way of learning' and, consequently, there can be no generalizations about teaching. Viewed from an evolutionary perspective, the idea that any species could have evolved in such a manner that fundamental processes, such as learning, are not similar across the species as a whole, is implausible. Nevertheless, the idea of the 'individual child', the emphasis on differences between children and the intertwining of moral and empirical claims about individuality are established and influential strands within the culture of British primary education and are manifested in a number of pedagogical aspirations, *one-to-one teaching* and *differentiation* being two important cases.

One-to-one teaching, when the teacher works with an individual child, was seen by the Plowden Committee as the ideal teaching and learning situation. The Committee's advocacy of small group teaching was a compromise adopted in recognition that, with 30 or more children, a regime of one-to-one teaching was not possible. Thirty years on, concern about increased class sizes is often expressed in terms of the adverse effects on one-to-one teaching, still reflecting the view that it is in this kind of teaching that the best quality learning takes place in the classroom. However, the evidence, consistently emerging from classroom observation studies over the last 20 years, paints a different picture. It indicates that teachers typically spend more time in one-to-one interactions with children than doing anything else, but the average child only gets 2 or 3 per cent of her/his time in this sort of contact. Teachers are busy in one-to-one interactions; children are not. The tragedy is that even if class sizes were halved and each child's one-to-one attention doubled as a consequence, it would still occupy less than five minutes of the typical classroom hour in the average child's classroom experience. It could be, of course, that the effects of these brief exchanges are wholly disproportionate to their duration, but the evidence does not seem to support this proposition either as the educational quality of exchanges in these episodes appears not to be high. Conversations tend to be brief and about routine matters and task management: 'Try to use a ruler for those lines . . .'; 'Miss, have we got any high gauze?'; 'Have you finished your work? . . . Good, now I want you to . . .'. There are also indications that progress is poorer and distraction is greater where teachers devote more of their time to one-to-one work than most. Despite this evidence and the inescapable arithmetic of dividing the attention of one teacher between 30 children, let alone 40, the aspiration to teach children as individuals and belief in the necessity to do remains robust among teachers and parents.

A second manifestation of the 'each child is unique' culture is a concern with differentiation. Differentiation, the matching of tasks to each child's current level of competence or understanding, and possibly to their preferred way of working, has been a hallmark of good practice in the eyes of HMI throughout the 1970s and 1980s and continues to feature prominently. Like the idea of one-to-one teaching, differentiation emphases the differences between children. It has not been a controversial goal, even though it is generally experienced as difficult to achieve in a normal primary classroom context.

The essence of the idea of differentiation is that learning proceeds from current understanding or competence — an unexceptional, even fundamental, idea. However, the way in which the concepts of *ability* and *attainment* become muddled in use, can result in differentiation being understood as requiring the matching of tasks to ability which, therefore, has to be assessed or estimated. If ability or attainment is understood as fixed, the concerns outlined earlier about low expectations and the setting of tasks which occupy but do not support learning become amplified. Evidence[3] from classrooms indicates that although teachers tend to recognize and deal with situations where they have given a child work which is beyond them, they are less likely to notice children for whom they have set work that is contributing little to their learning, so long as they are not misbehaving.

In summary, the culture of primary education properly values each child as an individual and places an emphasis on the responsibility that a teacher has for each and every child in their class. However, this professional ethic needs to be untangled from empirical claims about the ways in which children learn, which are not unique; indeed, if children did not have much in common, not only would research on teaching and learning be impossible but it would also be impossible for teachers to learn from their experience. So, the proposition that 'learning is likely to be much the same sort of process for all of us' has to be accepted if the possibility of research informing practice is even to be entertained. Research into teaching and learning *has* to assume that there are consistencies in the processes, but unless this idea is also accepted throughout education, evidence of relationships between aspects of teaching and learning will remain of interest only to researchers.

'All Teachers Cannot be as Good as the Best Teachers'

In one of his occasional forays into education, the famous American psychologist B.F. Skinner noted the propensity of educationalists and policy makers to urge *all* teachers to use the methods used by the best teachers (Skinner, 1965). At first glance, this is not at all an unreasonable idea: if they are the best teachers because of the methods they use, using those methods should make all teachers 'best' teachers. The problem is that although some methods can produce remarkable results in the hands of a small minority of teachers, when they are used by others the outcomes can be very variable and even very poor. One early British study of teacher effectiveness amply illustrated this point. The single most effective teacher in the project employed methods which were reported as less effective within the sample as a whole. She appeared to use approaches which had been enthusiastically advocated as 'good practice' but, it seems, turned out to be just too complex and demanding for all but the most exceptional to manage well.

Research in which teaching strategies are compared in their effects on children's progress will rarely show that *all* classes, let along *all* children, taught using one strategy make greater progress than *all* those taught using an alternative approach. The differences which emerge are usually differences in the *average* level of progress made by classes taught in the different ways. As with all averages, there will be a range around them: some of the classes make greater gains than others taught using the same approach. In addition, some of the classes taught using the more effective strategy will generally make less progress than some using another, overall less effective, strategy — just as it can happen that a minority of teachers using a less effective (on average) strategy produce learning gains greater than any of the teachers using the more effective (on average) strategy. Such a pattern should not be a surprise, but it does have important implications.

If the quality of learning is to be raised throughout the primary education system by seeking improved teaching methods, the approach has to develop and disseminate strategies which, *in the hands of most teachers*, have the greatest benefits for children's learning. Trying to improve teaching by identifying and disseminating what the very best teachers do is a waste of time, Skinner argued. Rather, we should concentrate on identifying what can be done to best effect by the remaining 95 per cent. There are two main reasons for this. First, identifying the key factors in the way individual teachers achieve their outstanding results is a highly complex research exercise. Secondly, even if this was possible, these teachers' special mix of judgments and skills are likely to be so complex that most other teachers could not acquire the expertise within a training programme of reasonable scale. Strategies which can be effective in the hands of the few should therefore be passed over in favour of those which can be effective in the hands of the many.

This line of argument has implications for policy-makers, teachers and educational research. Ideas about 'good practice' need to be cast with an eye for what is realistically achievable for most teachers working in conditions largely as they currently exist. To support these development of evidence-based accounts of 'good practice', research must similarly focus on identifying 'what works best for most'. The proposition that 'all teachers cannot be as good as the best' is therefore not a call for mediocrity as it might at first appear but a reasoned and necessary focus for policy, professional judgment and research if primary teaching is to develop and enhance learning for all children. There are indications in all three spheres that this view is developing.

The Organization and Conduct of Educational Research

For teaching to become a research-based profession it is not only important that there is a culture of beliefs about teaching which incorporates the four propositions outlined above, there also has to be a developing body of appropriate research to support innovation and evaluation. The series of studies referred to earlier has provided a valuable basis for the initial development of primary education as a research-based profession, but if it is to be sustained and teaching is to improve on the basis of evidence, research activity of this kind must continue and must be substantially focused on the relationships between teaching activities and learning outcomes. As we noted earlier, concern that this sort of issue has not been central to the educational research agenda has been expressed by some for decades. The fact that it is being expressed again now, at the same time as there is a determination to raise standards of achievement in primary schools and developing advocacy of the idea of teaching as a research-based profession, justifies some optimism that the research agenda will turn to focus more on questions of effectiveness in teaching. If it does not, the teaching profession will not have the option of considering evidence in determining teaching methods. There is, therefore, a responsibility among those who propose, fund and conduct research in education to focus on aspects of teaching and their consequences for children's education.

Concluding Comments

I have argued that conditions are now better than they have ever been for primary teaching to move from a history in which changes in methods have arisen solely as a consequence of the convictions of those with influence to a future in which evidence plays a greater role in the development of classroom teaching. The use of evidence is only part of the change for, as I have indicated, there are aspects of the profession's view of the nature of teaching which need to become more generally established if the idea of an evidence-based profession is to become more than rhetoric.

If it happens and teaching becomes more like medicine in its view of and relationship to research, it will not be a dramatic transformation. Beliefs and convictions about what is best will not wilt in the face of contrary evidence any more than they do in other fields, including medicine. Research studies will always have flaws and be susceptible to challenge on methodological grounds, especially when their findings cause discomfort. But, as David Hargreaves argued in his TTA lecture, without evidence against which to test the validity of claims about 'what works', the teaching profession will always be in a weak position to justify current methods or to contest politicians' claims that other methods would be better (Hargreaves, 1996). Until evidence is both sought and routinely employed in professional discussion and decisions, changes in primary teaching methods will not warrant description as progress. It is time for progress.

Notes

1 I have in mind particularly the ORACLE project conducted by Galton and colleagues, Mortimore et al.'s Junior School project, Croll and Moses' One in Five research, Alexander's study of primary education in Leeds, the PACE project at Bristol and the substantial body of intervention research concerned with classroom behaviour management.

2 Concise summaries of this research can be found in Croll and Hastings (1996) and Gipps (1994).

3 The clearest evidence of this was provided by Neville Bennett and his colleagues in a study of 'matching' in the classrooms of highly-regarded KS1 teachers (see Bennett et al., 1984). In addition, reports from HMI have low expectations and underestimation as recurrent themes.

References

ALEXANDER, R. (1997) *Policy and Practice in Primary Education*, 2nd ed, London: Routledge.

AUSUBEL, D. (1953) 'The nature of educational research', *Educational Theory*, **3**, pp. 314–20.

BENNETT, N., DESFORGES, C., COCKBURN, A. and WILKINSON, B. (1984) *The Quality of Pupil Learning Experiences*, London: Lawrence Erlbaum Associates.

BOURNE, J. (ed.) (1994) *Thinking Through Primary Practice*, Milton Keynes: Open University Press.

CROLL, P. and HASTINGS, N. (eds) (1996) *Effective Primary Teaching: Research-based Strategies*, London: David Fulton Publishers.

GALTON, M. (1995) *Crisis in the Primary Classroom*, London: David Fulton Publishers.

GIPPS, C. (1994) 'What we know about effective primary teaching', in BOURNE, J. (ed.) *Thinking Through Primary Practice*, Milton Keynes: Open University Press.

HARGREAVES, D. (1996) 'Teaching as a research-based profession', Teacher Training Agency annual lecture.

NATIONAL COMMITTEE OF INQUIRY INTO HIGHER EDUCATION (1997) *Higher Education in the Learning Society, Report 10 Teacher Education and Training: A Study*, London: HMSO.

SIMON, B. (1981) 'Why no pedagogy in England?', in SIMON, B. and TAYLOR, W. (eds) *Education in the Eighties*, London: Batsford, reprinted in SIMON, B. (1985) *Does Education Matter?*, London: Lawrence and Wishart Ltd.

SKINNER, B.F. (1965) 'Why teachers fail', lecture to Philosophy of Education Society, New York, reprinted in SPRINTHALL, R.N. and SPRINTHALL, N.A. (eds) (1969) *Educational Psychology: Selected Readings*, New York: Van Nostrand-Reinhold co.

13   Standards: The Case of Literacy

Julie Davies

Context

A dictionary will define 'standard' as: 'the degree of excellence required for particular purposes; the measure of what is adequate; a socially or practically desired level of performance' (Chambers, 1980). In the educational context, that is translated into the levels of attainment; attitudes and values. The popular use of the word 'standard' is not dissimilar. It is taken to denote an actual level of performance which is acceptable. It is this notion of standards that politicians and the public have in mind when they speak about falling standards: What they claim to see is a fall in actual performance levels dropping as a result of inadequate schooling and poor teaching. It was, in fact, the desire to raise standards which was the motivation behind the introduction of the National Curriculum. It was the then DES that claimed: 'There is every reason for optimism that in providing a sound, sufficiently detailed framework over the next decade, the National Curriculum will give children and teachers much needed help in achieving higher standards' (DES, 1989, p. 2).

Under the provisions of the Education Reform Act 1988, all maintained schools are required to provide 'a balanced and broadly based curriculum which:

> promotes the spiritual, moral, cultural, mental and physical development of pupils at the school and of society;
> prepares such pupils for the opportunities, responsibilities and experiences of adult life'.

Here was the focus for standards: the generally accepted view that the education system should support the central characteristics required from citizens in the society in which we live.

One of the fundamentally important ways that schools can achieve this is by ensuring the continued existence of a literate and numerate population. Being able to read and write is both a means and an end to enhancing life both materially and intellectually. It not only develops the individual, *per se*, but also the individual as a member of society, and as a citizen able to reflect critically on much that is written for pleasure, in employment, and the discharge of social relationships. Learning to read is one of the most important and empowering skills that anyone will acquire from schooling. Society recognizes this and consequently expects that schools will ensure children become not only literate but numerate as well. The economic benefits to the nation of the acquisition of literacy and numeracy skills are vital as the Secretary of State for Education and Employment asserted:

> Poor standards of literacy and numeracy are unacceptable. If our growing economic success is to be maintained we must get the basics right for everyone. Countries will only keep investing here at record levels if they see that the workforce is up to the job. (DfEE, 1997)

This is broadly the context against which to consider the issue of standards: an issue which is broader than immediate concerns would have us believe.

Beyond the Immediate

The challenges faced in developing a rational view of standards for the twenty-first century are many but may be summarized as:

- the weight of history;
- intense national interest;
- lack of consensus on standards in the past or at present;
- politicization of the standards debate;
- rupture of the research/policy/practice continuum;
- resources;
- accepting the need to develop a national monitoring system.

How will historians of primary education view the preoccupation with standards in the final decade of the twentieth century? Each year the issue of standards fills the media as the league tables of school performance are published. Test scores at the individual child level are relayed to parents; the school's overall results are reported to the public, to governors and education authorities. Results at local authority level are reported to the Department for Education and Employment and yet again reported by the media. The reported results are crudely summarized as 'x' per cent above the expected level and 'y' per cent below. The discussion that these figures generate centres on whether standards are rising or falling and for whom, followed by why some children are still below an expected level. Scapegoats — teachers, local authorities, 'trendy' educationalists and parents — are blamed.

Educational historians of twentieth century primary education may well see dissatisfaction with the performance of primary schools as measured by the national tests as a phenomena which dominated much of the nineties. Dissatisfaction has been expressed at different levels and resulted in policy initiatives which have a direct impact on teaching and learning in primary schools. Dissatisfaction is expressed spasmodically throughout the year but reaches fever pitch when the annual national test results are published.

Whatever the results they are rarely deemed satisfactory and targets are set which expect future cohorts of children to achieve even higher standards than their predecessors. There are targets set at present, for the primary education system to achieve by the year 2002. The Prime Minister, the Secretary of State for Education and Employment, Members of Parliament, local politicians, Her Majesty's Chief Inspector, the Teacher Training Agency as well as the media rail against the claimed low standards achieved by schools.

The next step is the search for solutions. The solutions have taken many forms, some curricular, some organizational, some cosmetic, some radical, some ephemeral. The historian will have a rich source on which to work. Solutions to drive up standards in reading, which had an immediate impact on children's work in school, include the National Curriculum for English with its programme of study and level descriptions and the national assessment system. Summer schools for literacy which involve year 6 children who are deemed to be able to benefit from these schemes (not those with the lowest literacy scores necessarily) are being increased 10-fold because of their perceived (but not proven) success. The literacy hour which each school is obliged to teach each day from next year is another solution being offered. Solutions which have affected the structure of the educational system include a National Curriculum for Initial Teacher Training which deals with students' own knowledge of English as well as prescribing what they must teach to children. The debate about low standards, in this case of class control, also led the Government to encourage schools to take over teacher training because of the perceived inadequacies in the training institutions' ability to turn out the right calibre of new teachers.

All in all, the central Governmental emphasis during the eighties and nineties has been on a deficit model of primary education the upshot of which was drastic remediation through policies aimed at driving up standards. But has there always been this amount of dissatisfaction with standards in primary education?

An Historical Perspective

History sometimes helps correct the rosy view we may have of schools in the 'good old days'. The elementary schools of times past, thought to produce literate people on a shoestring budget, were, in their day, open to criticism. In 1912, *The Times* commented that most people, even educated ones, could not spell. It also reported the comments of a headteacher that reading standards were falling because parents no longer read to their children, and spent too much time listening to the gramophone! In 1921, the Newbolt Report stated that pupils could not spell or punctuate: employers complained that school leavers were poor in spelling, grammar and punctuation. In 1925, His Majesty's

Inspectors reported that pupils were 'far inferior to the previous generation . . . even the most intelligent having glaring faults, letters badly written, badly spelled; sums generally wrong'. In 1938, the Spens Report, dealing with the top 13 per cent who went to grammar school, found: 'Many pupils pass through grammar school, and even university, without acquiring the capacity to express themselves in English'. A review of post-war literature regarding standards in reading in year 6 children reveals a plethora of conflicting opinion. A comprehensive study of national surveys and standardized tests, though, found little change in standards since 1945, apart from slight rises around 1950 and in the 1980s (Brooks et al., 1995).

Each generation, thus, appears to have been dissatisfied with the educational standards of its time. The present preoccupation with standards may be a symptom common not only to our own day but also to times past.

A Way Forward

This review may be of some comfort but can we improve on history so that coming generations do not get so absorbed in these posturings? Can we learn the lesson from history that the standards debate may well always be part of our political and public agenda and will always be discussed in negative, deficit terms? Probably not. But there is a way of circumventing its usual tenor: for the Government, at least, to report objectively, or as objectively as is possible, and as a matter of course, on the nation's reading standards.

Such a change would need to be preceded by an acceptance that the findings of national measurements need to be grounded in procedures that are technically defensible and accepted by all groups in society. A corollary is that standards are a matter for all. If the right to read is claimed for all children, responsibilities for making resources available and using them efficiently by schools to achieve this end, are both collective and individual. The Government, politicians, school and community as well as the parent, teacher and child have their parts to play.

With this caveat, is it possible to assess objectively standards in reading, their improvement or decline?

Problems in Measuring Standards

Looking at the present position, we find a Secretary of State for Education and Employment stating that national testing was here to stay as a means of checking at intervals on levels of educational achievement and progress. There are challenges facing the development of the national tests for these purposes, even though ministers have repeatedly expressed confidence in how they are conceptualized and developed. The burden of their argument was that what is new about National Curriculum testing is that we now have the chance to measure children's progress against standards that are set nationally and held in common across England and Wales. In this way we can have confidence in the results. We can have confidence that our children are being assessed against objective external standards rather than being judged against the relative performance of their classmates.

This somewhat optimistic view that national tests provide reliable measures of the progress of pupils both individually and collectively, and enable comparisons to be made over a period of years has been recently challenged on several grounds. First, national test data are derived from cross-sectional studies. Such data cannot be as reliable as direct study of progress through longitudinal monitoring of the same groups of learners. Ideally, monitoring changes over time in attainment involves giving the same test to the same children of the same age at regular intervals. Performance evidence is then generated which is reliable or as reliable as possible. However, if the sample of children is cross-sectional (as in annual national testing) then there is a possibility that the samples might change so as not to be equally representative on different occasions (Brooks et al., 1995). Strictly speaking, true norms of progress are not available from cross-sectional monitoring.

A second condition which could affect reliability of the tests' data is that national tests are based on criterion-referenced measurement of children's performance on tasks to assess their ability to show a range of abilities across the level descriptions. These level descriptions are somewhat vague summations and, as such, difficult to test reliably. For example, to test whether the level 2 description best fits a child requires a common, detailed understanding of what the statements actually mean:

> Pupils' reading of simple texts shows understanding and is generally accurate. They express opinions about major events or ideas in stories, poems and non-fiction. They use more than one strategy, such as phonic, graphic, syntactic and contextual, in reading unfamiliar words and establishing meaning.

The apparent vagueness of this description makes the design of a test to measure it a difficult task. Also, the nature of criterion-referenced measurement is open to question. Some 50 or more definitions have been given in the literature. The definition most widely used describes criterion-referenced tests as being constructed to permit the interpretation of examined test performance in relation to a set of well-defined competences (Popham, 1978). The emphasis on 'well-defined', in contrast to 'poorly-defined', competences makes the subsequent process of test item writing easier and more valid and may improve the quality of test score interpretations. It is here that there have been criticisms centred on the national tests' reliability based as they are on judgments of somewhat vague poorly defined descriptors, which in turn make it difficult for the test constructors to develop content specificity to the extent which would allow the results of tests set to be interpreted in the intended way. The level descriptions on which national tests are based leads the sceptic to think of the latter as elastic rulers which can be reformed through interpretation at any time.

Thirdly, the use of national tests as both measures of end of stage attainment and as diagnostic indicators for future lesson planning also received criticism. This criticism is based on the view that trying to develop a test which is both diagnostic and prognostic will not serve either purpose satisfactorily. Formative assessment requires detailed observation of a child's strategies when reading, such that learning objectives can be set by the teacher, for example. This assessment, to be effective, needs to be ongoing and frequent. Summative assessment, as its name implies, is an end of stage test to see what has been achieved over a period of time.

To publish the results and place great stress on them as indicators of school and teacher effectiveness is to make the likelihood that they are reliable measures of what children attain in reading less likely, given the pressures to practise the test to inflate these very important scores. In addition, the eight-point scale of level descriptions on which the tests are based have been considered too gross to allow for precision in measuring attainment and progress.

Even if one accepts the principle that whatever exists, exists in some quantity and can, in principle, be measured, there are still considerable challenges to be faced in developing a national testing system. Assessing and improving standards in relation to literacy is far from simple. A great deal of research and scholarship has surrounded the nature of early reading, the conditions likely to enhance its development and its assessment. Even so there are issues that continue to remain complex and controversial. This fact alone should encourage some circumspection in the development of prescriptions for tests of literacy in young children Some go so far as to argue that because of a failure to appreciate that different types of reading test and assessment techniques address different formative and summative uses, the Government's current policy and practice in the assessment of reading attainment at Key Stage 1 is seriously flawed (Pumfrey, 1995). It is important and necessary to appreciate the great range of pupils' inter-individual and intra-individual differences.

For example, in a study involving the administration of reading test to a representative sample of 164 year 6 children, the mean reading comprehension score was found to be 101.43. What is important to note is that within the group, 17 per cent of the children scored below 85 and 10 per cent above 115 with the remaining children scoring between 85 and 115 (Davies and Brember, 1997). Average reading attainment levels conceal as much as they reveal. If what is needed is a plan of action for raising average scores, then the identification of the tail of poor attainers is needed, but is masked if reference is only to national average scores.

Of What Use?

Two questions concerning national tests need further public discussion. How useful are level description data in informing parents and the community about children's standards and progress? For example, what does the information that their child is a level 2c reader mean to parents? Can the data, at the same time, help the teacher in identifying what support is required and its effectiveness when provided?

Debate about standards will and should continue to take place, but should do so against a background of assured knowledge about how children are performing nationally. Conflicting views about standards continue to arise because there is not an effective system in place to collect and report such evidence.

It is argued that

> We do not have an effective system of monitoring educational standards throughout the UK. Arguments about standards will continue until such a system is in place. National Curriculum assessment is not best suited to monitor national performances; for this purpose, specially designed, regular surveys are needed, using representative samples of pupils.

It must be remembered that the national testing programme has spawned a £43 million a year industry. Not only must the large vested interest lobby which wants to see the testing continue be watched but also the interest of the nation. Value for money is as important in education as elsewhere and is difficult to quantify.

General Assessment Issues

There are major problems in making comparisons of national test results over time because of the changing nature of the test population and of what is being assessed. In addition, potential bias in tests and in the criteria used must always be kept in mind. What must also be acknowledged and discussed is that boys and girls vary in their approach to assessment tasks and in their performance in both class work and tests. Thus, the general point can be made that the context, method and language of assessment should be consistent with the children's preceding learning and experience of being taught. Their confidence in learning is also likely to be an important factor. Equal access for all children to different styles of learning and teaching which includes techniques to be used in the national tests is needed. In addition, national test designers need to ensure that a range of assessment techniques are used so that there is no bias against a particular group of children. Not only that but allowance needs to be made for the fact that schools make more impact on girls' than on boys' attainment (Powney, 1996). Put succinctly: 'The concept of equity in assessment implies that assessment practice and interpretation of results are fair and just for all groups' (Gipps and Murphy, 1994).

A review of research not only with reference to gender but to other sources of invalidity can be generalized more widely to include consideration of ethnicity, socioeconomic status and class. But this is not all. There are factors within the assessment itself, for example, item format and response mode, the gender and specialism of markers, as well as the test constructor's view of what counts as achievement. Add to these variables beyond control of the test constructors, such as maturational differences between the genders, school effects (especially for ethnic minority groups), teaching style and pressure of tests, motivation and self-esteem and expectation of self and society.

Assessment is clearly a very complex activity which can very easily produce invalid data. This should be borne in mind when national test results are relied on so heavily in any debate on standards.

Improving the Measurement of Standards in Reading

The valid assessment of pupils and their progress requires techniques which, if they cannot be found, must be invented. Improvement in measuring standards and progress in reading will be fostered if an understanding of both child development and the theory and practice of various assessment techniques are used in concert to develop an appropriate form of assessment. In addition, distinctions need to be made between formative and summative uses of test information with both individuals and groups. Tests must be chosen carefully, for fitness for purpose to provide specific information about particular aspects of a child's reading development. There is a wide variety of reading tests in existence including normative tests, domain-referenced tests, tests based on item response theory, informal reading inventories and a range of unobtrusive measures. These have been developed over the years to suit the assessment purposes needed at different times of a child's reading development. The theoretical bases and applications of these various approaches to assessment and their respective strengths and weaknesses need explicating to both the public and the teaching profession. It is important that the most suitable and effective measures are used for clearly defined purposes. The confusion of summative and formative purposes in the national tests is not, as has been argued earlier, in the interests of either.

A Way Forward

A way to lower the stakes of national testing and increase the reliability of results would be to abandon full-scale testing of all children in the assessment of national standards and progress in reading and to replace it by the monitoring of standards of a representative sample of the school population. Monitoring implies attempting to determine changes over time in attainment. Ideally, this involves giving the same test to equivalent samples of children of the same age at regular intervals. The performance evidence generated would be anonymous and national rather than tied to individual schools and would not result in league tables but would provide a consistent measure to keep the nation informed about standards and progress in the key basis skill of reading. Attempts were made to do this by the Assessment of Performance Unit but abandoned in favour of nationwide testing. The arguments against the APU approach were both technical and political. The technical sophistication demanded needed to take into account the issues raised earlier, any of which might invalidate the collection of the data (but the national test design and analysis are equally subject to these). The political perspective, on the other hand, was that teachers should be held responsible for the standards and progress of the children they taught and that this would be achieved through publication of national test results at the level of the child and school.

The desire for improvements in literacy needs no argument but what to do about it does. Clearly research findings must play a part. So must the use of pilot studies to try out in practice which are the best ways of raising standards before their wholesale implementation in primary schools. The school, its classrooms and pupils represent crucibles in which both theory and practice can be tested and refined. What is needed in the early years of the next century is a more critical and sceptical view of changes introduced into primary schools in pursuit of higher standards. These should be based on a rigorous pilot testing period.

Research already has much to say about factors which affect attainment in reading all of which which should be taken into account in any measurements of reading attainment. Attainment in education is influenced by environmental factors within the home, such as the composition of families, their occupational and financial status, and their ethnic origins. These influences act on each individual and interact within families. No single factor is all-important. What matters is the cumulative advantage or disadvantage accrued from the interplay of several factors which affect children's school attainments. Below are just some of the variables associated with increased risk of high and low attainment at age 11 and which need to be borne in mind both when constructing tests and and equally when interpreting them:

- eligibility for free school meals (which is an indicator of poverty);
- large family size;
- one parent family;
- semi-skilled or unskilled manual parental occupation;
- child's behaviour;
- incomplete fluency in English;
- ethnicity of family background.

Although these factors are not independent of each other, overall, poverty is the most obvious key feature and has a significant impact on reading attainments across gender and ethnic groups. This needs to be said repeatedly — not solely in the context of an excuse for lower standards in certain socio-economic groups but also in the discussion of how standards may be measured reliably.

If a rise in attainments is deemed desirable in all groups then certainly a redistribution of the country's resources towards the more vulnerable groups is called for. If even a level playing field was called for, it is in the assessment of reading.

How To?

This would involve not only a redistribution of resources but also regular measurement of children's progress from a baseline assessment on entry to school and throughout their school lives, showing the value-added component of the educational process. This value-added component rather than average scores would become the criterion of achievement and national policy. But to be complete both value-added and background variables would be taken into account. This would give politicians and parents an understanding of how both school, teachers, family and community factors interact in the child's progress.

Such multilevel modelling techniques which take proper account of the structure of data (collected at the individual child level to include background factors as well as test results and at the school level to include such items as teaching and learning and assessment strategies) should be used more widely on national samples so that the net effects of individual pupil background characteristics (for example, ethnic group) are correctly estimated while controlling for the impact of other background factors (for example, sex, age, social class etc.) and school membership. In this way, something of the reality of standards would be apparent.

Conclusion

Standards in reading will continue to be an important and controversial topic both at Governmental and local level. Efforts to raise standards of reading are many and various: literacy hours, phonics for all, summer schools, changes in initial teacher training courses. These are centrally determined policy and practice initiatives. They have not come from the schools and teachers. One that has proposes to raise standards in the basics, including reading, by reducing the content of the National Curriculum. Practitioner response to ways to raise standards in reading need to be considered carefully by policy-makers. The creation of Education Action Zones in areas of low standards also allows the schools in those areas to apply for release from teaching the full National Curriculum so that the basics may be the main focus.

Continued central control of policy and practice in primary schools has cast teachers in the role of implementers and technicians. Implicit in this approach is that as long as the content and methods are prescribed and teachers are trained to use them then standards will be safe. A dubious proposition. An educational system is as good as its teachers — not the curriculum and methods it prescribes. For the next century we will need teachers of quality who can interpret the curriculum and select methods in the light of the learning needs of the children in their classes. From such teachers will come rising standards of reading. What is needed is to identify and retain them. We must, at the very least, ensure pay, working conditions and status are equivalent to the other professions.

What has happened in the nineties has been teacher flight from the classroom: a decade of increasing teacher dissatisfaction, low morale and high stress in the face of severe criticism of their professionalism and expertise. Teachers' feelings of inadequacy in the face of a highly prescriptive curriculum, content-heavy, and assessment-onerous has been obvious and unhelpful. If the measurement of standards and progress are to be undertaken with sensitivity to all the variables involved, children and teachers would benefit and so would the nation at large.

References

BROOKS, G., FOXMAN, D. and GORMAN, T. (1995) *Standards in Literacy and Numeracy: 1948–1994, National Commission on Education Briefing*, New Series 7, Slough: NFER.

CHAMBERS (1980) *Twentieth Century Dictionary* (revised edn) Edinburgh: Clarket Constable.

DAVIES, J. and BREMBER, I. (1997) 'Monitoring reading standards in year 6: A seven year cross-sectional study', *British Educational Research Journal*, **23**, 5, pp. 615–22.

DEPARTMENT FOR EDUCATION AND EMPLOYMENT (1997) *Shephard Welcomes BBC/Basic Skills Agency Numeracy Campaign*, 6/97, London: DfEE.

DEPARTMENT OF EDUCATION AND SCIENCE (1989) *Aspects of Primary Education: The Teaching and Learning of Mathematics*, London: HMSO.

GIPPS, C. and MURPHY, P. (1994) *A Fair Test? Assessment, Achievement and Equity*, Buckingham: Open University Press.

GOLDSTEIN, H. (1987) *Multilevel Models in Education and Social Research*, London: Charles Griffin and Co.

POPHAM, W.J. (1978) *Criterion-Referenced Measurement*, Englewood Cliffs, NJ: Prentice-Hall.

POWNEY, J. (1996) *Gender and Attainment: A Review*, Edinburgh: Scottish Council for Research in Education.

PUMFREY, P.D. (1995) 'School effectiveness and early literacy: Accountability', paper presented at the Joint European Conference, University of Kent.

SAMMONS, P. (1995) 'Gender, ethnicity and socioeconomic differences in attainment and progress: A longitudinal analysis of student achievement over 9 years', *British Educational Research Journal*, **21**, 4, pp. 465–85.

14   Accountability and Quality Assurance

Peter Tymms

Introduction

There can surely be no argument about the need for accountability within primary education. But, as always, the devil is in the detail and there is a need to be clear about: who should be accountable? for what should they be accountable? what are the consequences of setting up accountability systems? what types of systems should be constructed? how does monitoring relate to accountability?

These questions can only be answered in a limited way by defining roles, constructing syllabuses, creating systems and passing laws. Some of the answers must lie in a careful look at the ways in which the educational system operates. For example, it might seem reasonable to hold schools accountable for the achievements of their pupils, but once we realize that achievement levels are partly dependent on entry levels and that these entry levels vary from class to class, and from school to school, our position shifts. Instead it seems proper to think of accountability in terms of the progress of similar pupils in different schools. This relative progress of pupils, is, unfortunately, now called 'value-added'. Common sense would suggest that value-added would refer simply to the progress of pupils. For example, one expects to be able to apply it to one of the major achievements of our schools — the teaching of reading. We could say that schools have added value to our pupils by teaching them to read. This, however, is not the way in which the term is currently used by school effectiveness researchers, the Qualifications and Curriculum Authority (QCA, formerly the School Curriculum and Assessment Authority SCAA), or the *Times Education Supplement*. Their meaning of the term 'value-added' is the progress of pupils relative to other pupils with similar starting points. This is the meaning that will be employed in this chapter.

Within the Performance Indicators in Primary Schools (PIPS) project we have looked carefully at value-added measures and found schools to be an important factor in the progress made by pupils. This reflects the findings of many other studies. One particular aspect of the PIPS analyses has been to look at the differences in the educational achievement between girls and boys. Inevitably we found an overall difference between the sexes. But we need to ask: to what extent were these differences attributable to the school that the pupils attended? For example, were there some schools in which the boys and girls were making equal progress; some in which the boys progressed more rapidly; and some where the girls made more? Again although the answer to these questions is 'yes', for accountability purposes we need to ask a more probing question. Was it statistically possible to identify individual schools with a boy/girl difference that differed from average? This has not been possible and has never been shown to be possible for primary schools. Almost always schools that do well with one group of pupils do well with others. This holds whether the groups are identified on the basis of sex, ethnicity, ability or affluence. So, accountability procedures should concentrate on gross differences rather than on differential performance. This is not the orthodox view and we have seen a considerable effort across the educational world to address the 'underachievement of boys' for example. But in any accountability exercise we need to ask who is responsible for this so-called underachievement. If we find, as we invariably do, that the discrepancy between boys and girls is constant across schools, then individual schools must not be held responsible for this general feature of society in the 1990s. Its causes must lie in system-wide features such as the national curriculum, or the assessment procedures, or maturational differences or parental attitudes or other reasons. Schools, teachers and headteachers must only be held accountable for things over which they have direct influence.

Empirical studies can also help to answer the question about who should be held accountable. Pupils are taught in classes that are nested within schools which themselves operate within LEAs. With this kind of structure one can ask about the relative importance of teachers, schools and LEAs in the progress of pupils. It has already been noted that a *school* effect is generally found in relation to value-added. In the PIPS data we find that the *teacher* effect is greater while the *LEA* effect is smaller. This is hardly surprising. Pupils are taught by teachers and it is perfectly conceivable that teachers within a single school have different individual effects which will average out to give a school effect. It is also quite reasonable to suppose that schools within a single LEA have different impacts on their pupils. This fits well with the view of education composed of loosely coupled units, each of which has a degree of autonomy, and each of which operates within the confines of a larger grouping.

To summarize the argument so far: in the paragraphs above three points are being made. The first is that empirical studies must be used to inform accountability systems — teachers and schools must not be held accountable for things over which they have little or no control. The second is that the progress of pupils is most related to that which they most closely experience — teachers first, schools second and LEAs third. The third point is that teachers and schools, whilst variable in their effectiveness, tend to have a similar impact on all the different groups of pupils under their control.

Although empirical studies should be used to help inform accountability systems it is no less important that the systems themselves are thought through clearly. One conclusion that can be reached is that accountability must be reserved for impact, or outcomes, not for methods, processes or style. We may know that there is a positive relationship between a particular teaching method and pupil progress but this does not tell us that if particular teachers adopted this method that their results would automatically improve — adopting a recommended style may actually cause harm. Nor does it mean that teachers who use a recommended teaching method are necessarily doing a good job. To judge a teacher by style is unfair, it is their impact that matters. One of the best known thinkers in education is Michael Scriven the originator of the formative/ summative distinction. He has emphasized the point about not judging teachers on the basis of style with the following argument. It is well known, he says, that crime rates are much higher in the USA amongst blacks than amongst whites. But a jury would be quite wrong to take this knowledge into account when reaching a verdict. Judgments must not be made on the basis of association — it is against natural justice. So it is in education, teachers must not be assessed on the basis of associations between styles and outcomes.

The purpose of this chapter is to set out some general points relating to accountability and quality, and to point to various ways forward. One imperative must be to establish an acceptable quality assurance system. That is to say, procedures need to be in place which are designed to ensure quality and this necessarily includes accountability. This must involve both the checking of quality and the taking of action when the need arises. The next section outlines a possible way forward.

The author has been involved in developing two parallel monitoring systems for primary schools within England. The first is a Professional Monitoring System (PMS), and it was set up for confidential use within schools. The second, an Official Accountability System (OAS), is being set up at national level and will involve the publication of data for parents and others.

The PMS is PIPS which has grown rapidly since its start in 1993, more than doubling every year for the last four years. It now covers around 2000 schools. PIPS assesses the academic progress and self-esteem of pupils from when they enter school at the age of 4, until they move to secondary school at 11. Schools, or local authorities, buy into the system, presumably because they see its value in providing quality data to help them to help themselves. The schools' results are confidential to the schools unless there is an agreement with the local education authority (LEA). Schools are referred to by code names and great efforts are made to guard the information from the press. The PIPS system developed from the remarkably successful 'A' Level Information System (ALIS). ALIS, PIPS and other PMSs are run from the Curriculum Evaluation and Management (CEM) Centre within the University of Durham.

The OAS is being set up through the QCA and involves the use of statutory assessments at the ages of 7 and 11. A two-year Value-Added National Project (VANP) which has recently been completed with SCAA looked at the possibility of 'value-added' scores being published in addition to the raw results at the end of KS2. Value-added in this context refers to the relative progress which schools make with their children between the ages of 7 and 11. The project also dealt with the possibility for value-added scores for secondary schools and systems more generally.

Although PIPS and VANP both aim to provide very similar information the perception of the systems by teachers, their origins, the ways in which they are run and their possible impacts differ enormously.

Differing Perceptions

In a survey of one LEA in 1995 primary headteachers were asked how they felt about 'value-added information being made available to you confidentially'. More than 80 per cent of the 105 respondents said that they would find it 'Beneficial' or 'very beneficial'. By contrast when asked to respond to the possibility of 'value-added being given to the press' about two-thirds thought that it would be 'harmful' and another fifth that it would be a 'nuisance'.

The differences could hardly be more dramatic and are further emphasized by the actions of schools during the 1993/94 school year. Many heads within England broke the law and refused to carry out national assessments. At the same time there was a rapid growth in the involvement of schools in the PMSs, for which they had to pay. In view of the striking differences in action and perception one might reasonably wonder why it is that there is any pressure for OASs at all. To understand that one needs to look at the thinking behind the systems that are evolving.

The Origin of Monitoring Systems

Monitoring has a long and diverse history and the recent rapid growth in accountability systems doubtless has many causes. One source can be traced back to the development of public choice theory during the fifties in the United States. A useful account of this approach is given by Scheerens (1992). The essence of the theory is that bureaucracies hold within them individuals who may not always work toward the main aims of the bureaucracy. They may, for example, have their own aims and goals, which include personal advancement. If this is accepted then the way forward is clear. Individuals and groups must have clearly defined roles and their performance must be checked. People and institutions must be held accountable to well-defined performance standards. Competition is also seen as having a major part to play. Whatever the rights or wrongs of the theory there can be little doubt that this perspective has had a major influence on the current educational scene in England. The publication of test results, linked to parental choice legislation, aims to produce a more efficient schooling system. Competition, changed incentives, extensive inspection, enhanced feedback on outcomes and increased school autonomy are all in place to a greater or lesser extent and national monitoring schemes are now being extended to include value-added measures.

The monitoring systems designed for professional use (PMSs), on the other hand, have grown despite, or perhaps because of, these reforms. Their origins can be traced to early school effectiveness studies. They generated information on school differences which were then given to the schools. A key feature of the systems at Durham is a clear theoretical base founded on notions of feedback within chaotic and complex systems. Central to this view is the perceived motivation of individuals within the educational system. Teachers and headteachers participating in monitoring schemes are seen as wanting their pupils to learn, to enjoy their work and to have a high quality of life. They are making 'rational choices' that often put themselves second to the pupils. In this approach the education profession is viewed as working hard to produce good outcomes and being helped by high quality information. The information is needed because the system in which the individuals work is so complex, and the consequences of an individual's actions often remain unknown. Further, individuals or groups often have no knowledge of their comparative success. The theory suggests that, if teachers and schools knew the impact of their actions, and how well they were doing in comparison to others, they would be better placed to do the job that they are already striving hard to do.

Features of Official Accountability and Professional Monitoring Systems

Stemming, as they do, from very different rationales, it is to be expected that OASs and PMSs would be run in different ways. Some of these differentiating features are explored below.

Security of the Data

An OAS aims for accountability in the sense of linking performance measures to parental choice, public exposure and other consequences. If it is to work efficiently it must ensure, not only that it covers the whole system, but also that checks are put in place to maintain compliance and to ensure the integrity of the data. The Education Reform Act, within England, has established an extensive structure to test almost all pupils at the ends of the Key Stages. The publication and verification of these results also involve a complex and expensive series of checks.

The fear for an OAS is that if a tight structure is not in place some schools will not participate, or others might find ways to manipulate the data and avoid accountability. Others might change their practice in educationally undesirable ways to shift their indicators. An example of this is taken up in the next section. Within PMSs the information is for the school, not the public. Feedback is designed to fill a knowledge gap within schools not to encourage competition or to hold schools to external account. This is taken to the point where schools are given code names. Each school can see its own data against a backdrop of comparable schools but the information remains private to the school and hence the need to manipulate the data is eliminated. Of course, one still wants quality assurance in the data collection, but the need for expensive and demoralizing legislation is not necessary.

Ways of Reporting Data

As has already been noted, during 1997 the statutory test results for 11-year-olds, the end of Key Stage 2, were published. Prior to this the Department for Education and Employment (DfEE) set out proposals for publication in which the plan was to record the percentage of pupils with a grade 4 or above. There are limitations to this approach and a suggested alternative was outlined by the author in a response submitted to the DfEE:

> *Means not percentages*
> The first and most important point is that the tables would be much stronger if they reported the *average KS2 level* of pupils for whom there are results as opposed to the per cent of eligible pupils who achieved level 4 or above.
>
> 1 To report the percent above a certain level is to use a corrupting indicator (see Fitz-Gibbon 1995b pp. 18–20). A head who wishes to improve his or her school's position in the tables will set out to move pupils from level 3 to level 4. There will be no advantage in working with the non-reader who has no hope of a level 4 and little point in stretching the high flyer who is guaranteed a level 4.
> 2 The information available to parents and others is more informative if it is based on means rather than on percentages. For example, using the per cent approach, a school with 20 pupils in Y6 all at level 4 would apparently be equivalent to a school with 10 pupils at level 4, five at level 5 and five at level 6. The point being *that an average takes into account the individual levels of each pupil.* Cut-off scores can blur differences and encourage mediocrity.
>
> In short the use of averages would have the effect of raising *standards across the board,* of providing the public better information and of shifting the debate about educational standards into a higher gear.

The informal response of the DfEE to these points was that the information was not for the internal improvement of schools but for parents, who it was thought were much happier with percentages! Publication has now gone ahead on the basis of percentages. This decision encapsulates some of the driving forces of OASs. There is an imperative to publish in order to maintain competition, and hence accountability. Schools are seen as entities that must be goaded to effectiveness via the actions of external agencies. So forceful is this view that decisions can actually be made to provide corrupting data in order to communicate with the public.

By contrast, great efforts have been made within PIPS to ensure that everything that is fed back to schools can be easily understood, and that misleading, or corrupting, information is not released. The aim is to help schools help themselves. An approach that contrasts sharply with the DfEE approach.

Data Reliability

No monitoring system would find biased data useful, and an interesting issue arises when it comes to the reliability of school-based measures. If an OAS is to publish a figure describing a school, then common sense dictates that such a figure should be very secure. It is intended, after all, to form the basis of parental choice, teacher accountability and so on. Within VANP calculations suggest that for a primary school in England data would have to be available on around 30 pupils before a sufficiently reliable figure for a school's value-added score could be calculated. Furthermore, in some schools there is a very high mobility rate amongst pupils suggesting that the data for some quite large schools would be unreliable because so few pupils can be matched. These constraints suggest that an OAS involving value-added scores could not cover an important proportion of primary schools.

On the other hand, within a PMS data can be fed back even with small numbers of pupils. The data is confidential and the teachers can assess the information whilst bearing in mind the uncertainties surrounding it and taking into account their wider professional knowledge of the local situation. For example, data on pupils who have spent some of their time at different schools is still of interest to teachers, but should not be published as part of the school's value-added score. PMSs can report information of low reliability to schools that can help to construct a broad picture of the school when integrated with other information.

Possible Impact

It is probably safe to claim that our schools aim to educate all children and yet OASs set up competitive situations in which there are meant to be winners and losers. Losers in this context are schools with falling roles and empty classrooms with all that that can mean in terms of demoralization for staff and deteriorating provision. OASs are not aimed at improvement for all — some will go to the wall. There is to be sacrifice for the common good. By contrast PMSs take the view that all schools can improve and that high quality information can help. Schools are such complex organizations with evolving good and not-so-good parts to all of them that to allow some to go to the wall must surely be counterproductive. Within the PIPS project we never find a school in which the indicators are all bad or all good. Sometimes reading is going well in year 6 whilst the attitudes of pupils towards maths in Y2 is giving concern. Sometimes, progress in the reception year is a worry when all seems well in Y2 and so on. The idea of a 'failing school' is simply not supported by careful research.

A Compromise

It is tempting to suggest at this stage that it all comes down to values. If one believes one set of assumptions about human nature then the way of OASs is the one to follow, whereas another set of assumptions might lead one down the PMS path. A researcher would surely respond by suggesting that examining assumptions about human nature is not an intelligent way to proceed and that what is needed is more evidence about the impact of OASs, and PMSs on pupils and schools. It would be quite true to say that we have little information on the impact of educational indicators and we could surely do with more experimentation in this area.

A third approach would be to compromise, and such an approach appears to be developing within the England. It rises from the growth of interest in the on-entry assessment of pupils. These are assessments designed for children when they first arrive at school at the age of 4–5-years-old. There are many systems within the England that have sprung up in the last few years to do this, with about half of all LEAs involved in such work in 1996.

Rumours abound concerning the possibility of national exams for 4-year-olds and the tension between PMSs and OASs has become very apparent. Legislation has now been passed that requires universal assessment on entry but does not specify the system to be used. It does, however, describe principles that must underline the assessments. Schemes are to be accredited and schools can select the assessment of their choice. This provides a clear focus for local schemes. One might predict that enforcement of such a scheme will ensure the development and encouragement of excellent on-entry assessments around the country.

This compromise approach solves many of the problems inherent in the tension between OASs and PMSs. It allows for local development, encourages experimentation and even permits failure and yet ensures that all schools fulfil a perceived need for monitoring. It may not satisfy the hard-edged positions of those who would advocate an OAS, nor would it be seen as an ideal way forward by those who would prefer pure school autonomy but it should avoid the pitfalls of both.

The PIPS baseline assessment is the most widely used on-entry assessment in the UK. It is grounded in research and has been developed with teachers and LEAs over several years. Because it is an adaptive assessment it can cover the very wide range of starting points fairly quickly, is very reliable and forms the best basis for looking at value-added up to the end of KS1 of any baseline assessment. And yet we in the PIPS project do not suggest that it is adopted as the only assessment across England. This is because such a move would stifle developmental work, would force us to work with conscripts not volunteers and would remove the possibility that we might learn from other developments around the country.

Although there is room for compromise, and although we do need more research, and although values are of the essence, the world is so complex and changing that we cannot hope to decide conclusively how to run things on the basis of values or research findings. What is needed are carefully formulated decisions which can be changed in the light of new information. As things evolve new structures will be needed and new ways forward will have to be sought. The challenge is to make sure that the monitoring systems produce good information. The information can then be used to help with the need for informed change and monitoring systems can monitor themselves.

Accountability and Monitoring

There are to be many benefits to be derived from PMSs and there are clear dangers in OASs in terms of impact on individuals and on systems. These dangers are taken to an extreme with the present inspection system established within England. The public shaming of schools and individuals with its disastrous impact on morale, recruitment and on the lives of conscientious dedicated professionals is becoming unacceptable. There are a number of reasons for this. Partly it is the result of draconian legislation which puts the law behind fallible judgment. Partly it is the result of the dedication of OFSTED to the publication of perceived problems and partly it is the result of a system which mistakenly assumes that internal processes rather than outcomes provide important information on the effectiveness of schools.

But we cannot maintain an educational system operating solely on the basis of voluntary monitoring systems. There must be checks and balances. There must be inspections. There must be accountability in the sense that where things are not going well action must be taken and pupils must not be allowed to receive poor quality education.

The way forward is clear and is outlined below in a series of interrelated points.

1   A vital nationwide monitoring system will shortly be in place. This follows the completion of VANP and will provide for many schools fair and detailed information on the progress of their pupils.
2   Value-added measures cover a limited number of outcomes and time points, schools should be required to demonstrate how they monitor quality within their institution. This could involve joining a project like

PIPS but there are other alternatives. The essential point is that all schools should be active in this area.

3 The inspection system must be completely revised. Its *modus operandi* must be restructured and, at the minimum, it should be based on the following principles:

(i) inspections should be unannounced;

(ii) inspections should only report on factors which, it has been shown, can be judged reliably;

(iii) the public dissemination of reports should be played down. Reports should be made available to parents (including prospective parents) on request;

(iv) a mechanism should exist whereby judgments can be questioned;

(v) inspection, as a whole, in England should be apportioned a realistic sum from the national education budget. The present budget should be cut to a tenth of its present funding level.

Conclusion

Primary education needs to have effective quality assurance systems in place. These systems should be based on a clear understanding of the way in which the educational system operates. Some of this understanding comes from empirical evidence about the workings of the system and some must come from clear thinking. Such considerations lead to the conclusion that accountability systems must concentrate on outcomes, not style, processes or planning. Further, the most important units within the system are the teachers; schools are of secondary importance followed by the LEAs. The data also suggest that for each unit its greatest impact can be seen on pupils as a whole. Concentration on the results of sub-groups (boys/girls, high/low ability etc.) will divert attention away from the major issues.

Monitoring systems designed for professional use are far more acceptable to schools than top–down accountability structures and they also have a number of advantages. An important advance will be the establishment of value-added information on a nationwide basis but this should be run carefully and must be supplemented by other monitoring procedures. It is suggested that schools should be required to operate quality assurance systems but that they be free to choose which system they use. The inspection system also needs radical reform to move away from the massively overpriced damaging structure that it is at present, to a lean, incisive and, above all, fair system.

But whatever way the system evolves and however schools react the world will change. Any quality assurance structure put in place will alter the system itself and it may then be necessary to make changes. Not only do we need to monitor the educational system but we also need to monitor the impact of monitoring procedures themselves.

References

DEMING, W.E. (1986) *Out of Crisis: Quality Productivity and Competitive Position*, Cambridge: Cambridge University Press.

FITZ-GIBBON, C.T. (1995a) *Monitoring Education: Indicators, Quality and Effectiveness*, London and New York: Cassell.

FITZ-GIBBON, C.T. (1995b) *The Value-added National Project General Report: Issues to be Considered in the Design of a National Value Added System*, London: SCAA.

LEWIN, R. (1993) *Complexity: Life at the Edge of Chaos*, London: Dent.

SCHEERENS, J. (1992) *Effective Schooling: Research, Theory and Practice*, London and New York: Cassell.

TYMMS, P. (1996) 'Theories, models and simulations: School effectiveness at an impasse', in GRAY, J., REYNOLDS, D., FITZ-GIBBON, C. and JESSON, D. (eds) *Merging Traditions: The Future of Research on School Effectiveness and School Improvement*, London and New York: Cassell.

TYMMS, P.B. (1993) 'Accountability — Can it be fair?', *Oxford Review of Education*, **19**, 3, pp. 291–9.

TYMMS, P.B. (1997) *Value-added Key Stage 1 to Key Stage 2: Third Primary Technical Report*, London: School Curriculum and Assessment Authority.

TYMMS, P., MERRELL, C. and HENDERSON, B. (1997) 'The first year at school: A quantitative investigation of the attainment and progress of pupils', *Educational Research and Evaluation*, **3**, 2, pp. 101–18.

Notes on Contributors

Titus Alexander is an independent educator and author who works in all phases of education. As a research assistant at the University of Surrey he developed a course in *Learning to Learn*. He was a community worker in Brighton and London, a Principal Lecturer in the ILEA and then Adviser on Community Education for the London Borough of Waltham Forest. He is an accredited OFSTED Inspector and co-author of *Riches Beyond Price: Making the Most of Family Learning,* and *Home School Policies.* He has many other publications to his credit most recently, *Unravelling Global Apartheid: an Overview of World Politics,* published by the Polity Press.

Alan Blyth taught in schools in the post-war years, and then in colleges and in the universities of Keele and Manchester. In 1964 he was appointed to the Sydney Jones Chair of Education at the University of Liverpool, where he is now Emeritus Professor of Education. His early interest was in the sociology of primary education; his doctorate at Manchester was on the ecology of social groups in the middle years. Most recently he has been mainly concerned with aspects of humanities in the primary school curriculum, and most of his published work has been in this field.

Jim Campbell is Professor of Education and Director of the Institute of Education at the University of Warwick. He taught in primary and comprehensive schools before undertaking research into curriculum development at the Universities of Bradford and London. He was for many years editor of *Education 3–13* and for a time chair of the Association for the Study of Primary education. He has written widely on primary education most authoritatively on teachers' work but also on the primary school curriculum. His most recent book published by Longman is *Curriculum Reform at Key Stage 1: Teacher Commitment and Policy Failure.*

Colin Connor taught in primary and middle schools before taking responsibility for the coordination of the Primary Post-graduate Course at Homerton College in Cambridge. He now lectures at the University of Cambridge School of Education where he is primarily involved in in-service education with teachers in primary schools. His research interests are concerned with curriculum development in the primary school, assessment, evaluation, children's thinking and teacher development. He has published widely in each of these areas.

Peter Cunningham is Senior Lecturer in Education at Homerton College where he is engaged in the initial training and continuing professional development of teachers. His interest in primary education is as a parent, a governor, researcher and teacher, having formerly worked in primary schools in Oxfordshire and Leicestershire. His *Curriculum Change in Primary Schools since 1945* (1988) arose from an enquiry into the progressive ethos of the counties in which he taught. He subsequently co-directed funded research projects on the training, professional identity and practice of elementary and primary school teachers in the twentieth century. He is currently writing a book on this.

Julie Davies was a primary school teacher and headteacher for 13 years. She is currently Lecturer in Education at the Victoria University of Manchester where she is course leader for PGCE Primary English and History. Her research interests include the impact of the National Curriculum on childrens' reading and mathematical attainments, childrens' self-esteem and their attitudes to school. Her Ph.D. thesis centred on these themes and she has published widely in these areas. She has recently completed a book on teaching History in the primary school.

Mary Jane Drummond is a lecturer at the University of Cambridge School of Education. She taught in a number of infant and primary schools in London and Sheffield before moving to Cambridge. Her abiding interest is in young children's learning and her book, *Assessing Children's Leaning*, was published in 1992 by David Fulton.

Nigel Hastings is Professor and Dean of the Faculty of Education at Nottingham Trent University. He has published widely in primary schooling.

Chris Husbands is Reader in Education at the University of Warwick. He taught in schools in London, Norwich, and Hertfordshire. His research interests are in educational management and teacher development. He co-edited *Consorting and Collaborating in the Educational Marketplace*, (Falmer Press, 1996), and recently completed, with Anna Rendry, *Professional Learning: History Teachers in the Making*, (Open University, 1998).

Andrew Pollard is Professor of Education and Director of Research at the Graduate School of Education, University of Bristol. He is also co-director of Bristol's integrative programme on Culture and Learning (CLIO). He taught in Yorkshire primary schools for 10 years, and having entered teacher education at Oxford Brookes University gradually became more involved in research. For 10 years he was responsible for the development of research at the University of the West of England. He was director of the National Primary Centre (South West) from 1988–93. His present research focuses on the Identity and Learning

Programme project (ILP), a longitudinal, ethnographic study of children's experience of schooling and on tracking the impact of legislation on practices in primary schools (PACE). His books include *The Social World of the Primary School* (1985), *Reflective Teaching in the Primary School* (1987, 1993, 1997), *Changing English Primary Schools?* (1994), *The Social World of Children's Learning* (1996) and *An Introduction to Primary education* (1996).

Colin Richards was a primary teacher in Birmingham and Warwickshire before becoming a lecturer, first at Worcester College of Education and later at the University of Leicester. He was the fist editor of *Education 3–13* and is again its editor. He is the author and editor of many books and articles on primary education. In 1983 he joined HM Inspectorate and inspected both primary and secondary schools as well as teacher training institutions in the North East of England. In 1987 he became Staff Inspector: Curriculum 5–16 and in 1990 became Staff Inspector: Primary Education. From 1992 to 1996 he was OFSTED's specialist adviser for primary education. He now holds a Personal Chair in Education at the University College of St Martin in Ambleside, Cumbria. He is also Honorary Professor of Education at the University of Warwick, Visiting Professor of Education at the Universities of Newcastle and Leicester and an educational consultant. He is Chair of the Association for the Study of Primary Education and a secondary school governor.

Geoff Southworth has been a school teacher and headteacher. He worked at the University of Cambridge School of Education where he was a lecturer in primary education and management and conducted research into primary school cultures, whole school curriculum development, headships and deputy-headships. He is presently Professor of Education: School Development at the University of Reading.

Philip Taylor is Emeritus Professor of Education of the University of Birmingham where he was Head of the Department of Curriculum Studies for 25 years and Dean of the Faculty of Education for nine. While at the University he founded the Primary Schools Research and Development Group which publishes *Education 3–13* and conducts research; the most recent of which, 'The Primary Professional', is timely and has been well received. He has also published widely from books on the sixth form to the expertise of primary school teachers together with many articles in academic journals. He also founded and edited *The Journal of Curriculum Studies* now in its 22nd year. Before joining the University he was the Minister's Adviser on Examinations at the Department of Education and Science and Director of Research for the Schools Council. He has also taught in primary and secondary schools. He is currently engaged in research into constraints on teaching.

Sir Malcolm Thornton is a former River Mersey pilot who began his political career in local government in 1965, continuing until his election to Parliament in 1979. He was leader of the Wirral MBC from 1974–77 and, between 1977–79, was Chairman of both the Education Committee of the Association of Metropolitan Authorities and the Council of Local Education Authorities. He was PPS to Patrick Jenkins from 1981–84 and served on the Education Select Committee from 1985 to 1997, being Chairman from 1989. He was knighted in the Birthday Honours list in 1992. He is married to Rosemary, a primary head teacher, and has a son.

Pat Triggs is a Research Associate in the Graduate School of Education, University of Bristol. She taught English in secondary schools for 10 years and had three children before entering teacher education at University of the West of England (and working in primary school classrooms). She was Associate Director of the National Primary centre (South West) from 1990 to 1993. She is currently working with Andrew Pollard on the Primary Assessment, Curriculum and Experience Project (PACE) and continuing longitudinal tracking of pupils from this study in a new comparative project involving schools in France and Denmark.

Peter Tymms after taking a degree in the natural sciences taught in a wide variety of schools from Central Africa to Easington before starting an academic career. He was Lecturer in Performance Indicators at Moray House, Edinburgh before moving to Newcastle University and then to Durham University where he is presently Reader in Education. His main research interests are in monitoring, school effectiveness and in research methodology. He is Director of the PIPS project which involves monitoring the progress and attitudes of pupils in some 2000 primary schools.

Author Index

Subject Index